ANY GIRL CAN RULE THE WORLD

Susan M. Brooks

Fairview Press
Minneapolis

Published by Fairview Press, 2450 Riverside Avenue South, Minneapolis, MN 55454.

Library of Congress Cataloging-in-Publication Data
Brooks, Susan M., 1960–
    Any girl can rule the world / Susan M. Brooks.
       p.   cm.
    Includes bibliographical references.
    Summary: Provides information and resources for teenage girls who want to do more with their lives, such as becoming a political activist, investing in the stock market, or producing a cable television show.
    ISBN 1-57749-068-1 (alk. paper)
    1. Teenage girls--United States--Life skills guides--Juvenile literature. 2. Self-realization--Juvenile literature. 3. Self-esteem in adolescence--United States--Juvenile literature. 4. Sex role--United States--Juvenile literature. [1. Teenage girls. 2. Sex role.] I. Title.
HQ798.B72   1998
305.235--dc21   98-2519
                                                    CIP
                                                    AC

FIRST EDITION
First Printing: April 1998

Printed in the United States of America
02 01 00 99 98   7 6 5 4 3 2 1

Cover design: Laurie Duren

Publisher's Note: Fairview Press publishes books and other materials related to the subjects of social and family issues. Its publications, including *Any Girl Can Rule the World,* do not necessarily reflect the philosophy of the Fairview Health System or its treatment programs.

For a free current catalog of Fairview Press titles, please call 1-800-544-8207, or visit our Web site at www.press.fairview.org.

DEDICATION

This book is dedicated to Jenna, the girl who has ruled my world for the past 17 years.

ACKNOWLEDGMENTS

The biggest nod goes to all the girls who read, and liked, my 'zine, *REAL Girls*. Not one word of this book would have ever been written if it weren't for the cool letters you wrote to me to keep me going for "one more issue."

Also, thanks to John, who is a great guy (and who sometimes tries harder than any guy I've ever known to understand what it's like to be a girl); Mom; Dad (who I wish were here to see me succeed); Steph; my old friend Melissa, who is somewhere out there; my oldest friend, Sean, who was with me all those years that I hated being a girl and who stuck it out with me longer than anyone else; and to all the folks (most of them receptionists) from the many organizations listed in this book who provided info. A special thanks to all the librarians at reference desks throughout Los Angeles and the Bay Area (especially Berkeley), who gave me information I thought I'd never find. (Hot tip: Next to girls, librarians are by far the most undervalued resource in this country!)

Finally, thanks a bunch to Jess, who edited my words as only another girl could (and did a great job of making sense of stuff that didn't seem right before); and hello to Em (who I know will turn out to be a great *grrl)* and Amanda (who already has!)

Love to my best friend, Stig. Stigman, I miss you. xoxo

CONTENTS

INTRODUCTION

So you're probably wondering, what's all this about ruling the world? Didn't that idea go out with the Cold War and bomb shelters? I mean, isn't total world domination a little passé?

Yes and no. First of all, this book isn't literally about ruling (as in "my army can whip your army") the world and its people. It's not a manual on how to build weapons and infiltrate foreign governments. The kind of world domination we're talking about is a little more subtle; it's also a little more local, as in, my own backyard.

A few years ago, I was talking with a friend who was about to adopt a son. We were discussing the general state of the world—crime, environmental destruction, all those things that can give you doubts about bringing children into the world. I asked him how he felt about that, and he told me that the only way left for him to make a better world was to raise a good man. I love the simplicity of that thinking.

It was that premise, changing the world one girl at a time, that was behind my 'zine, *REAL Girls,* and the 'zine was the seed that grew into this book. Both give you something to get your hands on—something to do other than your hair or makeup, and something to think about other than how you don't measure up to some top model or TV star's glamorous life. What I like best, though, is sharing information—real information about how to get things done—because it's not enough to get you all excited about doing something without giving you the details you need to do it yourself. Reading about a girl who's made a documentary about kids at her high school is fine, but it can also be frustrating because you might want to do the same thing, but you don't know how. You'd need to find out the mechanics of where you'd get the cameras, where you'd get your video shown, stuff like that. Information doesn't just give you ideas, it gives you tools!

I'm sure you've heard that we are supposed to be living in the Information Age. If that's true, we are in serious trouble. Most of this so-called information seems to be commercial messages intended to get people to buy something, or worse, buy into something, usually for the benefit or profit of someone else. If you think about it, very little of the information you're given every day really benefits you and improves the quality of your life. The information for sale can be political—maybe a news clip about how Senator Joe Blow really has women's interests at heart (even though he's working behind the scenes to slash aid to this country's poorest citizens: women and children). Maybe it's a ten-second sound bite on the evening news about the tireless and selfless efforts of the paper industry to save our nation's dwindling forests (despite the fact that only 5 percent of the first-growth forests in the U.S. remain intact).[1]

Or the information they're peddling could be about a product some company wants you to buy. These messages start first thing in the morning when your clock radio goes off and they don't let up until you turn off late-night TV (believe it or not, we're each hit with about 3000 commercial messages per day).[2]

The product for sale could also be cultural. Are you part of the Pepsi generation or an MTV baby? Whole industries are based on the fear that we're not pretty enough, thin enough, blond enough, or hip enough. Corporations spend hundreds of millions of dollars trying to make us feel that, without their product, our lives are kind of pointless and incomplete.[3]

How do you fight that kind of manipulation and maintain a sense of self when everyone around you is trying to tell you who you should be? To give all those people a taste of their own medicine, you just, well—do it. Do something creative like writing your own magazine or forming an all-girl punk band. Do something important like forming a feminist activist group or organizing an anti-fur rally at school. The cool thing about stuff like this is that it not only makes you effective, it really does make you happy.

Being happy is the key, because if there's one thing I really believe, it's that a happy girl is a powerful girl.

A powerful girl? Wow, what a concept! That must be a pretty scary thought to some people. I'm not talking about the kind of power that comes from being Xena the Warrior Princess, or Tank Girl, or Sailor Moon (no, I am definitely not talking about Sailor Moon! By the way, have you ever wondered why powerful girls appear only as comic book characters and superheroes?). Just try to imagine what the world would be like if girls all over the world put down their pom-poms and stood up to claim their power instead of handing it off to corporations, politicians, and advertisers. What would that mean for you if you were one of those girls? For one thing, you'd no longer be shamed into losing weight or buying two dozen shades of lipstick. You wouldn't let your teachers ignore your raised hand (or your boss pass you up for a promotion you really deserve); you wouldn't let guys take advantage of you in any way whatsoever! And you would never again let anyone silence the voice inside you.

By doing things with your life and your mind—becoming active in local politics, volunteering in a community daycare center or animal shelter, expressing yourself through your own music and writing—you'll create a world for yourself where you are in charge.

You'll begin to see your value to the world, and you'll probably be kind of surprised to find that it has nothing to do with how pretty you are or what size jeans your butt can fit into. You'll discover that you can identify and solve problems; you'll find out that when you face a challenge, you meet it; you'll be delighted to learn that when you express a feeling or emotion and share it, lots of others feel just like you do. Best of all, you'll bond with about a billion other people who are searching for a way to improve their lives and their world. Just like you.

That's what this book is all about—helping you reclaim your personal power—power to make your own decisions, to find your place in the world, to have a voice in your life and your world.

The Time Is Right to be a Girl

That may sound like a feminine protection commercial, but it's not all that corny. It really is a great time to be a girl. Your brand of feminism is a lot different from that "have-a-nice-day," Bee Gees-induced stupor in which I spent most of the seventies. I was just as motivated to change my world as you are, and I felt just as much *grrl* angst (although I didn't have such a cool name for it) as you do. In retrospect, maybe one of the reasons I let so much pass me by is that I was just too naive. Now that I'm older, I know life isn't just one big Coca-Cola commercial.

When I hit the workplace, I saw promotions, raises, better offices, better assignments, and better jobs pass me up on the way to some more "deserving" and more "appropriate," more anatomically correct person (namely, a man). If I knew then what I knew now—yeah, you've probably heard that before, right? Well, if I did know then what I know now, I would have gone to trade school and become an aircraft mechanic; made friends with more women; learned how to fix more things; started my 'zine about two decades sooner; listened to different kinds of music and not watched so much TV; had more pets; learned how to write a scathing letter to the editor; learned how to save and invest money; learned how to stay away from jobs I hate; learned how meat gets from Farmer Brown's pasture to my dinner table; given more of my time to others who needed it; not spent so much time acquiring things; voted in every election; read more newspapers; learned sooner how to completely dissect a magazine that is supposedly written for the liberation of women—and made more of a difference in my world (and everyone else's)!

If I knew then what I know now, I could have written this book twenty some years ago. But you don't have to wait so long to learn how to organize a national boycott, how to find a job working in the environment for the entire summer, how to get a paid internship with NASA or the EPA, or how to mobilize other women into the political equivalent of an army of pissed-off red ants.

All I was missing then was what you have now: knowledge. Information. The stuff that winds you up and makes you go. That's what this book is all about. And what this book doesn't give you directly, you can find for yourself with the army of resources at the end.

Girls are thinking, creative, political people who care about the world and its inhabitants. We're interested in politics, animal rights, the environment, and social issues like homelessness and poverty in our communities. From browsing the deluge of mindless magazines at your local newsstand you'd think the only thing girls (or women) care about is where our next date is coming from or how high we can get our butts in the few weeks left before bikini season starts.

> Lesson #1 in ruling the world: If you want something done, you've got to do it yourself. That's what this book is all about. It's a pro-active, pro-girl guide to total world domination, sort of like the mental equivalent of dynamite. And it's all based on a simple principle:
>
> information = knowledge
> knowledge = power
>
> It's easy to see:
> *information equals power.*

Why Should I Want to Rule the World?

"Okay," you're saying to yourself, "ruling the world sounds cool for some people, but it's not exactly for me." Sure, you're concerned about the world, but the list of reasons you wouldn't make a good world ruler far exceeds the list of reasons you would. You're not a joiner. You're not an overachiever. You don't have money, you don't have connections, you have enough to worry about in your own life, right? I mean, really, why would anyone such as yourself have any interest in ruling the world?

Q: Are you okay with making only about 75 percent of what a guy doing the same job as you earns? [4]

Q: Can you live with the fact that 40,000 children starve to death every day? [5]

Q: Are you comfortable living in a culture where beauty and thinness is so important that 9.3 percent of ninth-grade girls report vomiting or taking laxatives (and 9.2 percent report taking diet pills) to lose or control their weight? [6]

Q: Are you content to sit by the sidelines knowing that in the U.S., 95 percent of our first-growth forests have been cut down in this century alone? And that of what remains, over 80 percent is already pegged for logging? [7]

If you answered no to any of the above, then maybe you should rethink all the reasons you wouldn't make a good world ruler. When you start thinking about the state of the world and what it's going to take to change it, you're probably going to realize that you're the perfect girl for the job!

What Does it Take to Rule the World?

It doesn't take a billion dollars to rule the world, or your own army, or your own country. Believe it or not, you don't have to be Xena the Warrior Princess to take the upper hand in your world (although it would be cool to adopt a more Xena-like presence in everyday life). You too, can achieve TWD (Total World Domination) in just four steps:

1. Become a strong political force
2. Manipulate the economy
3. Shape your culture
4. Care for and maintain your new world

Become a Strong Political Force

Learning how to pull the political strings of your government—whether you have a taste for local power or the industrial-strength stuff in Washington, D.C.—should be number one on your list of Things I Must Do Today to Achieve World Greatness. But how does someone who might not be old enough to vote (or who isn't much interested in voting for anyone in The Dwindling Pool of Appealing Candidates) reach such a goal?

There are tons of ways to get active, politically speaking; this book has a few to get you started. Contrary to what you've been led to believe, political greatness is not about money or connections or ancestors; it can be achieved by anyone with an itch to change the status quo.

Manipulate the Economy

You know money is important, you've heard it makes the world go 'round, but how important is a fat bankroll to human happiness? Driving around in a great car or wearing the latest fashions has nothing to do with happiness. But, as politically incorrect as it sounds, it's true: Money is power. But not power to keep your fellow earthlings down; not power to grab all the greatness for yourself and leave everyone else in the cold. Having money gives you the power to change the world—not just for your own benefit, but for everyone else's as well. Start a co-op organic garden in your community; fund scholarships for girls from low-income and at-risk families; build your small business into an empire that is ecologically sound and animal friendly. You can do all these things, and more, once you learn how to become a little more financially independent.

Shape Your Culture

Culture is nice, but what does it have to do with how the world is run? Often, it's not enough to be a charismatic politician or a savvy investor; sometimes the people who get the most attention are those who appeal to our love of music, of well-acted plays, of good reading. If you don't like a culture, then go ahead and create your own culture. Write songs, play an instrument, write Pulitzer-prize winning articles about the state of our nation and our people. Step up and become the voice of your generation—before someone else steps in to speak for you.

Care for and Maintain Your New World

Because you're a modern girl who cares not just about yourself, but about the other little Earthlings who share your planet, you'd naturally want to learn a little about the care and maintenance of your new world, right? Herein lies all you need to know to keep your brand-new planet shiny and in good working condition for generations to come. Forego that minimum-wage summer job at the local junk food palace in favor of a job outdoors, healing our forests, rivers, and communities. Make an unwanted animal's stay in the pound a little easier to handle. Change your place in the world forever.

Meet the Challenge

Become a strong political force, learn to manipulate the economy, shape your culture, and you too can hold the world in the palm of your girl hand. And once you have us all right where you want us, don't forget to take care of and maintain your new world.

Don't be scared. If you aren't sure you can go right into ruling the world, then start small and move forward at your own pace. Just know this: Once you start to make positive changes in your life—get a better job, make extra money, teach a child to read, save a dog's life—it's a sure bet that you'll soon develop a taste for changing the lives of others as well.

Mostly, you should have fun with this book, and although that should go without saying, it never does. There are a lot of really cool things in here; I've given you many great alternatives to Must-See TV. And even if you don't plan on using your experience in calling a national boycott to rule the world, or if the only reason you want to intern with NASA is that it sounds like a neat summer job, that's okay.

Although the information you'll find within each chapter is pretty complete, it's not intended to be a blueprint for whatever you're trying to accomplish. Rather, what you find in here is meant to just plant the seed. Take the parts that appeal to you, forget the parts that don't, and make whatever sense you can of the rest. Then set yourself loose on the world.

Endnotes

1. "Voting Green," by Jeremy Rifkin and Carol Grunewald Rifkin, and David Fishman in *E: The Environmental Magazine,* Jan./Feb., 1990.

2. "Turn Off Your TV," *Adbusters,* The Media Foundation, at http://www.adbusters.org/.

3. In 1996, Nike spent over $356 million in advertising and Estee Lauder spent $164 million on cosmetics advertisements. Incredibly, Estee Lauder, in a ranking of the top 100 spenders, came in second to last.

4. Education Information Branch, Bureau of the Census, 1992.

5. John Robbins, *Diet for a New America* (Stillpoint Publishing, 1987).

6. 1995 Youth Risk Behavior Survey (YRBS).

7. "Voting Green," by Jeremy Rifkin and Carol Grunewald Rifkin, and David Fishman in *E: The Environmental Magazine,* Jan./Feb., 1990.

PART ONE

BECOME A STRONG POLITICAL FORCE

The first step in any serious bid for world power starts with politics, and coincidentally, this is an area where girls (and women) are poorly represented. From our earliest days, we're programmed not to make noise, not to make waves, and not to make change. When boys in your class are running for class president, you are encouraged to run for treasurer. You know the deal: A boy who is aggressive is a go-getter; a girl who's aggressive is—well, asked to tone it down.

Close your ears to all that noise, because its time we joined forces and got wise about the big bad world of politics. How to become a mover and shaker is no great secret, and it basically involves asking yourself two questions:

 1. What are the decisions to be made?

 2. How am I going to make them?

The real secret is how some people can sit back and wait for others to do all the work. When two out of three adults living in poverty in the U.S. is a woman; when women are still paid less than seventy-five cents for every dollar earned by men (and women of color are paid even

less);[1] when 25 percent of the world's homeless population is made up of young women,[2] it's time to stop waiting for change and start making some of your own. A strong political agenda, and more importantly, the knowledge and resources to make that agenda a reality, is the cornerstone of control.

American women have a rich history of stirring things up, politically speaking, but you wouldn't know it from most history books. Ask any elementary school student, "Who freed the slaves?" and most will tell you Abraham Lincoln. Not that there's anything wrong with giving the man his due, but we should remember the pioneering efforts of women like Sojourner Truth[3] and Harriet Tubman,[4] who were born slaves and risked their lives to pave the way to freedom—not just for themselves and their own generation, but for yours as well.

Fighting for women's right to vote is another example of Girls Getting Things Done. You might be wondering how to become politically active before you're old enough to vote, but did you know that before activists like Elizabeth Cady Stanton[5] came along, the only thing women could vote on was what to cook for dinner? It seems like the only homage paid to groundbreaking women like these is the occasional commemorative stamp or coin (even the Susan B. Anthony[6] dollar, issued in 1979 in remembrance of one of our original *grrls*, hardly made a dent in our collective consciousness).

It's no coincidence that the soldiers on the front lines of both these battles were women. And after those victories were won, they moved onto other issues like social reform and rights for the oppressed and disadvantaged. Surprised? Don't be. It just proves what women have known all along; when you want to make a change in your life and your world, you pretty much have to make it yourself, because few of the men (at least on this planet) seem to be very preoccupied with the question, "How can I make things better for women?"

Sure, things have changed a little over the past couple of hundred years, but how much? One thing that hasn't changed a whole lot is that men are still making

most of the decisions. Women are still abysmally underrepresented in government—from the local to the national level[7]—and women who do rise from the ranks to become a strong political force, like Madeline Albright (U.S. Secretary of State) and Janet Reno (U.S. Attorney General), find themselves subject to the unforgiving scrutiny of the media, who focus not on their accomplishments, but on their weight, their choice of hairstyle, or their wardrobe.[8]

So how do you take the reins of a world power like the United States? For those of you who said, "Marry the president," shame on you! Why strive to be Hillary when you can be Bill (figuratively speaking, of course)? Even if you don't want to run for student body council, even if it's years before you're old enough to cast a vote in an election, you can still raise your political voice and be heard by the people who are pulling the strings in your state's and nation's capital. In fact, armed with a little information and a lot of nerve, there's no reason you couldn't become a champion puppeteer yourself.

Want to stir things up on a local, national, even international level? Great! Where do you want to start? How you choose to get involved depends on a couple of things, like where your interests lie and how active you want to be. There's something for everybody—for example, you can work to change the system from within by becoming an intern with a federal agency like the CIA or the Secret Service, or you can go your own road and form a political activist group of your own,

> I don't know about you, but I'm ready for a change.

WHAT COULD YOU DO WITH JUST A LITTLE BIT OF EFFORT?

with your own agenda! If your demons are more of the corporate type, you can harness the awesome political and economic power of a boycott.

Set your goals and go. Do you want to equalize the pay scale between men and women? Level the political playing field so all people, all cultures and races, are represented equally in their government? Increase opportunities for the disadvantaged? The choices are waiting to be made—you just have to know how to make them happen.

Endnotes

1. U.S. Department of Labor statistics.

2. The Third Wave's Web site (http://www.feminist.com/3wave/htm).

3. Truth was born Isabella Van Wagner in 1779, and did not gain her freedom until 1827, after most of her 13 children had been sold. She changed her name after experiencing a vision. Truth is the first black to win a slander case against a white person.

4. Born in 1820, Tubman (nicknamed "Moses") began life as Araminta Greene. Tubman escaped from slavery and became part of the Underground Railroad, an effort that helped other blacks escape to freedom. She was so effective in her work that rewards for her capture peaked around $40,000.

5. Stanton joined the women's rights movement after being excluded from an anti-slavery convention because she was a woman. Working with Susan B. Anthony in the fight against slavery, the two formed the Women's Loyal National League, and later the National Women's Suffrage Association. She was also an early feminist author, having written *The Women's Bible* in 1895, and in later years, her autobiography, *Eighty Years and More.*

6. Susan B. was one of our original *grrls;* she gained public notoriety in 1872 after being arrested for voting in a national election (she was fined $100, but refused to pay because no women were allowed on her jury).

7. In 1997, women made up only 11.5 percent of Congress; only 21.5 percent of state legislators are women.

8. Even "*Ladies' Home Journal's* Unforgettable Women of 1995" claims to honor women of that year; and a glance at the table of contents ("Points of Light," "Washington Women," "The Best in Business") gives the impression that it does. But the editors also felt compelled to include an article entitled "Fashion Fiascoes," in which women of all backgrounds, including politics, are judged by their appearance.

Chapter One

FORM AN ON-CAMPUS ACTIVIST GROUP

You know what they're saying about you, don't you? About you and "your kind." They're saying that you're apathetic; that you'd rather watch MTV and play video games than get involved in your world. They say you're a bunch of slackers. Those are pretty harsh words coming from a generation who hit their activist peak three decades ago.

When you read in *Time* magazine that "Thirty years after the Summer of Love, the flower children's kids envision— nothing,"[1] you might feel like not only is there no point in voicing an opinion, there's little point to having one in the first place. If nobody else in your generation cares about anything but the premiere of the latest *Real World*, why should you? For one thing, if you're one of those people who believe everything you read, then you should be a little more careful about what it is you're reading. The same month that *Time* was spewing about your generation's apathy, *E: The Environmental Magazine*, was highlighting the efforts of a dozen or so young people who are busily making change in their lives, their communities, and their world.[2] A sampling of "slack":

In 1996, Adam Werbach (only 23 years old) was voted the youngest president of one of this country's oldest environmental organizations, The Sierra Club. Werbach also started The Sierra Student Coalition while still in high school.

Angela Brown of the international Youth Task Force began her career in activism at age 13, when she organized community protests against a landfill. Ironically, one of her recent campaigns is targeting *Time* magazine for their use of chlorine (I wonder why the writer at *Time* neglected to mention Angela and her pioneering efforts?).

Danny Seo started his campaign at age 12, when he formed Earth 2000 to save a 66-acre forest from development. When he was 14, he organized protests against animal dissection, resulting in a California law that allows students to refuse to take part in dissection without harming their grade. When he was 17, his letter-writing campaign against fur was instrumental in getting some clothing chains to stop selling it.

What about you? Were you born to shop, or born to lead? You can express your activist tendencies in lots of ways: write letters to save the oceans, boycott cosmetic companies that engage in animal testing, put yourself on the line for gender equality in your high school sports programs—whatever your cause, there's a way to act on it. And one of the best ways to get everyone else excited about your cause is to form an activist group at your school.

Why an On-Campus Activist Group?

Schools aren't exactly shining models of democracy in action, are they? To be fair, they're not supposed to be. The decision-making process that school administrators and teachers follow often excludes student voices entirely; even when students do take part in forums like student government, they often represent a minority of the student body. You've probably felt, at least a couple of times, that your opinion about what goes on in the hallways, classrooms, and on the playing fields of your school just doesn't matter. Believe it or not, you can wield tremendous power on your campus. All you need are some people and some momentum behind you. You may not think you can do much on your own, but when you join forces with others and take action, you can change history.

Kids not much older than you are now, on campuses all over the country, altered this country's destiny by organizing student demonstrations against the Vietnam War. Students protesting the Gulf War started the University Conversion Project (which grew into the Center for Campus Organizing), a student activist organization dedicated to working for peace and justice. Besides, do you really want to sit around and wait for the student body president to take care of the problems you think are facing your school? What if she or he doesn't see things your way? What if your opinion isn't the popular one? What if your agenda is simply too radical for the pedestrian politics of student government?

Then change the status quo, or better yet, create your own. If you think your school's policies and programs tend to favor boys, form a feminist group. If you're fed up (literally!) with the mystery meat that your school dishes out, organize a vegan group and demand that the cafeteria start offering non-meat alternatives. If you think minority students are underrepresented, work to achieve a more balanced environment.

Before you put forth the effort of organizing and sustaining a political activist group on campus (know this: forming an activist group consumes a lot more time and energy than forming an opinion does), be sure that a similar group isn't already in existence. If you are interested in women's rights and there's already a feminist group at your school, it might be best to join their ranks rather than form a competing group that could, in the long run, actually hurt your collective cause. While you're looking around for groups whose efforts you might be duplicating, also keep an eye out for groups that might be sympathetic to your cause or a natural ally—for instance, a vegetarian group might join forces with an animal rights group.

There's a lot to do to form and run an activist group, so you're going to need some help. Get some friends together who share your views and extract promises in blood from them to put in some long hours for a good cause. This might be the easiest part; you probably have some friends who share your views on gender bias, racial equality, animal rights, or whatever issue you've decided to take on. Get together and start knocking around some ideas. It might seem small in comparison to the Mideast Peace talks or the Beijing Conference, but that's how all great movements had to start. Try to get people who are as committed to the project as you are; it would be a huge drag to get your campaign going and end up running the thing entirely by yourself. Plus, if you're unable to create any momentum for this group, not only will you end up doing most chores alone, but the group will most likely fizzle out completely after you graduate.

Next, find out your school's policy about student clubs and groups. The rules governing on-campus activist groups vary from district to district. Some schools are very restrictive, while others encourage true diversity and democracy. Your school may require you to have a faculty advisor, or there may be some other way that you need to become "accredited." Ideally, you wouldn't need the school's approval for your group; in fact, you may think that having the school's official seal of

> **Political activism is to world domination what silicone is to *Baywatch:* you simply can't have one without the other.**

approval might be a minus rather than a plus (you're probably thinking it's like selling out, right?). But taking such an isolationist approach is a little idealistic. The truth is, sucking up to The Man is going to provide you with some useful perks, like free photocopies or meeting space. Do some soul-searching, then strike a balance.

Once you have a few people interested, immediately try to attract more! Don't wait to plan your first meeting. If you spend too much time alone (or with just one or two others) drafting a mission statement, coming up with a name, and deciding on an agenda, then this group will quickly become "mine" instead of "ours." It's really important that the group remains a collective, a collaboration of ideas and thoughts. People are not going to want to join a group to do your bidding; they join to become part of the process.

Your First Meeting

Your first meeting is really important: It's there that you'll present your ideas for a group to a bunch of others who may (or may not) decide to join you. This is an opportunity to get other people's opinions and feedback to help shape your group's goals. It's also your best chance to take advantage of the excitement and anticipation surrounding your group's debut.

Where you meet depends on a couple of things: If your school has given the nod and you are "official," then you can probably reserve the auditorium, cafeteria, or a large classroom. If you have a faculty advisor, he or she can probably handle these details for you. If your school doesn't encourage student-run activist clubs or groups, that doesn't mean you have to abandon your ideas. It just means that you can't use school property to achieve them. Meet at someone's house or a public place instead.

Once you have a meeting place, schedule the meeting and advertise it! Advertise it all over the place, and when you're done, advertise it some more (have you gotten the idea that advertising is important?). Get some artistic friends to make posters and post their efforts all over the school and even off school grounds, if you can. Create and photocopy flyers and post them in the cafeteria, the library, on bulletin boards, and in other high-traffic areas. (Put some in the bathroom stalls; people will be sure to read them there.) Keep your posters and flyers simple—include the day of the meeting, the time, and the location. Write just a couple of sentences about the purpose of the meeting.

This is your debut, and you know what they say about first impressions. You may never generate as much excitement for your group as you do the first time out, so take advantage of it! You want to get as many people as possible, and one guaranteed way to pack the room the first night is to have free food. That might seem like a cheap, manipulative tactic, but it works!

Obviously you don't want to buy tons of food—like a six- or seven-course meal—you probably don't have the budget for it, anyway. But you can have a potluck, or if you know anyone whose

If you feed them, they will come...

parents own a restaurant, ask them to donate some food (maybe a couple of pizzas). Even chips and dip can lure some people to come and see what all the fuss is about. If you go to a warehouse grocery store, you could pull this off for less than twenty bucks. If you end up paying for the food yourself, try and recoup some of your expenses by asking people to donate a buck on the way out. If your attendance is high enough, you could end up with more than you shelled out.

Don't be choosy about who comes to your meeting; invite everyone, even school administrators (even if they don't let you meet on school grounds) and teachers. Get people involved in other student clubs to announce your meeting to their members. Ask the principal if you can announce your meeting on the PA system; get it mentioned on the school radio station, if you have one. The more of a buzz you create about a group, the more potential members you'll attract and the more effective you'll be in the long run.

Deciding what to do during your first meeting is kind of hard for beginners. To make it as easy on yourself as possible, prepare some notes ahead of time. Keep it simple. Just explain the situation as you see it, and describe why your concerns are important to you and the other founding members. Find examples or analogies that will make this issue important to other people, too. Imagine that everyone in your audience is thinking, "Why does this matter to me?" Anticipate the questions they might have and come up with good answers.

You obviously have a lot of passion for this subject, or else you wouldn't be trying to rally others to help you with your cause. But when you start speaking in public and debating topics, you have to know when to use emotion to get a crowd behind you, and when to keep emotions out of it. When you talk about how you feel about animal rights, about the impact that it has on you and your life, it's okay to get heated up and emotional. Really effective public speakers develop a talent for whipping a crowd into a frenzy using pure emotional energy. But when you start laying out arguments in favor of your cause and people start asking you pointed questions, like, "Why is it wrong to eat meat? Aren't people at the top of the food chain?" don't respond by yelling about how animals feel. Come up with logical, reasonable answers to opposing viewpoints and practice your responses. You're much more likely to sway people by proving that you've thought this out completely and that you've arrived at your position with good reason.

The key to holding effective meetings is to have a clear agenda. Eventually, the group should decide on future agendas together, but you'll have to draft the first meeting's agenda by yourself, or with a few cofounders. Decide what you want to talk about and how much time to spend on each topic. If you're going to need to vote on any proposals, allow time for that.

Before the first meeting, elect someone to take the minutes, or notes, of the meeting, and someone to facilitate. The notes are important because you need to

> Without a good idea of what you want to accomplish during each meeting and a plan for how you want to get things done, you run the risk of letting meetings ramble on until everyone gets tired and leaves. You won't get far with meetings like this.

keep track of issues discussed, resolutions passed, and agendas for future meetings. The facilitator is responsible for keeping the meeting on track, sticking to the agenda and not letting everything get out of hand. She also makes sure that everyone who wants to speak, does.

Because of the nature of the facilitator's responsibilities, try to choose someone who is not overtly opinionated or pushy, or the discussion will always revolve around what she wants to talk about.

If you've never chaired a meeting before, it might take time and practice for you to become really efficient at it. It's common for new groups to spend the first few meetings just talking, debating, even arguing with one another until they run out of time. As the leader of the group, it's your responsibility to keep the discussion moving in a positive, productive manner. If people start arguing or if you feel the discussion is going in circles, break in and move on to the next topic.

By the end of the first meeting, you should have decided on a name, drafted a mission statement, and agreed on plans for the next meeting. You should have also chosen a new facilitator and/or assistant, if that's the method of self-government that your group has chosen. Keep your name simple and easy to remember. A good example of an effective and catchy name is YES!, which stands for Youth for Environmental Sanity. Acronyms work well because they're easy to remember and look great on posters.

Draft a Mission Statement

Your mission statement is simply a description of what you are trying to accomplish. Don't confuse your mission statement with short-term goals. An example of a mission statement for a student vegetarian group is "To promote a better understanding of the health benefits of a meatless diet and to encourage a more humane, nonviolent lifestyle." An example of a short-term goal is "To hold a rally and pass out flyers that describe the suffering and pain of animals raised in factory farms."

Let everyone participate in the formulation of your mission statement. Even though you're responsible for starting the group and the mission is probably your

> When you're trying to think of a name for your group, remember that descriptive names like
> **STUDENTS AGAINST SEXISM**
> and
> **VEGGIE STUDENT UNION**
> work really well.

brainchild, be flexible or you'll be a one-person group. The mission statement must be representative of the group as a whole or people will not support it. Make your mission statement no more than two paragraphs. Say who you are, what you do, and why you do it.

Taking Action

Once you're having great, efficient meetings, what's next? As you've obviously guessed, being an activist involves way more than sitting around talking about things: It means acting on your beliefs. How do you decide what kind of action to take, and how do you follow through?

The first step is to set some long- and short-term goals. When you're formulating goals and tactics, ask these questions:

Q: What is our goal? What do we want to change?

A: Our goal is to keep the girls' athletic programs at school from shutting down.

Q: What has to happen in order for this to change?

A: The school administrators have to reverse their decision to make budget cuts to the programs.

Q: How can we make this happen?

A: We can convince them to reverse their decision by getting community support behind us.

That's a simple example of setting goals and figuring out what to do. Now that you know the what, next comes the how. That means developing a strategy. To come up with a strategy for achieving your goals, start brainstorming with the group. Get some butcher paper or big pads of paper and, at your next meeting, start writing down long- and short-term goals, tactics (or methods) to achieve those goals, and who will be responsible for what.

There is a high potential here for getting overwhelmed, especially once you start writing down all the things you want to accomplish. This is another way that members lose interest. It's like facing Mt. Everest—it can be so intimidating that a lot of people find it's easier to go back to apathy. In the above example, part of your strategy might be to organize a letter-writing campaign or petition drive.

If your list of goals starts to look like a shopping list of needs for a small country, don't be intimidated. The whole idea of working in a group environment is to take advantage of everyone's ideas and plant as many seeds as possible. Just because someone comes up with an idea doesn't mean you all have to rush right out and make it happen. It's better to start with a huge pool of possibilities and narrow it down than to be staring at a blank piece of paper with nowhere to go.

Make it easy on yourself and start small. Set some reasonable, short-term goals that the group feels are challenging

but still within reach. If you start out with the goal of ending racism, you will probably never feel that you have succeeded. If you start with a goal of reducing the number of racially motivated hate crimes on campus, you've significantly improved your chances for success. Plus, a few small victories—reducing the number of hate crimes from five to two in a school year—can really inspire a group to take on bigger issues.

As you start outlining goals, agree on a timeline. Then ask for volunteers for specific tasks. If nobody volunteers, you're going to have to make some assignments. Ideally, everyone would volunteer for everything all at once, leaving no dirty work to you. However, we've all been struck with that how-do-I-totally-disappear posture when someone asks for volunteers. Do some coaxing. Get people to understand why they are the perfect person for a task.

How to Keep Attracting New Members

An on-campus activist group always needs a constant supply of new members—people move on to other interests, they get busy with schoolwork, they graduate. But you have an edge over other noncampus-based groups. Since you're on campus, you have a steady pool of potential recruits every year when new students arrive. Here's a few more ways to attract new members and keep the ones you have.

Set up a table, or assign some canvassers, at fall registration. That way you can meet freshmen as soon as they hit the school grounds. Freshmen are always anxious to fit in; this is the perfect time to invite them to join your group.

Create a newsletter to give updates on your group's progress to everyone on your mailing list. Always be on the lookout for new names to add to the list.

Organize nights for group members to just hang out together; give them a chance to get to know each other a little better and build some solidarity.

Keep your meetings consistent: same place, same time. If you find that attendance for weekly meetings is kind of low, switch to meeting every other week and see if more people show up.

Planning for Your BIG Event

Events are the best way for you to get your group in front of people and attract some support—maybe even some new members. Lots of events are perfect for a campus activist group: fund-raisers, speakers, panel discussions or debates, demonstrations, a film or video screening, and concerts are a few ideas.

Planning an event like one of these takes a lot of energy and patience, but especially endurance! Be sure you have lots of people to help and most important, be sure to use them. Lots of activists, even seasoned ones, can get carried away and try to take on too much responsibility for themselves. The success of your event depends on how well it's planned and how well that plan is carried out, so don't get hung up on being "the important one."

Decide up front what you want to accomplish at the event. Do you want to sign up 25 new members or collect $500 in donations? Be clear up front about what you hope to gain or you may leave the event feeling like you accomplished nothing.

Once you know what you want to do, assign specific tasks to people and work out the logistics of the event. Who is going to run the information booth? Who's going to collect signatures and who will take care of the money? Who will get the speakers or the band lined up? Where will you put the tables? Make sure you have all of these details worked out well in advance.

Critique your event afterward with the whole group. Nobody likes to hear criticism, but you have to be able to look at your efforts objectively. If the concert you threw for animal rights was packed and everyone had a good time, but you collected only a dozen signatures and maybe twenty bucks, then you can't really call it a success.

Fund-raisers: Any and all of the ideas here could, and should, be turned into a fund-raiser—all you have to do is have a cover charge or ask for donations. You might turn off possible attendees by making people pay to get in, and that kind of arrangement might not work at all for your event. But if you ask people who are already there to chip in toward your cause, you'll probably make more money. Set up a table and staff it with a well-informed group member and a big stack of information sheets. The key to fund-raising is to take in more than you're going to spend. If you plan on having food and drinks, find someone to donate them. Otherwise, you may end up barely subsidizing your events, or even losing money. No matter what kind of event you're holding, you'll need plenty of informational materials on hand.

Speakers: Get someone who can speak with authority on your subject. If your group is about feminism, invite someone from the local NOW chapter. If you're advocating vegetarianism, get someone from a local animal rights group to talk about the health benefits of a meatless diet. Book a couple of speakers to add a little variety to the evening. Ask your speakers to limit their time to under a half an hour, but if you have only one (really fabulous) speaker and want to allow her more time, break up the evening with a short intermission, and always remember to schedule a question and answer period.

Panel discussions/debates: To make a panel discussion interesting, you need people with differing, even opposing, views. It would be dull to load a panel with half a dozen liberals who all have the same opinions on affirmative action. You need a little spark between your guests to make it informative and engaging for the people attending. That doesn't mean you have to take the tabloid TV talk-show tactic of exploiting people and setting them up for confrontation. Don't book the leader of a local animal rights group with a member of the local sport hunting association. You'll only stir up trouble for everyone, including yourself.

Demonstrations: Ask your parents if they remember "Hell, no, we won't go!" This is probably the most memorable slogan of the anti-war demonstrations in the sixties. Nonviolent demonstrations are a great way to attract interest in your group and

REMEMBER THE ADVERTISING

Leaflets describing your group's work, plus a contact name and phone number. To keep costs down, design them four to a page, two-sided, and photocopy them on light-colored paper. One ream (500 sheets) will make 2000 leaflets. You might get permission to use school equipment to make copies, especially if you have a faculty advisor. Otherwise, get someone's mom or dad to run the copies at the office.

A couple of big signs with your group's name and the name of the event on it. Make sure that your signs can be easily read from up to twenty feet away. Don't put too much text on your signs, but don't forget to include contact information here as well.

Clipboards to hold your petitions, if you're collecting signatures or compiling a mailing list (or both). Make sure you write down the names and addresses of everyone who attends your bash. This is essential in creating a mailing list of potential and current members. As your group becomes more organized, you can start using direct mail to contact members and solicit more donations.

Announcements of your group's next meeting. You can put this on your signs, your leaflets, your information sheet, anywhere it will fit! Make sure you announce it to the crowd at least a few times during your event. Whether you're holding a demonstration, a concert, or a film showing, keep promoting the group and encouraging people to show their support and join.

your cause. Your school might not allow on-campus demonstrations, so be really clear with everyone up front about the rules and consequences of holding one. You could demonstrate in front of the school; or maybe your demonstration would be more effective at another location, like the school board offices. Check with local police before you plan a big demonstration and find out if you need any permits. If your demonstration has nothing to do with school, don't feel that you have to hold it there. Hold an anti-fur demonstration at the shopping mall where fur is sold, or hold a demonstration against your city's homeless policies at city hall where you'll get the most visibility.

Film/video screenings: If you have the facilities and equipment to show a film or video, chances are you won't have any difficulty finding something to show. Whether your group is fighting racism, animal testing, rape, or poverty, there are hundreds of larger organizations that provide educational materials free of charge to schools and other groups. Check out the resources at the end of this book for some ideas on who to contact; if they can't supply you with a film or video, they will probably be able to direct you to someone who can. Just make sure that you have the right equipment before the night of the big event, or you could end up in a really embarrassing situation.

Concerts: Every high school out there (and lots of junior highs) has at least a couple of decent garage bands floating around. The band won't cost you a dime (they'd probably be happy to do it for the exposure) and you could attract a lot of people who might otherwise not be caught dead at a political rally. Don't fill the evening with only bands, though; include a couple of speakers as well, and make sure that you have tables set up to hand out information or collect signatures or donations (or both!).

How's it Going?

The bad news is that everything so far is the easy part. The good news is that you're getting better at this all the time, so maybe what's left won't be so tough after all. You've got the group. You've mastered the meetings. You've planned the events. You've raised the cash. So are you making a dent yet? Sometimes it's hard to tell if you're making any progress toward your goals, even if your events and meetings are going well. If you've been working toward specific goals, like increasing funding for girls' athletic programs, it's easy to tell if you've been successful. But if you're working toward a larger issue, like environmental protection, it's probably not very clear whether your group has had any effect—positive or negative.

Make frequent status checks on the progress of your group's mission. It's important to follow through on your goals—short- and long-term—and give members regular updates about how things are going. Remember, the goal here isn't to raise money or to produce a blowout demonstration; those are means to the end, but they're not the end product.

It's easy to have lots of initial enthusiasm for a project like saving the world, but it gets harder to maintain this level of intense excitement as time goes by. Maybe someday your grandchildren will be reciting slogans that you penned;

maybe someday you'll be leading entire nations to victory. After all, that's the idea behind world domination, isn't it?

If taking on the entire planet is too much right now, feel free to narrow the scope of your quest for power. Start small, like with your school. After you have learned how to lead a group like this to victory, maybe you should consider bigger and better things—student council, city government, state legislature...could the presidency be far behind?

Meet the (New) Girls Next Door: Young Activists Bent on Making Change

You're probably pretty familiar with the standard, Hollywood-issue stereotypical activist—pissed-off, in your face, unreasonably shouting their demands and blocking entranceways to save the whales, the spotted owls, and anything else they can think of, right? Unfortunately, lots of people still share this misconception about activists. Here are two real grassroots activists who could be the girl next door to break these stereotypes. They're living proof that what's really going to change our world aren't the politicians we elect or the wars we win, but the girls (and guys) who are working to better their own communities—and eventually yours as well—by living that big fat golden rule of change: Act, don't react!

Liz, All-Around Activist on Overdrive

Liz D. is only 19, but she's spent the last several years on activist overdrive, and it doesn't look like she's come close to hitting her peak. "Technically, I started reaching out to my community as an activist when I was a senior in high school," she says. "I was appalled at how horribly women were treated when they found the courage to bring their rapists to court." That year, Liz formed a group called WARPED (Women's Alliance for Respecting Peace, Education, and Diversity). Using guest speakers from local Seattle Rape Relief and the Seattle Young People's Project, Liz led discussions for campus girls on topics like women in sports, sexual harassment in school, abortion rights, and homosexuality. Liz was also one of the founding members of MONSTER (Mobilizing Our Neighbors and Sisters to Eradicate Rape). Working with other women is one of the driving forces that Liz says helps her succeed. "I found a support network of active women (young and old) who showed me by example how important it is to help one another. For better or for worse, I live by those examples."

After high school, Liz went to school in New York and really blossomed. She taught self-defense, organized a Young Women's Alternative Health Forum, became the president of an on-campus queer club, and found time to produce two 'zines, *Cafe Fallopian* and *Succulent 65*. Her plans for the future include starting a monthly women's health seminar on campus to address eating disorders and body image. She also plans on staying active in anti-rape campaigns. As far as advice for newcomers, she offers these words: "Just remember that you can't do everything on your own, and that it's okay to seek support and help from those around you. I spent so much time trying to prove to everyone that I wasn't 'weak' that I wore myself out and was of no use to anyone. I still have that tendency, and I still spread myself too thin. Stay healthy and think strong!"

Tovah W., Founder, Vegetarian Youth Network

Barely 18 years old, Tovah's already got over five years of solid activist experience under her belt, and she admits that she doesn't go for the kind of hard-hitting scare tactics that tend to put some people off. "To me," she says, "living your life in accordance with your values and beliefs is one of the biggest forms of activism. I've made a lot of people think twice about the way they view things and the thoughtless things they do and say just by being myself and setting a good example."

Truth is, Tovah is not nearly that passive, and there are times when she gets tired of waiting around for change and gets out to make it herself. "I'm a strong believer in every girl's ability to make change in her world," she says. Like any truly rad girl, Tovah not only talks the talk, she walks the walk. When she was only 13 years old, she founded the Vegetarian Youth Network, where she "attempts to make a small contribution to end the lack of support that many young people feel when they choose to be vegetarian." Though the group has future plans for publishing an introductory booklet to living veggie, they organize and educate primarily through their Web site. "It is definitely a non-professional, grassroots organization, but we have reached a lot of young people, which makes me happy," she says.

In addition to the veggie network, Tovah co-founded the Gay-Straight Student Alliance while she was still in high school, and eventually got the group sanctioned by her school so they could become an on-campus presence. "The Alliance was created to put an end to the isolation that so many lesbian, gay, bisexual, and SS (Straight and Supportive) students feel," she says. "We provide resources, emotional support, and a forum to discuss personal as well as school issues." For more information about what's Tovah's up to these days, contact her at Vegetarian Youth Network, P.O. Box 1141, New Paltz, NY 12561; or visit her site at http://www.geocities.com/RainForest/Vines/4482/.

Endnotes

1. "It Ain't Us, Babe," by James S. Kunen, in *Time* magazine, Jan. 1, 1997. In this two-page article, Kunen interviews a handful of teenagers in Greenwich Village and makes the extreme generalization that kids today just want to drink, smoke, and have sex.

2. "Just Doing It! Generation X Proves that Actions Speak Louder Than Words," by William R. Buck and Tracey C. Rembert, in *E: The Environmental Magazine,* Sept./Oct., 1997.

Chapter Two

ORGANIZE A BOYCOTT

Boy • **cott** (boy cot): v., to engage in a concerted refusal to have dealings with (as a person, store, or organization) usually to express disapproval or to force acceptance of certain conditions.

If you've ever been angered by the business practices of an irresponsible company, or wished you could do more than just return a product made by a company you don't like, if you've ever dreamed of finding a way to hold corporate America responsible for their actions, this is the place for you!

Boycotting is one of the best opportunities for would-be rulers to flex their muscles, socially speaking. Unlike amassing enormous wealth to turn the economic tides or scratching and clawing your way to a position of great political prestige, boycotting requires no money, no experience, and no connections. Plus, a successful boycott will bring you both economic and political clout—more of the stuff that girls on their way to ruling their world can really use.

In practical terms, a boycott means that you refuse to give your money to any company that engages in practices you find objectionable, for whatever reason. You probably already do this on some level; maybe there's a store you don't shop at because they treat young workers unfairly, or a line of clothing you won't buy because of their sexist advertising.

When you purchase a company's products or services, you are supporting that company's beliefs and their value system, which includes their employment practices, their stand on animal testing, sex discrimination, the environment, and everything else they do and say in the name of making a buck. Whether or not you agree with what they do doesn't matter. What does matter is that even if you don't approve, you have suspended that disapproval long enough to whip out your checkbook or credit card and ensure that they can continue to go about their business.

So when you decide to not buy Preteen Sexpot Jeans (aside from their

If you have a gripe against a company, you don't have to settle for a little anonymous grumbling to an uncaring customer service center, and you don't have to wait for someone else to spring into action:

YOU CAN CALL A BOYCOTT OF YOUR OWN.

incredibly obnoxious name, you don't like the fact that they use young girls as sex objects in their magazine advertisements), you are making a conscious choice to not support this company. When you tell a few friends about Preteen Sexpot Jeans and you get them to stop buying their stuff as well, you've started a sort of mini-boycott. When you publicize your complaint and move enough of other people's money out of the Preteen Sexpot Company's bank account and into their competitor's—so much money, in fact, that this company announces that it will not only change its name, it will use more "mature" women in their ads—then you've spearheaded a successful boycott, and you've had your first taste of real power.

You'll occasionally hear about boycotts in the news (McDonald's, Walt Disney, and RJ Reynolds are three companies that are virtually always the target of a boycott, but there are hundreds of others called every year). Some boycotts may be on a smaller scale (or may have a smaller publicity budget) than the ones that garner most of the media's attention, but they have just as much conviction and passion behind them.

Don't think for a minute that one girl can't make a difference. Two of the most successful boycotts in recent years were started by people who might be even younger than you! A group of teenagers in New Jersey had a huge impact in a war waged against McDonald's for the fast food chain's use of environmentally damaging Styrofoam containers. After renaming the chain's icon "Ronald McToxic" and giving him a lot of bad press, they made all the difference in the world in getting McDonald's to change their ways. Now McDonald's wraps burgers in McPaper.

An even younger group—fifth graders!—organized a boycott against H.J. Heinz, the parent company of StarKist Tuna. They protested Heinz's sloppy fishing practices that claimed the lives of countless dolphins. The students were extremely organized in their campaign and even got other schools involved. Soon, they had scores of kindergarten classes writing to StarKist and asking, "Why are you killing dolphins?" As a result, StarKist is now one of many companies that sells dolphin-safe tuna.

Boycotts can also have a great political impact—in 1955, tens of thousands of people boycotted the racist public transportation system in Montgomery, Alabama; this is one of the factors that helped launch the civil rights movement.

Today's young people are tomorrow's consumers. Successful companies know that if they lose the faith of a young buyer before he or she has grown to be a full-blown consumer, that consumer has been lost to the competition for good. A boycott is more than one girl voicing a complaint: A boycott can be very threatening.

While it may seem that a girl's efforts won't be very effective against a company whose annual sales top a cool billion or so, most companies who got that big built their bottom line on a solid reputation, and that means creating as little controversy as possible. So if your boycott exposes a company's bad business practices and gives them a bad image, they will probably be more receptive to your demands than you might think.

Speaking of demands, it's important to know what yours are. Remember, the whole point of a boycott is not to punish a company for wrongdoing, but to encourage them to change their ways. While you might prefer it if the Preteen Sexpot Jeans Company would disband, liquidate their assets, and give the money to girls' sports programs, it's unlikely they would concede to do that. That could be seen as an unreasonable demand. A more reasonable demand would be to stop using young girls in their advertisements, or stop putting those models in sexually suggestive poses.

Your reasonable demands, when met, must end the boycott. That's the company's motivation for stopping. If you vow never to buy Preteen Sexpot Jeans for as long as you live, and you vow to forbid your children, and your grandchildren, and all future generations from buying said jeans, then what's the point of conceding to your demands? You have to give the company a way out, otherwise you're just griping, not working for change.

The Old One-Two

Armed with this information, you're contemplating upping your one-woman battle against the Preteen Sexpot Jeans Company into a full-blown boycott. Great! How'd you like to put a little extra something into that swing of yours? Not only can you affect the Preteen Sexpot Jeans Company directly by refusing to buy their products, you can also hit them indirectly by boycotting companies that appear to endorse their sexist ways—that is, the magazines that carry these incredibly offensive ads or the stores that carry their merchandise. It's the one-two punch: First a left, then a right, and you've doubled your chances for success!

This multi-level strategy works for just about any boycott, and works especially well when the second boycottee is a smaller, local business. Say you don't like the fact that a huge cosmetics company still participates in animal testing. Fine. Organize a boycott against them. But why stop there? You can increase your chances for success by also boycotting the local markets that carry this company's products. Maybe a huge cosmetics company won't give you and your boycott the time of day (animal rights activists have been fighting Procter & Gamble for

A group called Animal Emancipation, Inc., in Santa Monica, California, had been barely making a dent in Coors Beer's extensive sponsorship of rodeos. So a few years ago, they decided to focus on a more local, grassroots effort: they organized a boycott against a local business that sponsored the next rodeo that came to town. Was it successful? You could say that—that particular business never sponsored a rodeo again.

years), but a store that depends on the continued patronage of its community for survival will.

Although there are many reasons to call a boycott, all will fall into one of two categories: a complaint against something the company is actually doing (for example, dumping toxic waste in your city's rivers); or for their support of another company's activities (for example, sponsoring a TV show that glorifies violence against women). There's no material difference between the two—you want them to either stop their behavior or stop supporting someone else's behavior, and you structure each boycott in basically the same way.

Four Steps to a Successful Boycott

These guidelines will help girls who are starting a boycott from scratch. Before you choose to take that action, however, you should find out if there is an existing boycott against this company. A boycott is a pretty tiring undertaking, and it might be easier just to join a boycott that someone else has organized, especially if you're new to this activist thing. The best place to find out if your boycott's already been called is a magazine called *Boycott Quarterly* (see the resource section for more information). This magazine is strictly about boycotts; aside from the really helpful in-depth articles on current boycott issues, it lists a comprehensive directory of current boycotts. It also gives you brand name information, in case you don't know who owns Lay's potato chips, for example. If you check out *BQ* and discover that nobody's gotten on the

Preteen Sexpot bandwagon yet, then you're ready to begin.

Planning and organizing a successful boycott can be broken down into four steps:

1. Research: Check out not only the company, but also the activity they participate in or sponsor.

2. Make contact: Write to the company and ask them to stop.

3. Issue an ultimatum: Stop by this date or you will call a boycott.

4. Act: Call the boycott and get the word out.

Although the process looks pretty straightforward, it's not quick. You're probably not going to change the world—or even your little corner of it—overnight. In fact, it could take several months to get a boycott off the ground, and several years before you could call it a success. But don't let that turn you off. If ruling the world were that easy, everybody would be doing it. And just think of where the rest of us might be if no other girls had the patience or the resolve to live their convictions. Beauty products manufacturers would still test on animals, we'd still be wrapping our veggie burgers in Styrofoam, and the rainforests would probably be paved over with convenience stores. So hang in there!

Research

The most effective weapon that any boycotter can have on her side is the truth. So before you make accusations and call a boycott against any company, it's important to be sure you have your facts straight. This is serious business—after all, you're gambling with the financial future of the company itself, as well as the future of the people who work for that company or own stock in it. You can't base a boycott on rumors. You need facts, and lots of them, if you want total strangers to change their buying habits and get behind your cause.

In the case of the Preteen Sexpot Jeans Company, there's not much debate. Those offensive ads are plastered throughout every single magazine on the newsstand, so it would be pretty hard to deny their sexist tendencies.

In most cases, all you need to do to confirm a rumor about a particular company's involvement in any practice is to call them and ask them if it's true. Most product labels carry a toll-free customer service phone number. Use it, it's free. Call them up and ask them straight out, "Do you do this?" They may not want to answer such a pointed question, they may send you into a sort of voicemail hell where you're transferred to departments of all kinds, but you'll probably get an answer eventually.

If there's no phone number available, or if all you have is a brand name and not the legal name of the corporation, hit the library. You can find information for virtually any company in the country by referring to *The Directory of Corporate Affiliations.* This is a gold mine for boycotters—it lists parent companies, subsidiaries, all affiliations, and even lists companies by brand name. It will also give you detailed contact information on the principals of the company, like president and vice-presidents of marketing, PR (public relations), and advertising.

If you don't get a straight answer, or you suspect you are not being told the truth, then you have to dig a little deeper. There are a number of magazines and newspapers devoted to the (often objectionable) business practices of corporate America. You can also find a wealth of information by skimming past issues of magazines like *BusinessWeek, U.S. News and World Report,* and *The Wall Street Journal.* Most libraries keep extensive archives of these titles and more—they're usually stored on microfilm or some other compact, easy-to-reference medium.

> People are more likely to listen to what you have to say if you know what you're talking about.

Don't underestimate the importance of research. It's vital to arm yourself with as much information as you can about the company's history, because the more knowledgeable you become, the more convincingly you will be able to speak on the subject.

Once you determine that the company you're researching does indeed participate in the activity you don't like, find out as much as you can about the issue—whether it's animal testing, harmful advertising, or the destruction of the rainforest. You need to become an expert on your gripe.

The reference materials at the library (back issues of newspapers, magazines, etc.) will bring you lots of good general information, but if you really want hard-hitting facts, passionate articles, and explicit photographs, your best bet is to contact a special interest group or organization that specializes in the subject matter you're researching.

For example, if you want some really detailed information on animal abuses (whether it's testing, circuses and rodeos, or wildlife extinction), your first stop should be an animal rights organization like People for the Ethical Treatment of Animals (PETA) or In Defense of Animals (IDA). In your fight against the Preteen Sexpot Jeans Company, or any company that is displaying sexist and questionable advertising, you could try the women's studies department of a local university, a women's group like the American Association of University Women (AAUW), or even a media watchdog group like Media Watch or AdBusters.

Use your imagination when trying to think of sources for material. If you have a computer and a modem, get on the Internet. You're already connected to virtually thousands of sources using just one or two keywords. Check out the yellow pages in the phone book, too. One or two good contacts could lead you to a gold mine of potential activists and informants.

Gather as much info as you can, and start a file of any related articles or clippings you discover. Your job here is to build a case based on facts, not emotions, that any company would have a hard time either denying or ignoring.

Make Contact

You're on a roll! You're determined to bring decent, credible, and respectful advertising to the jeans community, and you're going to start with the Preteen Sexpot Jeans Company. Great! By now you should have a pretty good collection of material on the company and what they've done. You have facts and figures on teen self-esteem, on eating disorders, and the influence of media on young women. You've found lots of examples of their lame advertising—ads that have appeared in everything from *Tiger Beat* to *Mirabella*. You're ready to make waves.

Your strategy is deceptively simple: Write and ask them to stop. Sound too easy? Remember, even large, multinational companies are run by people, and often, these people don't mean to upset anyone. The head marketing whiz at the Preteen Sexpot Jeans Company might not be a bad guy after all; he might actually think his company's ads are kind of cute. He may be surprised to hear that women across the country would like to strangle him with his own jeans. It's up to you to let him know—gently (at least at first). The point of your letter is not to put them on the defensive, but to convince them to change their ways. So express an understanding that the company is in business to make a profit.

Let the company know that you don't like what they are doing. The people in charge may not even realize that they have offended anyone.

Make your letter brief and to the point, but include all relevant information (see pages 29 and 30 for sample boycott letters). The tone should be professional

---

DON'T FORGET TO WRITE

A statement that you disagree with their policy on X activity.

Facts and figures that they might not know. This is not the time to be shy: If you have statistics on how women under the age of eighteen are the victims of violence and sexual aggression, include those figures. For all you know, the person you are writing to is not even aware of the effects of his or her company's activities.

Alternative ways of doing business. Don't just criticize, give them options for change. If you were writing to the Preteen Sexpot Jeans Company, you could include ads from successful competitors that don't feature prepubescent girls in sexually suggestive poses. Remind them that Levi's jeans have been around for more than 100 years without the benefit of Kate Moss' wiggling behind.

---

and businesslike. You don't want to come across as a fanatic—don't ramble on for five pages about how everyone in the company is going to perish in hell for what they're doing. Don't scrawl the letter in lavender ink and dot your i's with frowning faces. You want to show that you're an intelligent, responsible, mature girl who knows what she's talking about and who deserves to be taken seriously.

Don't write to customer service, but go straight to the top to the people who can change things for you. Address the letter to the Chief Executive Officer (CEO) and send a copy to a couple of Vice Presidents—try the VPs of the marketing, public relations, and advertising departments. (You can find this information in *The Directory of Corporate Affiliations.*) Send the letter by registered mail, and keep a copy for yourself.

Issue an Ultimatum

Your next move depends on a couple of things: first, did you get a reply? If yes, how do you feel about the company's response? Are you satisfied with it or are they blowing smoke in your face? It will take probably a month, if not more, to get a reply to your first letter. Sometimes mail gets routed through several people (not to mention several departments) before it ends up on the desk of the person to whom it was addressed.

Give the company at least thirty days to respond, and if you still haven't heard anything (or even if you received a response that you don't like), start drafting your second letter. Like your first letter, the tone of this one should be businesslike, but much firmer. If you think of your first letter as a request, your second one is a demand.

Include a copy of your first letter and reference it. Tell them that you have already written to them once and have not received a reply (or that their reply was unacceptable). Repeat your evidence and restate your demand. Then issue your ultimatum: Either stop these practices immediately (give them a specific deadline), or risk a boycott. Never threaten anyone, and don't cuss them out! Just have your say and see what happens. Again, send the letter by registered mail and keep a copy for yourself.

Act

The wait for a response is a real nailbiter, isn't it? Still, it's exhilarating to think that you might be responsible for turning the tide in corporate crimes against humanity (or the animal kingdom). If you've succeeded with just a threat, consider yourself lucky, and celebrate! If another month or your deadline has passed since you sent your second letter and you still haven't heard anything, or if the company has no intention of giving in to your demands, you're ready to call your boycott.

There will be a lot to do once you begin a boycott, so enlist as many friends, relatives, and innocent bystanders as you can find to help you. You have press releases to write, people to contact, financial futures to influence—you'd better get to work!

There really isn't any one thing you need to do to make your boycott "official." You don't have to register it with any agency, and you don't have to file any papers. There isn't anyone in particular who has to be notified, other than the company you've called the boycott against (but there are some people you'll definitely want to notify).

The proper sendoff for a boycott involves two steps: preparing an information packet, and publicizing the boycott as much as possible. Public relations is the key to getting people behind your cause, and good PR involves educating as many people as possible about what you're doing, why, and how they can help.

Once you've created your press materials, you're ready to spread the word. Your goal is the buzz: you want to create it, and you want to maintain it. You want to keep people talking about your boycott until they've told two friends, and the friends have told two friends, and so on.

Why? Because the most successful boycotts are those with the most supporters (and thereby do the most damage to the company against whom the boycott is called), and the ones with the most supporters are the ones that people know about.

What to Put in Your Information Packet

A list of allegations against the company that led you to organize the boycott in the first place. Give the history of their practices, and include as many factual references as possible.

Evidence you've found of the detrimental effects of this activity.

A list of your demands, which, when met, will end the boycott.

Contact information (name, phone number, and address) of the person at the company who you've contacted, and contact information for yourself. While it's important that potential supporters be able to get in touch with you, you also need to protect your privacy. Avoid publishing your home address, and if possible, use a P.O. Box. They're only $40 a year at the post office. If you can't get a P.O. Box, arrange to receive mail through your teacher at a school address, or through your parents' work address.

A list of all subsidiary companies and products manufactured by the company. You can get this information from any brokerage house, or from the company itself by asking for a prospectus. You can also find this information in *Boycott*

Quarterly and *Shopping for a Better World.* Include names of companies that may be supporting this activity, even indirectly. This would include names of magazines that carry the company's ads, stores that carry their merchandise, and so on.

Your information packet can be as simple or elaborate as you want. You can photocopy and staple your materials, or you can design a whole package with graphics, color, and photos, depending on how creative you want to get, and how much time you have on your hands (or who owes you some serious favors).

If you're stuck for ideas or want to see how other people do it, get information packets from other groups. These will give you some great ideas about how to arrange your stuff and might even give you information you didn't have. The best way to contact other boycotters is to browse the listings in *BQ* and find a group that's working on a boycott similar to yours, then give them a call and request an information packet.

Creating Your Press Release

A press release is vital for effective PR. It relates all the essential information about your boycott in one page, and provides information on how the media or potential supporters can contact you (see page 31 for a sample press release). Most press releases are written in a certain format: the sentences and paragraphs are short and read like a newspaper article.

Spend more time writing your press release than you spend on any other component of your information package. You don't have to write volumes on your work (only a couple of paragraphs is all you need), and for the cost of a first-class stamp you can get your message out to TV stations, newspapers, magazines, or any groups or individuals who would be interested in what you're doing.

LOOKING GOOD

Design some simple letterhead to copy your press release onto.

Type your press release, double-spaced. In the upper left-hand corner, type the date; below that, type FOR IMMEDIATE RELEASE. In the upper right-hand corner, type the name and phone numbers of contact info for your group.

Start with an eye-catching headline centered above the text.

Indent the first line of each paragraph at least half an inch.

Write in the third person; never use words like "I" and "myself."

Answer the five W's of journalism (who, what, when, where, and why) in your first few paragraphs.

Explain your boycott and your reasons for it. Use only facts, not opinions.

Include a few details about the company's actions and the detrimental effects of these activities.

End your press release with "-30-" or "####" or "END" at the bottom. Try to fit all your information on one page. If you must go to two pages, type "-MORE-" at the bottom of the first page and one of the ending symbols at the bottom of the second.

SPREADING THE WORD

Design a small information piece (about the size of a business card) about your boycott. List only the essential information—who the boycott is against and why, a list of their products, and your contact information. Make a few hundred copies and leave them on car windshields or attached to front doors.

Get on the Internet. Just one keyword, like "animals," "women," or "amnesty," can lead to literally tens of thousands of groups that would be natural allies for your cause. Even if you don't own a computer, there are lots of net set-ups in libraries and coffee shops.

Get students at your school involved. Form an on-campus political activist group or organize a letter-writing campaign. Get other schools involved, too, like the students who successfully boycotted StarKist Tuna. Get a teacher to help you make contact and organize a letter-writing campaign or some other protest.

Get your boycott listed in a directory like *Boycott Quarterly* (see the resources at the end of this book for more publications that list boycotts). Check out your local bookstore or music store for mainstream and alternative magazines that might publish your boycott details.

Leave copies of your press releases in coffee shops, music stores, libraries, laundromats, anywhere where people will read it. Make sure you have information posted in stores that are frequented by people who might support you—for example, if your boycott is against animal abuse, leave copies in pet shops. If it's about sexism, leave copies in women's bookstores.

Send your press release to all the local TV and radio stations in your area. Most of them will love the novelty of a young woman calling a boycott—you'll probably get lots of press.

Write a letter to the editor of a local newspaper. If they won't print your boycott info word for word, discuss the larger issues about why you called your boycott; this will allow you to sneak in a couple of words about your efforts. They may even print your contact information.

Think about how you're going to get the attention of the media (TV, radio, newspapers, and magazines). Start small at first—you probably won't get very far with a national network TV news show, but the local news might be interested in running a short story on a local boycott organized by young women.

Make a list of all the local news sources you can think of, and look through the yellow pages to come up with more. Once you have a phone number, get a contact name. If you don't have a real person's name on the envelope, your press release probably won't make it very far. The switchboard operator can usually tell you all you need to know to get your materials to the right place. "To whom should I send a press release? What is her/his fax number/mailing address, etc.? What is the editor's name (for magazines and newspapers)?"

Contact *Boycott Quarterly* next. If you provide all the essential information, they'll print your boycott and contact information in their directory. Don't stop there, though; there are lots of other magazines and newsletters that may publish your boycott info—mostly based on the subject of your boycott. For example, *The Bunny Hugger's Gazette* prints boycott information against companies who are accused of animal rights abuses. *Ms. Magazine* prints boycott information against companies who are accused of sexism and racism. Check out your local newsstand and find other magazines targeted to the groups you're trying to reach, then send them a press release.

Your possibilities for exposure are endless; all you need is a little creativity! Don't stop at traditional outlets like TV and radio stations, newspapers and magazines (although those are great places to start). Make at least 100 copies of your press release and hand them out to people, tack them up on bulletin boards, leave them in music stores and bookshops, or splatter your school with them. Eventually, you'll learn to target specific groups and people to get the best results.

While you're thinking of ways to spread the word even further, remember this: Instead of focusing your energy trying to change the minds of people who don't agree with you, spend your time finding and organizing the people who already do agree with you!

Hang in There

Organizing a boycott is really a lot easier than most people think. The hardest part isn't organizing it, but keeping it going once the initial momentum has worn off. You need to stay focused for your boycott to be long-lasting and effective. You may start off with a bang and then slow down a little, and you may even get dissatisfied by the slow progress of your boycott and be tempted to chuck it. But resist! A boycott can be a slow, steady process, but it can also change the world, and that is a proven fact.

Just be patient, get as much coverage as you can, and above all, keep everyone talking about your boycott for as long as it takes. Like Zach Lyons, publisher of *Boycott Quarterly*, says, "even a 1 percent shift in the market [YOU are the market] is devastating to any company."

Activism in America's Heartland

Acting for social justice isn't just a coastal thing, you know. Armed with her *grrl* tendencies and a growing concern for modern social injustice and general ill will, Jennifer Perry made it her business to educate the population of Grand Rapids, Michigan, about things like U.S. corporations' treatment of third-world workers, the plight of the homeless in our own country, women's and gay's rights, and the rights of workers everywhere.

One of Jennifer's more visible attempts has been to educate the students and citizens of Grand Rapids about the international boycott against Nike. As a junior at Aquinas College, she recently organized an on-campus educational effort to get some of the students involved with the boycott. "I had an informational table set up with Nike sweatshop details and a video with interviews of Indonesian workers," she says. "There was a letter to Phil Knight [Nike's CEO and, according to Forbes 400 Richest People in America, 1997, the 17th richest man in America, worth $5.4 billion], which I had supporters sign. I also had volunteers pass out leaflets to everyone as they entered the cafeteria building. By the end of the day I had the letter signed by 200 students and teachers. If the letter doesn't make too much of a difference, hopefully the community's awareness level has increased."

Jennifer's activism goes well beyond boycotts. She's also found some cool local groups with which she can work on a grassroots level—groups like the Institute for Global Education and the West Michigan Environmental Action Committee—and she became totally inspired to work for social justice after taking a service learning trip to Oaxaca, Mexico, with 13 other students from Aquinas. "We lived and worked among the poor for two weeks," she says, "and I must admit that the experience changed my life. I made a vow to return to the States and fight for justice for those who could not."

Jennifer says that her information table about the Nike boycott certainly caught people's attention. "One boy claimed, 'Man, this isn't my style.' When I informed him that he ought to make intelligent purchasing decisions, he claimed that Nike shoes are the only ones that fit him. Comments like this help keep me motivated to change things."

The key to successful activism? She says its all in your perspective. "Many college students live their happy little college lives and don't care about many issues outside of where they will go to party on Friday night. Everyone needs to leave his or her comfort zone. It's frustrating at times to get through to kids who don't know or care that their tennis shoes were made by the sweat of exploited Indonesian women."

Sample Initial Contact Letter

March 1, 1998

Mr. Joe Blow
Chief Executive Officer
Preteen Sexpot Jeans Company
123 Main Street
New York, NY 10001

Dear Mr. Blow:

I have been noticing for several years that your company uses very young looking girls in sexually suggestive poses in advertisements for your jeans. The facts and statistics regarding date rape and sexual aggression toward young women are well documented (please see attached fact sheets that I have enclosed). I'm sure you're also aware of the link between sexually suggestive images, such as your ads, and these alarming acts of aggression.

I urge you, as the president of the Preteen Sexpot Jeans Company, to do anything within your power to change the direction of your company's advertising campaign. Several of your competitors, Levi Strauss is one example, have extremely successful and well-known campaigns that do not rely on these tactics. It's the Preteen Sexpot Jean Company's responsibility to respect their customers (young women) and not continue portraying them in a demeaning way. As a concerned buyer who spends up to $150 per month on clothing, I urge you to reconsider your ad campaign and start using models who are not so young-looking, and not put in such sexually demeaning and suggestive poses.

Sincerely,

Your Name
Your Address

cc: Miss Myra Maines, Vice President—Marketing
        Mr. Hugh Jass, Vice President—Public Relations

Sample Second Letter

April 1, 1998

Mr. Joe Blow
Chief Executive Officer
Preteen Sexpot Jeans Company
123 Main Street
New York, NY 10001

Dear Mr. Blow:

I wrote to you on 3/1/98 (see attached copy) regarding the demeaning way in which you portray girls in advertisements for your jeans. As my first letter stated, this kind of sexist advertising has proven to have a very negative impact on young women's self-esteem and their safety, as the attached fact sheet on the link between sexual aggression and sexist images in the media shows. I gave you several examples of how your company could stop these practices and still compete in the market. However, I have not received a response from anyone in your company.

If you do not respond to my letter in 30 days, I am prepared to call for a boycott against your products, and against any magazines that carry your ads, as well as stores that carry your merchandise.

Sincerely,

Your Name
Your Address

cc: Miss Myra Maines, Vice President—Marketing
         Mr. Hugh Jass, Vice President—Public Relations

Sample Press Release

GIRLS AGAINST SEXISM
123 Main St.
Anytown, CA 94545

May 1, 1998   Contact: Your Name
FOR IMMEDIATE RELEASE   (510) 555-1212

GIRLS BOYCOTT JEANS COMPANY FOR SEXIST ADS

A group of Bay Area young women are calling an immediate boycott against the Preteen Sexpot Jeans Company for the company's practice of eroticizing young girls in their advertising.

"It's dangerous to portray young girls as the objects of sexual desire," says Amy Smith, organizer of Girls Against Sexism, a local activist group comprised of high school aged women who are committed to erasing sexism in media. "Images like these put all women, especially young women, at risk of sexual violence."

G.A.S.'s boycott includes all products manufactured by the Preteen Sexpot Jeans Company: Sexpot Jeans, Classic Sexpot, BabySoft Tees, and the entire Naughty! line of women's clothing. They will continue to boycott the company and to work to educate other women—and men—about the dangers of eroticizing young girls, until the company agrees to pull these ads and start using more mature-looking women in their ads.

G.A.S. also urges a boycott against local stores that carry the Preteen Sexpot Line and magazines in which their ads appear. For a complete list of local stores and national magazines that are supporting the Preteen Sexpot Jeans Company products, write or call G.A.S. at the address/phone above.

-END-

Chapter Three

FIND A GOVERNMENT INTERNSHIP

Starting your own country from scratch is hard work, and you need a lot of supplies. For one, your own continent (maybe just a big piece of unoccupied land would do, but you might as well get a whole continent). Plus, you need a national flag, a national song—oh, and those zillion other details like a social security system, health care for your citizens, some form of legal tender, an entire political system, and a brand new White House.

This is not exactly something you can squeeze in between your Feminist for World Reform meetings and all-nighters spent writing the next great American play. That's okay, because you really don't need your own country to launch a political campaign to change the world—it's much easier to concentrate on change from within. A smart way to become the political force you want to be is to create a kind of Frankenstein government. Take the parts that do work (like the democracy and voting thing), then take the parts that don't work very well (like military spending and social security), tweak them a little, and put the whole thing back together. With luck, what you'd end up with is no monster, but a monstrously

effective government that you were simply born to rule.

This is where your girlness comes in handy. Historically, our government has always been run by men. While we don't want to come right out and say that they've made a mess of things, in the back of every girl's mind has always been the sneaking suspicion that, given the chance, we might do better.

So you're not old enough to run for president, and you're not ready for the huge responsibility of being on the city council or the school board? No problem; there's a comfy in-between option here. There are lots of great internship, volunteer, and employment training programs for high school and college students in all branches of the government, from the spy vs. spy operations of the CIA to the partisan politics of the National Democratic or Republican committees. By working within these agencies you can not only observe government, you can become a part of it. Besides, a lot of these internships are cool jobs with cool organizations. You may think that you'll settle for just any old job, but sitting in the typing pool day after day or spending hours doing nothing but photocopying and filing gets dull fast. If the work, or the people you work for, are even somewhat interesting, that can keep you coming back every day. Can you think of any cooler job than working for NASA?

In addition to opportunities with federal agencies, you'll find information on some internships with a few non-governmental agencies. Although these organizations are not officially a branch of any government office, their work greatly affects American politics—the American Civil Liberties Union (ACLU) and the Feminist Majority are a couple of examples—and should definitely be right up there for consideration when you're deciding how to get your feet wet, politically speaking.

All these positions offer extremely valuable job training and benefits, opening doors for high school students, graduates, and college students that otherwise might be locked up tight. Some are designed to simply broaden your horizons and give you some inside perspective on your government, and others are designed to lead you into a permanent, full-time position once your internship is up and you've graduated from school. But even if you don't plan on a career with the Democratic National Committee or Environmental Protection Agency, you'll pick up valuable skills that will help you land the job you do want.

Why Intern When You Can Find a Permanent, Full-Time Job?

An internship with the government opens a door that at times is pretty hard to nudge. Civil service jobs are very competitive. Because the benefits and the opportunities can be so much better than in the private sector, there's usually a long list of qualified applicants for every opening. Plus, most agencies hire from within; that is, people who are already holding government jobs often get preference when another position opens up. Interning sort of brings you into the family, granting you distant cousin status or something like that, and allows you to get around some of those requirements.

An internship can also give your résumé a boost, which is especially helpful if you don't have much work experience. If you've been out looking for work lately, you know the catch: You need experience to get a job, but you can't get a job without experience. When you graduate, you'll probably find the job market to be a lot more competitive than you thought. Every year, hundreds of thousands of students graduate with a degree, believing they've got a ticket to instant employment. But what your counselor may not have told you is there could easily be over a hundred applicants for every job listed in the newspaper, and employers will be looking for any edge you might have over the competition.

Having an internship on your résumé, especially one in a related industry or position—or one that smacks of serving your country—could put you on the inside track.

Some internships pay nothing; some offer a pretty good salary, depending on who you're working for and what you're doing. Most federal internships offer at least a small stipend to cover bus or train fare and occasional meals. While it would be nice to make as much money as possible, don't choose an internship based solely on the wages. The experience and contacts that the position could give you would probably be way more valuable than a few extra bucks.

Agencies can pick and choose from a pretty large pool of qualified candidates for most internship positions. Some things make it easier to get an internship than a job, though: for example, potential employers won't be looking for work experience on your résumé, but they will be looking for a real interest in the industry. Most seek applicants with related coursework, like foreign studies or economics, on their résumés.

How Do I Apply?

Once you find an agency where you might like to work, contact their office for information on how to apply for an internship. Most have their own application procedures, but generally require some of the same information (see box).

Most agencies require that students apply well in advance of the start date; for example, if the position is open to high school seniors, you may be asked to apply during your junior year. If you think you

> ## HAVE YOUR PAPERS READY
>
> **A letter of introduction,** stating who you are and why you're interested in that particular internship.
>
> **A completed application,** which the agency will provide.
>
> **School transcripts.**
>
> **Résumé** (you may not need to provide a history of your work experience, but be prepared and write one in case you need it).
>
> **References** (personal and/or professional).

may be interested in interning for the government, do your research and request application packages and information as soon as possible. Some of the application periods are very specific, for example, in the "second semester of your senior year," so don't procrastinate or you could miss out on a really cool opportunity.

The sampling of internships here is just that, a sampling. There are lots more to be found with a little research and digging. A couple of excellent places to start are *Peterson's Internships,* an annual directory of private, non-profit, and federal internships, and *Federal Jobs: The Ultimate Guide* by Morgan Goldenkoft (ARCO Publishing, 1997), covering almost every agency of the federal government. Even if you don't discover the perfect opportunity in these books, you can always call your local elected official and ask for help—in fact, your local elected official may have an opening in his or her own office.

Internship Listings

American Civil Liberties Union

American Civil Liberties Union
c/o Internship Coordinator
ACLU National Headquarters
132 W. 43rd St.
New York, NY 10036
(212) 944-9800

Even though it's not an agency of the government, the American Civil Liberties Union (ACLU) has as much to do with protecting the rights of American citizens as the U.S. State Department does, maybe even more. If you happen to believe in the Constitution and what it stands for, you know that the work the ACLU does is essential in guaranteeing American rights. However, the ACLU is disliked by some groups because they're just as quick to defend unpopular causes (like the rights of prisoners) as they are to defend more accepted concerns (like children's rights). Some of the issues the ACLU handles, and projects that interns may work on, are AIDS discrimination, arts censorship, gay/lesbian rights, reproductive freedom, women's rights, rights in the workplace, privacy and technology issues, capital punishment, church-state conflicts, and immigration. No matter where you stand politically, an internship with the ACLU is a great way to learn about our constitutional rights.

Interns are paired with ACLU attorneys and help with just about everything, from administrative tasks like filing and typing to research for trial preparation and preparing applications for political asylum.

American Foreign Service Association

American Foreign Service Association
c/o Internship Coordinator
2101 E St. NW
Washington, DC 20037
(202) 944-5519
http://www.afsa.org

The American Foreign Service Association (AFSA) represents tens of thousands of active and retired foreign service employees of a few federal agencies (including the U.S. Department of State) in labor disputes and negotiations on working conditions, rights and privileges, assignments, and retiree pensions and benefits. In addition to representing foreign service employees, AFSA also works to promote and advance the diplomatic profession.

You'd think that since the job is all about foreign service, you'd get to work in some cool place like Paris or Brussels. However, most internships with AFSA are served in their Washington headquarters. AFSA also offers internships with the *Foreign Service Journal,* a monthly magazine produced by AFSA for its members. Positions with the journal are open to students majoring in journalism, foreign affairs, business, marketing/advertising, or political science. Duties include writing, editing, and designing and implementing a marketing campaign.

All positions require students who can write and communicate well, can work independently with little supervision, and can talk comfortably to a diverse group of people, from grassroots organizers to elected officials. Computer skills are desired, and Web experience is a plus.

Central Intelligence Agency

Central Intelligence Agency
c/o Recruitment Center
P.O. Box 12727, Dept. STU-I
Arlington, VA 22209-8727
http://www.odci.gov/cia

"The red cat is weeping in the garden. Repeat: The red cat is weeping in the garden" (that's code for something like "Women should be ruling the world"). If you're into espionage, this is about as cool a job as you could get. If planting bugs, deploying operatives, and trading secrets—all the things that go into collecting, processing, and analyzing information that might have an impact on national security—appeals to you, you might find your niche at the CIA.

The CIA Undergraduate Scholar Program is for high school seniors who are enrolled (or planning to enroll) in a four-year college after graduation. You must major in computer science, electrical engineering, economics, a non-romance foreign language (meaning they prefer Russian, Slavic, and Middle Eastern languages to French or Italian), or foreign studies. Although the program is primarily intended for minority students and students with a disability, anyone who meets the minimum requirements is eligible.

Interns earn an annual salary plus up to $15,000 a year for tuition, fees, books, and supplies for college. They work during summer break at a CIA facility but are required to maintain full-time college student status while enrolled in the program. Participants also must agree to work for the CIA after graduation from college for a time period equal to 150 percent of the length of the internship. The CIA pays for

TRENCH COAT NOT REQUIRED

Want to intern with the CIA? You must:

be enrolled in a four-year college

be a U.S. citizen

successfully complete medical and security screening, including a polygraph (lie-detector) test

maintain at least a 2.75 GPA (preference is given to those with a 3.0 or better)

be able to work in the Washington, DC, area

all transportation between school and the Washington, DC, area, and they also provide a housing allowance.

The CIA Student Trainee Program is for high school graduates who are enrolled in college. In this program, interns alternate schooling with employment with the CIA; that is, they work a semester, go to school a semester, work a semester, and so on.

Interns must spend a minimum of three semesters or four quarters on the job with the CIA prior to graduation from college. It's a chance for students and the CIA to check each other out (although they are probably way more adept at this than you are!); students can decide if they like working for the CIA without committing to a future with them, and the CIA can decide if someone has the potential to become a permanent employee. The typical starting salary for students in this program is $19,421–$21,641 per year (as of the writing of this book). The best time to apply is the fall of your sophomore year.

U.S. Department of State

U.S. Department of State
Office of Recruitment
Student Programs
P.O. Box 9317
Arlington, VA 22219

The State Department is one of this country's oldest federal agencies—established in 1781 by our first president, George Washington—and they've been keeping an eye on U.S. interests in foreign affairs for over 200 years. That could mean coming to the rescue of an American citizen who's come to find herself on the business end of a foreign police department's wrath, or monitoring the sale of nuclear weapons by U.S. companies to foreign-owned businesses and governments.

The State Department represents U.S. interests by maintaining over 250

MORE FOREIGN AFFAIRS

Issuing visas for entry into and passports for exit out of the U.S.

Negotiating treaties and trade agreements with foreign governments.

Fighting drug trafficking into the U.S.

Aiding foreign nations in establishing their own political and economic systems.

Helping the White House formulate and enforce U.S. foreign policy.

embassies and consulates in foreign countries all over the world. While there are lots of internships available right here on U.S. soil, there are also opportunities for student interns to travel and work in other countries (most overseas opportunities are available to undergrads and graduate students only). Interns working at offices in Washington, DC, and other locations inside the U.S. must provide their own housing; interns abroad are usually given free housing, sometimes in embassy apartments, sometimes within the embassy itself. Over 900 students are accepted into service with the State Department every year.

The State Department has three student programs: the co-op program (where students alternate school with paid academic-year and summer internships), the summer clerical program (where students work primarily in administrative support during the summer), and the student volunteer program (which offers a wide variety of unpaid positions every year).

Interns and volunteers must be at least 16 years old and must usually maintain a minimum GPA to serve. There are no other specific requirements as far as experience or knowledge for most positions; however, a working knowledge of Russian, Polish, Rumanian, Hungarian, Czech, Slovak, and Bulgarian languages gives you a distinct advantage. Interns must also be U.S. citizens, possess excellent writing skills, and have a true interest in foreign affairs.

You could find yourself sorting passport documents, collecting and delivering cables and telegrams from foreign embassies, or answering letters from the public. Although administrative work is a big part of all internships, many interns find themselves being asked to do things like conduct background research and prepare briefing papers. As with all internships, the difficulty and depth of your assignment depends on what type of experience you have and what level of education you've completed (there are programs for high school students all the way up to graduate students).

Even with the most mundane tasks like filing and typing, there is a level of intrigue in all government internships. For example, interns with the State Department are required to complete an orientation where they learn more about State Department missions, take the oath of office, and undergo a security briefing. Then they're shown how to open a safe (where sensitive documents are placed every night at quitting time).

Environmental Protection Agency

Environmental Protection Agency
c/o NNEMS National Program Manager
U.S. EPA (1707)
401 M St. SW
Washington, DC 20460
(202) 260-4965

Since its creation in 1970 by Richard Nixon, the Environmental Protection Agency (EPA) has labored to improve both the environment as a whole and the quality of life for every creature on Earth. As part of these efforts, the EPA created the National Network for Environmental Management Studies (NNEMS), a program that introduces students to jobs in environmental preservation.

The work is about as varied as the types of environmental issues that our planet copes with every day: air and water pollution, hazardous waste management, and the preservation of oceans and land are just a few. Specific duties for interns range from very tame administrative and clerical support that most offices need, to investigation of water and air pollution, to helping research and write reports and briefings (there's a lot of research work, so interns have to be motivated and able to work alone for long periods of time). Most of the research is very intensive, so a background in conservation or earth sciences will help.

There's also occasional travel, and all expenses are paid. Internships last 10 to 14 weeks, and almost 80 percent are full time during the summer months; the remainder are either full- or part-time during the rest of the year. One-year grants are sometimes offered. Positions with the EPA pay between $4000-$7000 for the duration of service.

Opportunities are available in the Washington headquarters, as well as at all EPA locations nationwide: Boston, New York, Philadelphia, Atlanta, Chicago, Dallas, Kansas City, Denver, San Francisco, and Seattle. Positions are also available with the Office of Research and Development at labs in Research Triangle Park, North Carolina; Duluth, Minnesota; Ann Arbor, Michigan; Las Vegas, Nevada; Ada, Oklahoma; Corvallis, Oregon; Gulf Breeze, Florida; and Athens, Georgia.

Federal Reserve System, Board of Governors

Federal Reserve
c/o Stay in School Program Coordinator
20th and C St. NW, Mail Stop 129
Washington, DC 20551
(202) 452-3880

Basically, if it has to do with money, it's under the jurisdiction of the Federal Reserve. If you're planning a career in high finance or just love the stuff, this is the internship that makes your world go 'round. The Stay in School Program is a way for students interested in business or finance to get a taste of big time bean-counting. It's not a full-time program, so it allows you to work and complete your studies at the same time.

The Federal Reserve's internship requirements are a bit less restrictive than those of some other federal agencies. You must be at least 16 years old (anyone under 18 must have a work permit); be enrolled full-time in an accredited school and working toward a degree, diploma, or certificate; take at least 9 credits each semester; and maintain a C average while employed. Most of the assignments are clerical—typing, filing, and answering phones—but they'll consider any interests that are reflected by your class schedule. The length of assignments varies, but the maximum you can serve is four years.

Interns work 12 to 20 hours a week during school and up to 40 hours during the summer. Students working for the Federal Reserve are not eligible for health or life insurance. You can earn sick leave and vacation pay during the school year; if you work only during the summer, you can just earn sick leave.

The Feminist Majority

The Feminist Majority
801 W. 3rd St., Ste. 1
Los Angeles, CA 90048
(213) 651-0495

1600 Wilson Blvd., Ste. 801
Arlington, VA 22209
(703) 522-2214
http://www.feminist.org

Founded in 1987 by Peg Yorkin and former NOW (National Organization for Women) president Eleanor Smeal, the original mission of the Feminist Majority was to encourage and support more women to run for office. Although this is still a priority for them, they now tackle other issues relevant to women and girls, like the fight against sexual harassment and the struggle for equal rights and equal pay. They've also launched other pro-women campaigns like Empowering Women and Rock for Choice.

Although the Feminist Majority isn't a federal agency, their work has a great impact on the political culture of this nation; if you're interested in a career in politics or women's issues, this would be a great place to get a feel for the kind of work you'd be doing and the kind of issues that you would face. Interns have monitored press conferences and congressional hearings; analyzed political policies as they relate to women's issues; and handled campaigns like the Feminization of Power, which works to place feminists in positions of leadership on campus or in public office. Interns also research and write papers. Your assignment will depend on their needs at the time you're available, and on your own particular interests.

Opportunities are available for part- and full-time work; the duration of positions varies from eight weeks to a full year. There's no pay for these positions, but the experience and networking skills you'll gain are extremely valuable, especially if you are interested in women's studies.

National Aeronautics and Space Administration

NASA
c/o Higher Education Branch
Mail Code FEH
Washington, DC 20546

So you don't yet qualify to be an astronaut-in-training? That's okay. You haven't yet conquered this world; there will be plenty of time to extend your sphere of power beyond our home planet. As you might guess, there are some very cool internships with the National Aeronautics and Space Administration (NASA), and so it should go without saying that these are some of the most sought after (meaning competitive) internships going. But it's not all learning to moonwalk; as you also might have guessed, internships with NASA are more academic, primarily in math, science, computers, and engineering (not many opportunities for those majoring in liberal arts).

Ever since we took those first tentative steps on the moon, we've been absolutely fascinated with what lies just beyond our reach. Interest in NASA flatlined a little in the eighties and early nineties, but ever since they brought back live pictures from Mars, it's a race for the galaxy once again (a race, I might add, that any girl could win). Think of NASA programs like one giant science

fair: most focus on robotics, earth sciences (biology, geology, environmental science), aerodynamics, biomedicine, biotechnology, space propulsion, and satellite communications.

The type of work an intern is likely to do depends mostly on the specialty of that particular site. For example, at the Goddard site, where the Hubble space telescope was developed, interns work in atmospheric and hydrospheric sciences. One of the most popular internship sites is the Johnson Space Center ("mission

---

MINIMUM REQUIREMENTS FOR THE NASA ASTRONAUT CANDIDATE PROGRAM

you must be between 58.5 and 76 inches in height

you must pass a rigorous physical exam that will take your body through G forces you never even knew existed

you must hold a B.A. degree in science or engineering

you must have 3 years of related work experience

Sure, it's possible (but really, finding three years of work experience related to moon tripping might be tough). On the other hand....

MINIMUM REQUIREMENTS FOR THE NASA INTERNSHIP PROGRAM

you must be 16 years old

you must meet minimum GPA requirements (that, thankfully, have nothing at all to do with the rotation of the planets) control" for piloted spaceflights and where astronauts are trained). There, interns have worked on projects like learning how to grow crops in space, dealing with problems of anti-gravity, and helping prepare experiments for space flight.

Although competition for a NASA internship is pretty hot, they offer a pool of over 200 programs from which to choose (some targeted for specific groups, like minorities and women); and they end up choosing a lot of people. Just one facility can employ up to 300 interns. Work is available at 10 facilities across the country.

In NASA's programs, you work hard and you play hard. Unlike a lot of other agencies, NASA really goes the extra light year to make interns feel welcome. They organize social get-togethers like dinner receptions, outings, and biking trips (you can even use the gym where one is available). An internship with NASA pays in more than just the warm-and-fuzzies: you can make up to $400 a week.

Political Parties

The Democratic National Committee
430 S. Capitol St. SE
Washington, DC 20003
(202) 863-8000
http://www.democrats.org/

Republican National Committee
310 1st St. SE
Washington, DC 20003
(202) 863-8560
http://www.rnc.org

The Reform Party
4500 Connecticut Ave. NW, #408
Washington, DC 20008
(202) 728-3935
http://www.reformparty.org

The Green Party
P.O. Box 100
Blodgett Mills, NY 13738-0100
(607) 756-4211
http://www.greens.org/

The Libertarian Party
P.O. Box 12075
Washington, DC 20005
(202) 462-4390

If you're going to work within our current system of government, sooner or later you're going to have to align yourself with one political party or another. Your two most obvious choices are those original political party animals, the Republicans and Democrats. In the spirit of true political groundbreaking, feel free to offer your services to any political party that strikes your particular fancy—whether you're going to lead the next generation of Nader's Raiders with the Green Party, or you're just another Jo for Ross Perot's Reform Party.

You can find party offices just about everywhere across the country; some are small, with only a couple of volunteer workers, and some are large enough that they have a staff of several people, including paid interns. You'll find most of the positions at headquarters, but even if you live on the West Coast, don't let a few thousand miles stand between you and your political dreams of grandeur. Call or write any of the headquarters listed on this page; they'll be able to direct you to an office close to your home.

Unlike many of the other internship positions listed in this chapter, these positions are unpaid (you know how it is, political bigwigging costs big bucks!), but they can give you valuable experience, not to mention adding a few gold stars to your résumé.

As far as the type of assignments you can expect, they vary wildly: at one office you could find yourself working in the legal offices; at another, you could snag a job dealing with media and press outlets or helping in the planning of the next national convention.

U.S. Secret Service

U.S. Secret Service
Personnel Division
1800 G St. NW, Rm. 912
Washington, DC 20223
(202) 435-5800

The Secret Service has a strange combination of responsibilities. Created by President Abraham Lincoln as an arm of the Treasury Department, the Secret Service's initial responsibility was to stop the rampant spread of counterfeit money at the close of the Civil War (between one-third and one-half of all U.S. paper money in circulation at the time was counterfeit), and monitor other political hot potatoes like the Teapot Dome oil scandal and government land fraud. In 1901, after President William McKinley was assassinated, Congress directed the Secret Service to provide protection to the president and his family. Today, the Secret Service performs both functions.

The Secret Service has several cool internship programs for students. Their Cooperative Education Program gives full-time students the chance to participate in a work-study program that is consistent with their field of study, or major.

Some of the positions available with the Secret Service are accountant and

---

SECRET AGENT GIRL

Want to get in with the Secret Service? You must:

be a U.S. citizen

be enrolled full time in an accredited education program

be enrolled in your school's Cooperative Education Program

maintain a 3.0 GPA

be enrolled in a field of study relevant to the position you're applying

submit to and pass a urinalysis screening for drug use

pass background investigation

pass a polygraph (lie-detector) test (in some cases)

---

budget analyst, computer specialist, criminal research specialist, electronic engineer, intelligence research analyst, management analyst, personnel management analyst, telecommunications specialist, and visual information specialist.

Working in the Coop Education Program, you'll most likely begin with clerical and administrative tasks; however, the level of involvement, difficulty, and sensitivity of assignment is progressive. The goal of the Secret Service's Cooperative Education Program isn't simply to provide a way to make some extra money, earn education credits, or give a student a summer job, it's to find people they can bring into full-time positions after their graduation.

Interns work 16 to 32 hours per week during the school year, but can work up to 40 hours a week during breaks. Student interns also get life and health insurance, sick pay and vacation leave, holiday pay, and awards and promotions. Positions last about two years. The salary interns make depends on their level of education.

Unlike other agencies, the Secret Service requires that students in this program sign a working agreement prior to beginning the program, stating the student's work and education schedule, program responsibilities, and requirements for becoming a full-time federal employment after graduation.

PART TWO

MANIPULATE THE ECONOMY

Rule number one in the great rule book of How to Be a Happy Person clearly states that money can't buy happiness. That said, remember (this isn't exactly a rule, but more like a footnote) that the world you're bent on dominating is a capitalist one. What that means is that money can buy lots of the things you'll need as a political and social force, whether your goal is to fund a new national day-care system for children of working parents, bankroll your new federal forest revegetation plan, or just buy a cool used car to tool around and visit your loyal constituency.

Searching for a meaning of life beyond $100 sneakers or a trendy $50 bottle of cologne is admirable, even essential, if you're to find true happiness, and a burning desire to improve your world is probably one of the things that led you to this whole world domination thing in the first place. But there's nothing wrong with developing a healthy respect for income (and learning how to increase yours), because when you start to see all the important things that money can buy, you'll wish you had more of it lying around in your savings account. Having a fat surplus of that crinkly green stuff will help you make change (no pun intended) that much faster.

How much easier would it be to build a no-kill animal shelter in your community if you had a few hundred thousand dollars laying around?

How simple would it be to make sure that no child ever goes to bed hungry again if you had an unlimited cash reserve with which to pay for hot meals?

With more money than you could count, can you even imagine how easily you could ensure that every woman, no matter what her economic status, is able to make her dreams come true through higher education?

Even if your goals are somewhat more personal—saving for college so you can become the premier rocket scientress of the twenty-first century, or taking a well-deserved vacation to some sunny spot before you tackle the social problems in your own community—learning how to manage your wealth is pretty important, especially for girls.

> Part of growing up is making your own decisions, right? You shouldn't give up the right to make choices just because you think that learning how to manage your money is hard, or boring, or both.

Most girls are never taught how to manage their finances. Many are never even taught the basics of economics; consequently, lots of women never grasp how easy it can be to achieve financial independence. They spend their lives relying on others to tell them when to spend, when to save, what to buy, and what to do without. Without the knowledge of how to make and manage money, many women end up living from paycheck to paycheck, never being able to afford the things they want or need and feeling more like slaves than employees. Being at the mercy of others who hold all the knowledge is a drag; girls of today want no part of that.

Money-making is no longer about lemonade stands, baby-sitting, or joining the typing pool. While it's true that women still make about 25 percent less than men working the same jobs, it's also true that the doors to some opportunities for women are flying open! This is a great time to be a girl—and really, with you at the helm, your world can only get better. Practice with your own bankroll. Learn how to turn a buck, then learn how to turn that buck into a few hundred more. Maybe right now you're working in small denominations, but master the principles of finance and investment, and before you know it, dollar bills will be bearing your geeky senior photo.

Whether you want to start your own business, find satisfaction building a successful career out of work you love to do, or forget that whole nine-to-five thing altogether and become a lioness of Wall Street, other girls have been there, done that, and paved the way. Following in their footsteps is a good way to start, and when you're ready to branch out and take your own path, you'll have all the skills, the tools—and most important, the courage—to make sure your path is not so rocky.

Chapter Four

WORK IN A NONTRADITIONAL JOB

For decades, it seemed like the only job opportunities available to girls entering the workplace right out of high school were secretary and waitress—oh, and housewife. And the only trade school opportunities for girls were in the stereotypical professions like hairdresser or beautician. Not that there's anything particularly wrong with any of those choices, but these few options don't give girls much choice. What about the girl who's always wanted to be an auto mechanic? Or an electrician? What about the girl who wants to build things—like houses—with her hands? And work outdoors?

After decades of being denied a fair chance to work in the blue-collar trades—at jobs like welder, carpenter, or mechanic—women are beginning to make their presence known in these and many other areas. Every year, more and more community-based organizations, schools, and private companies offer workshops to teach girls the skills they need to earn a living in a nontraditional career. The federal government has become involved, too, with dozens of programs designed to get women into a skilled profession that will provide security, income, and satisfaction. And while

women were once sorely unrepresented in blue-collar unions, there are now local and national organizations dedicated to improving opportunities and working conditions for women in a variety of positions.

I had always wanted to be an aircraft mechanic, but when I graduated from high school, the only opportunities I could find (outside of college, which didn't really appeal to me) were of the secretarial variety (99 percent of secretaries are women).[1] I never got used to pushing paper and fetching coffee, and so I spent the first few years out of high school skipping from job

47

to job. My parents and my bosses may have thought that I was lazy or couldn't focus, but I just wasn't interested in traditional "women's work."

That's not to imply that working in the trades is like some kind of stroll through a rose garden. It can be really hard work, and most of the time this work is physical, so you're not just using your brain, but your body as well. Plus, women are still facing problems like sexual harassment and unequal treatment (not to mention unequal pay). But over the past twenty years or so, the climate has slowly improved. Don't just wait for some other girl to change things, though, because the only way things will continue to get better is if we flood these industries with girls like you. Imagine, if half the workforce in your local carpenter's union were female, it would be pretty hard to ignore issues like child care leave, sexual harassment by peers, and disparity in wages.

What is Nontraditional?

The federal government defines "nontraditional" as any occupation in which women comprise 25 percent or less of the workforce, so the categories of jobs that could be classified as nontraditional are varied. A lot of people think nontraditional jobs are only in the trades (like construction, auto repair, and masonry), but nontraditional also includes professional specialties like engineering, forestry, and math and science occupations. Most trades jobs start at $7 to $9 an hour but can go all the way up to $20 to $30 an hour or more.

The opportunities are out there, and getting better all the time. These are good

> 2.3% of airline pilots are women
> 3.3% of mechanics are women
> 1.9% of construction workers are women[2]

jobs. They pay well, and—as lots of men have discovered—working with your hands can be immensely satisfying.

A lot of people think that the term "blue collar" means unskilled, but that holds about as much water as the misconception that girls can't do math. Certified plumber or electrician training often takes years, and usually combines classroom instruction with on-the-job training. Often, there's an extended period of apprenticeship.

The skills a girl learns while apprenticing are extremely valuable, and not just in that field. There's more to being a carpenter than just slamming a hammer; you need math skills and the ability to read a blueprint. In addition to knowing what kind of tools and materials are required on a certain job, it would help if you knew something about the culture of the environment where you'll be working. For that reason, all apprenticeships and training programs geared toward women cover a lot of areas.

Assessment of abilities and aptitude: It's important to get a good idea of your starting point—that is, at what skill level you're already at, before determining what kind of training you need. In some programs, the most basic literacy skills are taught to get a girl up to speed.

Physical conditioning: Any auto mechanic will tell you that, in her profession, a strong back is essential. Sitting on your behind all day isn't what trade jobs are about. Tradespeople need to be in excellent physical shape, so this area of training stresses nutrition, stamina, and strength.

THE THREE STAGES OF TRAINING

Pre-apprentice: A pre-apprentice spends eight to ten weeks in a classroom, learning about everything from how to handle sexual harassment on the job to the different names and uses of specific tools. A student is ready to become an apprentice once she has completed a pre-apprenticeship program. Most pre-apprenticeships charge tuition, but the fee can often be reduced by grants, scholarships, and financial aid.

Apprentice: Consider this paid, on-the-job training. An apprenticeship can last several years (from two to five), for good reason; this is where you become an expert. Apprentices work under the guidance of a highly skilled, experienced person (called a journeyworker) to learn more complex tasks related to the career. When you finish your apprenticeship, you get a certificate of completion that basically says you're a chick who knows her stuff.

Journeyworker: At this level, you've had years of instruction and training. You're no longer green—you're certified, skilled, and experienced. With time, you'll become a veteran journeyworker and maybe you will guide and mentor young, unskilled apprentices, the same way someone guided you.

Self-esteem: Unfortunately, this is something most of us lack, to some degree. Most girls grow up believing that these kinds of jobs are for men only, and if you want to work with a hammer all day or drive a forklift, there must be something wrong with you. Forget that! You know that you don't belong in the typing pool, and here's where you'll learn that you can achieve anything a man can achieve, and probably more.

Assertiveness training: Since the trades we're talking about are dominated by men, it's important for you to know how to handle yourself on a job site. This kind of training helps you learn to deal with things like sexual harassment on the job and the isolation a girl can experience working in a male-dominated industry.

Job hunting techniques and placement assistance: Finding a trades job isn't anything like finding an office job, where you would just cruise the want ads and send out a bunch of résumés. Most jobs are found through unions and other member organizations, so you need to know how to make important contacts for finding a job when you're ready, and how to apply for work.

Literacy skills: We all know that reading and writing are important, but here's where all those math classes pay off. Maybe all you need is a review, or maybe you need some serious tutoring; regardless of what level of instruction you require, your instructor will make sure you get it.

Hands-on training: How much fun can it be to bang some nails into a plank or screw around with some wires on a telephone pole? Lots! In addition, courses include the basics like names of tools and how they're used, work site slang, and stuff like that (thankfully, the skill of wolf whistling at passing women isn't taught here).

Emotional support: You can gets lot of different kinds of support, including emotional, once you finish training and enter the workforce. Some programs also offer mentoring programs, where a newly trained woman is guided by a more experienced mentor.

Eligibility requirements for pre-apprenticeship and full apprenticeship programs vary, but few have strict criteria. Plus, many programs focus on disadvantaged or at-risk women, high school drop-outs, displaced homemakers, single mothers, women on federal assistance programs, and women of color. So regardless of your background, chances are pretty good you'll find a place that's right for you.

What's really great about all of these programs is that, by gearing the classes toward women, they've put a whole new spin on the training. These aren't just "guy" classes with a few lessons on self-esteem and what it's like to be a woman. These programs have been specifically structured to ensure that women in the classes have an equal chance to succeed in the trades. The mechanical and hands-on training is the same training that a man would get, but the other parts—the counseling, assertiveness training, building a network of support—is all about being a girl. It's not about pretending you're a man.

Contacts

For assistance in getting into an apprenticeship program for women, or to learn more about a particular occupation, contact one of these offices.

Arkansas
Women's Project
2224 Main St.
Little Rock, AR 72206
(501) 372-5113

California
Gender Equity Program
City College of San Francisco
Campuses Division
33 Gough St.
San Francisco, CA 94103
(415) 241-2308

Colorado
Northeast Women's Center (NEWC)
2247 Oneida St.
Denver, CO 80207
(303) 355-3486

Connecticut
Preliminary Awareness of
Construction Trades Training
(PACTT)
c/o National Association of Women
in Construction (NAWIC)
125 Silas Deane Hwy.
Wethersfield, CT 06109
(203) 224-0666

Delaware
Womanpower
YWCA of New Castle County
233 King St.
Wilmington, DE 19801

District of Columbia
Wider Opportunities for Women, Inc.
(WOW)
1325 G St. NW, LL
Washington, DC 20005
(202) 638-3143

Florida
New Options Center
5603 34th St. W.
Bradenton, FL 34210
(813) 751-7922

Equity c/o Dade County Public
Schools
Robert Morgan Voc. Tech. Institute
18180 SW 122nd Ave.
Miami, FL 33177

Illinois
Pre-apprenticeship Tutorial
Chicago Women in Trades (CWIT)
37 South Ashland
Chicago, IL 60603
(312) 942-1444

Indiana
Gender Equity Projects
Smith Research Center, Rm. 126
2805 E. 10th St.
Bloomington, IN 47405
(812) 855-8104

Iowa
New Horizons Program
Iowa Western Community College
2700 College Rd., Box 4-C
Council Bluffs, IA 51502

Pre-Vocational Training Program
University of Iowa
C107 Seashore Hall
Iowa City, IA 52242
(319) 335-0560

Kansas
Career Assistance Network
Topeka YWCA
225 W. 12th St.
Topeka, KS 66612
(913) 233-1750

Louisiana
Electro-Mechanical Training Program
for Women
Governor's Office of Women's Services
P.O. Box 94095
Baton Rouge, LA 70804
(504) 342-2715

Maine
Women Unlimited
1250 Turner St.
Auburn, ME 04210
(207) 786-5259

Michigan
Secondary Sex Equity Program
Michigan Department of Education
P.O. Box 30009
Lansing, MI 48909
(517) 373-3388

Minnesota
Minnesota Women in the Trades
550 Rice St.
Women's Building
St. Paul, MN 55103
(612) 228-9955

Missouri
New Horizons
Non Traditional Careers
Mineral Area College
P.O. Box 1000
Flat River, MO 63601
(314) 431-4593

New Jersey
Gloucester Cty. Voc.-Tech. School
P.O. Box 186
Tanyard Rd., Deptford Township
Sewell, NJ 08080-0186
(609) 468-1445

Training for Trades & Technology
Bergen County Technical Institute
Career & Life Counseling Center
280 Hackensack Ave.
Hackensack, NJ 07601
(201) 343-6000, ext. 270

New York
Nontraditional Jobs for Women
(NTJW)
3940 Hickory St.
Seaford, NY 11783
(516) 485-5413

North Carolina
Sex Equity Program
Wider Opportunities for Women
Resource Center
c/o Central Piedmont Comm. College
1101 Elizabeth Ave. at Old Kings Dr.
P.O. Box 35009
Charlotte, NC 28202
(704) 342-6532

Ohio
Hard Hatted Women
P.O. Box 93384
Cleveland, OH 44101
(216) 961-4449

Pennsylvania
Tradeswomen of Philadelphia/Women
in Non-Traditional Work, Inc.
(TOP/WIN, Inc.)
3001 Dickinson St.
Philadelphia, PA 19146
(215) 551-1808

Rhode Island
Equity in Career Options and Ed.
Community College of Rhode Island
1762 Louisquisset Pike
Lincoln, RI 02865-4585

Tennessee
Coal Employment Project (CEP)
17 Emory Pl.
Knoxville, TN 37917
(412) 883-4927

Women in Trades (WIT)
YWCA of Greater Memphis
1044 Mississippi Blvd.
Memphis, TN 38126
(901) 942-4653

Texas
Vocational Equity Programs
c/o Texas Regional Service Centers
9600 Sims Dr.
El Paso, TX 79925-7225
(915) 595-5714

Vermont
No. New England Tradeswomen, Inc.
1 Prospect St.
St. Johnsbury, VT 05819
(802) 748-3308

Washington
Apprenticeship & Nontraditional
Employment for Women (ANEW)
P.O. Box 2490
Renton, WA 98056
(206) 235-2212

West Virginia
Women and Employment, Inc.
1217 Lee St.
Charleston, WV 25301
(304) 345-1298

Wisconsin
Women's Resource Bureau
Box 518
Rhinelander, WI 54501
(715) 369-4477

Wyoming
Expanding Your Horizons
c/o Laramie County School District
2810 House Ave.
Cheyenne, WY 82001
(307) 771-2216

Job Descriptions

Aircraft Mechanic

My personal favorite. I always thought it would be rad to be an aircraft mechanic and work on engines nearly as big as my house. Repairing a Volkswagen engine is cool, there's no doubt about that, but speaking as someone who likes to do things in a big way, it always seemed to me that a job that requires a ladder, scaffold, or hoist is just too cool.

What would I do?

Basically, this job involves the maintenance and repair of aircraft. Maintenance checks are done at regular intervals, based on things like the number of flight hours since the plane was last inspected. Mechanics also perform preflight checks to make sure everything is in good working condition—testing electrical wiring, landing gear, brakes, air conditioning, flight instruments, and any of the dozens of other functions and systems that have to be looked over before a plane can be given the green light to go. Mechanics who specialize in repairs perform diagnostics (based on input from the pilot) and then make necessary repairs. Because

an airplane has so many parts and systems, a mechanic could be working on a complex electrical system one day, and find herself elbow deep in a plane's hydraulics the next.

Airframe mechanics are certified to work on any part of the airplane, except the instruments, powerplants (engine), and propellers. They will check the fuselage (the body) and the wings for cracks and other problems, and make repairs. Powerplant mechanics are certified to work on engines and to do some work on propellers. Repairers (also called technicians) work on instruments and propellers. A&P mechanics (who have the skills of both airframe and powerplant mechanics) can work on any part of the plane.

What are my working conditions?

Less than glamorous, as you might expect (leave those press-on nails at home). Most mechanics work at or near the airport, usually in hangars, but sometimes outdoors, and sometimes in nasty weather, especially if they are repair specialists. There's a lot of heavy lifting, so you have to be in good physical condition. Because a lot of the repairs are needed immediately, and because the work that airplane mechanics perform is so critical, there can be a lot of stress, so drama queens need not apply. You also need to be able to handle a lot of responsibility and be able to think on your feet. The training you'll get is pretty technical, so it helps if you have an aptitude for math. It goes without saying that you should not have a fear of heights.

Over 60 percent of airline mechanics work for private airlines, like United or American; about 20 percent work for airline assembly companies (like Lockheed or Boeing); and 15 to 20 percent work for the federal government. The rest work for companies that maintain their own air fleet, or for small, private repair companies. Hours are pretty standard—a forty-hour work week (with some overtime) in eight-hour shifts.

How much training is required?

It takes some pretty intensive training to become an FAA-certified mechanic; this isn't exactly the kind of thing you can pick up in shop class or in your driveway, tinkering with your own machinery.

Most future mechanics enter an FAA-approved trade school after high school; there, candidates complete a minimum of 1,900 actual classroom hours of instruction. The total time spent in school is about 2 to 2-1/2 years for a combination of full-time instruction and hands-on training. There are only 192 FAA-approved schools in this country, so depending on where you get accepted, you may have to move away from home while attending school. The training is expensive, but there are lots of ways to finance your education through loans, grants, or scholarships.

What do I get out of it?

What do you get in return for all this hard work, heavy lifting, and intense pressure? Aside from the tremendous satisfaction of a job well done, this job has a tremendous impact on hundreds of thousands of people you don't even know!

The median annual salary for airplane mechanics is around $38,000, but as you gain more experience, you can make much more. Airline mechanics also get a great perk: reduced airfare rates for personal travel—not just for themselves, but for their families as well.

Who should I contact to learn more?

FAPA
4959 Massachusetts Blvd.
Atlanta, GA 30337
(800) JET-JOBS, ext. 190

Professional Aviation Maintenance Assoc.
500 Northwest Plaza, Ste. 1016
St. Ann, MO 63074-2209

Auto Mechanic

If you like the idea of working with your hands and you're not afraid of a little grease or sweat, but for one reason or another you are a little intimidated by the scope, the responsibility, and the training that you'll need to be certified as an aircraft mechanic, you might think about working on cars. It's a lot easier, quicker, and cheaper to become an auto mechanic, and one of the huge advantages of becoming an auto mechanic is that you can practice your skills just about anytime, right in your own driveway, using your own beloved automobile as a sort of guinea pig. That's kind of hard for aircraft mechanics to do (unless they happen to have a 747 parked in the carport).

What would I do?

Auto mechanics do all those things on your car that you pay someone else to do for you. But you too can become a pro at big tasks like valve jobs and tuning carbs, and small jobs like changing the oil or fixing brakes. Basically, an auto mechanic inspects, lubes, adjusts, repairs, or replaces things like belts, hoses, steering systems, spark plugs, brake and fuel systems, wheel bearings, and anything else that goes *ca-chunk* or *whoppety whoppety* when it's not supposed to.

Ren Volpe, Woman in Charge

Ren Volpe has been fixing cars for over ten years, and has been teaching women in the San Francisco Bay Area how to do the same for themselves for more than seven years. To date, over 500 women have learned the nuts and bolts of car care from her and discovered that it's not just much easier than they thought, it's actually fun! Look for her book, The Lady Mechanic's Total Car Care for the Clueless *(St. Martin's Press, 1998).*

How did you get into this profession?

I wanted to learn how to fix cars, but I didn't really have plans to be an auto mechanic. I graduated from college with a degree in philosophy and had no clue what to do next. I wanted to travel by car throughout the country, so I decided to go to trade school and see what I could learn. When I finally settled down after traveling, it seemed logical to get a job fixing cars. Now it's been ten years!

Do you work with many women?

For the past two years I've worked for myself, by myself, and all my customers, except for a few, are women. It's been great.

What are the skills you need most?

Most mechanics go to trade school, and keep going to school throughout their lives to keep up with changing technology. You must be physically fit, fairly strong (with a good back), have good hand-eye coordination, pay attention to details, be very patient, understand math, be able to read complicated manuals—and as a woman, be willing to work twice as hard as the men to get half the respect.

Do you ever experience discrimination and/or hassles from guys on the job?

Of course. Trade school was the worst, though. The nice thing is that the more experienced I get, the less it bothers me. Now that I've been around for a while, people get to know me personally and see what I can do, and it gets easier.

What's the pay like?

When I first started I was making $6 an hour, although at the time I was sweeping floors and cleaning parts. Journey-level mechanics make anywhere from $14 to $20 an hour, and master-level mechanics make $20 to $25. It also depends on where you live. Labor rates and pay rates vary throughout the country. You can make a good living anywhere, if you're qualified.

Do you think there are many opportunities for women in this field, and would you encourage other women to get into it?

Yes; lots of people would prefer going to a woman mechanic. Even if you go to school and fix cars only for a few years, the skills you'll gain are worth it. I fix stuff around the house—plumbing, wiring, and so on. I have a confidence in my abilities that I didn't have before I became a mechanic.

What do you hate about your job?

Broken bolts, wrong parts, defective parts, lost tools, dipping my ponytail into a pan of used motor oil, the chemicals and toxic fumes.

What do you love about your job?

How trusting my customers are, and how much they appreciate me. Most of my customers are women, and they are very easy to work with. I also love diagnosing something difficult: figuring out what's wrong and fixing it. I love the satisfaction of turning the key and going on a test drive after working on something for hours. I also love being the hero when I can help someone out on the side of the road, or solve an easy problem and get a car working in a few minutes.

This is a cool job if you like tools—you'll use power equipment like pneumatic wrenches, machine tools like lathes and grinders, welding and flame-cutting equipment to repair exhaust systems and other parts, jacks and hoists to lift cars and engines, and maybe even some pretty high-tech stuff like infrared engine analyzers and computerized diagnostic devices. You'll still use the old-fashioned tools like screwdrivers and wrenches, too, so it's safe to say that this is another job where long fingernails aren't exactly an asset.

What are my working conditions?

To check out the grunge factor encountered in this job, take a stroll down to your corner auto shop and shake the mechanic's hand. That's only a sampling of the grease you'll attract in a day's work. A mechanic's work can be hard; there will be lots of scraped hands and bumped knuckles (it's rumored that there's nothing as painful as a bumped knuckle in cold weather). There's a lot of lifting, too, so you have to be in good physical shape.

Most mechanics work in a shop; what kind is pretty much up to you. You can find work at small, local repair shops or gas stations with only you and one or two other mechanics, or go for a job at a huge car dealership that employs dozens of mechanics who may specialize in different areas—like engine work, transmissions, or electrical and computer systems.

How much training is required?

Although you can still become trained the old-fashioned way, through on-the-job training (or an apprenticeship) with a mechanic who's willing to take you on, the trend is toward formalized, classroom instruction at a trade or vocational school. You can also get good training in a community college program (most high school programs give great introductory lessons, but won't get you very far in pursuing a paid job). Some training programs are certified by the National Automotive Technicians Education Foundation (NATEF), an affiliate of the National Institute for Automotive Service Excellence (ASE). If you check out the classifieds, you'll probably see lots of ads looking for mechanics who are certified ASE. Certification by ASE is voluntary, but it will definitely help your career. Depending on the type and extent of training you would like, you could spend from six months to four years in school, in a combination of classroom instruction and hands-on work.

Most auto manufacturers sponsor programs at community colleges around the country to teach the latest automotive technology. Students split their time between classroom instruction and work at the dealership. This is a great opportunity if you plan on working for a dealer. Sponsored programs can take a little longer to complete than other courses (up to four years), but you can be assured that you've been fully trained by the time you finish and you're almost guaranteed the chance to continue your employment with the dealership where you trained.

It's possible to get a job as a mechanic without any certification, but you probably won't get as much training using diagnostic equipment or any of the high-tech tools that most new cars require. That's okay if you want to specialize in older cars,

---

MANUFACTURER-SPONSORED TRAINING PROGRAMS

ASSET Program, Training Dept.
Ford Parts and Service Division
Ford Motor Company
Room 109, 3000 Schaefer Rd.
Dearborn, MI 48121

Chrysler Dealer Apprenticeship Program
National C.A.P. Coordinator
CIMS 423-21-06
26001 Lawrence Ave.
Center Line, MI 48015
(800) 626-1523

General Motors Automotive Service Educational Program
National College Coordinator
General Motors Service Tech. Group
30501 Van Dyke Ave.
Warren, MI 48090
(800) 828-6860

---

but this might limit your opportunities for the future.

What do I get out of it?

Almost everyone, at one time or another, has become convinced that they, and they alone, have taken on the responsibility of putting their mechanic's kids through Harvard. Car repairs can be extremely expensive; that's a fact.

However, if you want to become a mechanic to make money, someone should have pointed you toward medical school a long time ago. While you can make a good living working on cars, the big bucks are usually reserved for shop owners and experienced mechanics who have built a reputation for superior service. The median weekly salary for beginning mechanics is about $500 per week. That's just a ballpark figure; actual pay can vary, depending on your training (an apprentice is liable to make less, maybe as little as minimum wage; an accredited beginner, more). Some mechanics earn commissions on top of salary as an incentive to do more work. There's really no cap on your earning potential; if you make a career of it and keep abreast of current technology by enrolling in continuing education courses (and if you develop a steadily growing pool of satisfied clients), you could end up with your own shop, sending your own kids to college on someone else's blown engine.

Who should I contact to learn more?
National Auto Tech. Ed. Foundation
13505 Dulles Technology Dr.
Herndon, VA 22071-3415

ASE
13505 Dulles Technology Dr.
Herndon, VA 22071-3415

Automotive Service Association, Inc.
1901 Airport Freeway
Bedford, TX 76021-5732
(general info)

Automotive Service Industry Assoc.
25 Northwest Point
Elk Grove Village, IL 60007-1035
(general info)

Accrediting Commission of Career Schools and Colleges of Technology
2101 Wilson Blvd., Ste. 302
Arlington, VA 22201
(directory of accredited, private trade and tech schools for auto mechanics)

Vocational Industrial Clubs of America
P.O. Box 3000
1401 James Monroe Highway
Leesburg, VA 22075
(list of public auto mechanic training programs)

Carpenter

Have you ever built a birdhouse from scratch? Or a go-cart, a bookend, or a paperweight? If you have, you know that working with wood is one of the coolest ways to spend second period because you end up with a tangible product—something you can hold in your hands and show everyone. If you've never had the chance to make something with your own hands, then you've missed out. Carpentry is a great career for girls who never even imagined they could get paid for doing something that's so much fun.

What would I do?
   Don't think this job is just about hammers and nails. Carpenters also lay out jobs, working from blueprints or other instructions; they cut and shape wood and other building materials, using both power and hand tools; and they assemble and install prefabricated pieces as well.

What are my working conditions?
   While it's true that working with your hands can be immensely more satisfying than slamming a keyboard all day (unless you're writing the book that will change the world), it can also be a lot more difficult. Aside from the prerequisite splinters and cuts, you'll be doing a lot of lifting, and could be forced to stand or kneel in one position for long periods of time. Accidents are common, because you'll be working with rough

materials and sharp tools in all kinds of weather. Don't let that scare you; as any girl who's ever made something from nothing knows, the end result is well worth a few bumps and scrapes.

You may think of carpentry as just building houses, but it can mean hundreds of different things—from building the foundation for a freeway project to hanging a French door in a new home.

How much training is required?

Most contractors and others who employ carpenters recommend that anyone interested in this line of work begin an apprenticeship program after high school, and most agree that this is the best way for a woman to enter the field (there are lots of training and apprenticeship programs specifically for women). The length of time you'll spend as an apprentice varies, but it's usually from three to four years.

Apprenticeships offer a combination of classroom instruction in basics like math, blueprint reading, first aid, and the use of tools, with on-the-job training in things like elementary structural design and common tasks like form building and outside and inside finishing. Apprentices also become familiar with the tools of the trade—both power and hand. Programs that are geared specifically toward women also include valuable information and guidance on things like sexual harassment at the work site, and how to find a job in a field that is still dominated by men.

You can get training and learn skills without enrolling in an apprenticeship program (working for a family business, for example, or by finding a company willing to put in the time and cost to train you), but the training you'll receive probably wouldn't be as comprehensive.

It also may not help you much in seeking work with other contractors, so your options for the future could be limited.

Math skills, good coordination, manual dexterity, a certain amount of physical strength, and a good sense of balance come in handy. It helps if you've taken courses in woodworking or shop, mechanical drawing, and math, and most programs and employers require a high school diploma.

What do I get out of it?

The average pay is about $500 per week, but again, that figure can vary, depending on who you work for, where you work, and what kind of work you do. It also depends on how much training and experience you have. It's important to remember that carpentry work is sometimes cyclical; there aren't too many opportunities for carpenters who specialize in new home construction in the dead of winter when there is two feet of snow on the ground. There are generally more consistent opportunities in regions of the country where the weather isn't so harsh. Other factors, like the economic climate of the country, also affect the opportunities for carpenters, so any edge you can get (like the formalized training you'd receive as an apprentice) can help a lot.

Who should I contact to learn more?
Associated Builders and Contractors
1300 N. 17th St.
Rosslyn, VA 22209

Assoc. General Contractors of Amer., Inc.
1957 E St. NW
Washington, DC 20006

Home Builders Institute
National Association of Home Builders
1201 15th St. NW
Washington, DC 20005

United Brotherhood of Carpenters and
Joiners of America
101 Constitution Ave. NW
Washington, DC 20001

Painter

What's to say? Painters paint, right? Sure,
but they do a lot more than swing a brush.
Painters can also be color and design con-
sultants—it's a neat occupation, really,
because it lets you combine trade skills
(the actual painting) with your wildly creative streak (the design and color-coordi-
nation part). Not many jobs let you
express so many different talents.

What would I do?

Before you can paint (the fun part),
you have to prepare your surface (the not
quite as fun part), which includes strip-
ping, sanding, and water/sand blasting
(this might actually be the most fun part).
The painter smooths the surface by filling
holes and cracks and sanding rough spots,
and mixes colors as needed. Painters also
have to know what kind of paint works
best for each kind of surface, and it helps
if they have some eye for color and design.
You'll need to know stuff like this when
working with clients and customers; it's

especially important if you want to have a
business of your own and do more than
just work for someone else.

Be a painter and
COLOR YOUR WORLD!

What are my working conditions?

Probably better than working as a
mechanic or carpenter, but still no cake-
walk. Painting may look easy, but it can
be strenuous; you'll be lifting, bending,
maybe even climbing, and you could be
required to spend long periods of time
with your arms raised overhead (that can
get tiring after awhile, so it helps if you
have lots of stamina and upper-body
strength). You can work part-time or
full-time, and the structure can be flexible: for example, you could work full-
time for one employer (like a contractor
or maintenance company) or on a job-by-
job basis, depending on what you prefer
(and if you don't mind risking a few periods of unemployment here and there).

What training is required?

Lots of painters learn their trade on
an informal basis; for example, starting
out as a helper or assistant and picking
up skills on the job. That's great if you
can get it, but one of the reasons these
jobs are classified as nontraditional is
because the opportunities for women are
reduced. Unless you have some pretty

good connections, it might be hard to convince a company to take you on; realistically, they'd probably give the chance to a guy. One way to beat this system is to enter an apprenticeship program that's designed for women where you'll be taught everything you need to know to become a journeyworker. An apprenticeship lasts three to four years, and includes real work experience along with about 150 hours of classroom instruction per year. Most apprenticeship programs require applicants to be at least 16 years old and have a high school diploma.

What do I get out of it?

When you first start out as a helper, you're usually paid about 40 to 50 percent of what experienced painters earn. That could average about $300 per week, depending on lots of factors, like the work you're doing and who you're doing it for. As you complete more training and gain experience, this pay rate, like the others in this chapter, will start to climb. Eventually, you can make a good living as a painter.

Who should I contact to learn more?

Associated Builders and Contractors
1300 N. 17th St.
Rosslyn, VA 22209

International Brotherhood of Painters and Allied Trades
1750 New York Ave. NW
Washington, DC 20006

Home Builders Institute
National Association of Home Builders
1201 15th St. NW
Washington, DC 20005

Electrician

Got fantasies about becoming the next Edison? Are you the kind of girl who likes to take appliances apart to see what makes them tick (or whir, or buzz, or beep, or whatever else they do)? If so, you might consider getting into electricity (figuratively speaking, of course).

What would I do?

Aside from amassing an enormous collection of bad puns about making connections, staying current, becoming a live wire, and so on, you'd install, test, and repair all kinds of electrical systems. You might install the wiring in a new home or office building, test automobile electrical systems, or repair a security system. Basically, if it has anything to do with AC or DC (voltage, not the rock band), it's in your court. An electrician uses a variety of tools—aside from the standards like power and hand tools, you also get to try out some cool equipment like oscilloscopes, ammeters, and test lamps.

What are my working conditions?

Generally, you'll be working indoors. Compared to some of the other positions described in this chapter, the conditions for an electrician are pretty good—not as strenuous as a carpenter or as messy as a painter—but there are drawbacks. For instance, you might have to work in small, cramped quarters, you might have to spend a lot of time on a ladder or scaffold, and there's always the danger of getting shocked by a live wire. But if you're thoroughly trained, and you're careful, you can greatly minimize your risk of getting hurt.

Most electricians work a standard 40-hour week, but as you probably have suspected, depending on who you work for, you could be asked to put in some overtime hours (nights and weekends are common, especially for emergency or repair jobs). Only 1 in 10 electricians is self-employed.

What training is required?

This isn't one of those jobs that's easy to pick up with on-the-job training or just tinkering as a hobby. If you want to become a certified electrician, you should seriously consider an apprentice program. There, you'll have a combination of classroom instruction (which is very important for learning basic and advanced electronics, code requirements, math, etc.) and hands-on experience. Apprenticeships last four to five years and must include 144 hours of classroom work and 8000 hours of working on actual jobs. The kinds of skills helpful to electricians are math; courses in electronics, mechanical drawing, and science; and good color vision (you'll often have to identify wires from their color).

What do I get out of it?

Fair is fair—it makes sense that the more training required to do a job, the more that job should pay, right? On average, you can earn more as an electrician (even as a beginner) than in any of the other nontraditional jobs listed here. Median weekly earnings are almost $600. With some training and experience under your belt, you could increase that to about $800. Electricians also work more consistently; because almost all their work is done indoors, they aren't affected by weather. And because there are lots of opportunities for electricians outside the construction trade, you're not

as vulnerable to downturns in the economy and housing industry.

Who should I contact to learn more?

Independent Electrical Contractors, Inc.
507 Wythe St.
Alexandria, VA 22314

National Electrical Contractors Association (NECA)
3 Metro Center, Ste. 1100
Bethesda, MD 20814

International Brotherhood of Electrical Workers (IBEW)
1125 15th St. NW
Washington, DC 20005

Associated Builders and Contractors
1300 N. 17th St.
Rosslyn, VA 22209

Homebuilders Institute
National Association of Home Builders
1201 15th St. NW
Washington, DC 20005

Vending Machine Repair Person

I've known lots of women who think this would be the greatest job—if for no other reason than they wouldn't be strapped to a desk in an office, watching the clock and waiting for something interesting to happen. It's a cool job if you like the idea of doing something mechanical, but aren't thrilled with the idea of spending years in an apprenticeship program.

What would I do?

Just what the title says. You drive around, visiting all those vending machines in office buildings, on school campuses, and just about anywhere else where someone's got a few extra quarters to spend. Aside from restocking, you'd also perform maintenance and upkeep, as well as make repairs when the things start spitting out cans of soda indiscriminately. Food and beverage machines don't have to be your only domain, though; you can also learn to work on video and pinball games.

What are my working conditions?

You'd be working indoors mostly, but even if you were working outside it wouldn't be for hours at a time. Some repairers work in a shop, while others do on-site servicing, driving to wherever the machines have been placed. There's usually a lot of driving in a job like that, and a fair amount of heavy lifting. You need to be comfortable (not to mention capable) of working on your own, and you need to have pretty good upper body strength.

What training is required?

Luckily, this is one of those jobs that doesn't take years of training and instruction. In fact, if you've taken a few courses in electronics or shop, you may be able to find a "trainee" position right out of high school. You can better those chances if you take a few related courses after high school in a trade or vocational school. Some vocational schools and community colleges offer a two-year program in vending machine repair.

If you want to spend the time and effort as an apprentice, there are programs available through the National Automatic Merchandising Association. You must complete 144 hours of home-study instruction on subjects like basic electricity, blueprint reading, customer relations, and safety. When you finish the program, you must pass written and performance exams to be certified.

What do I get out of it?

The average hourly wage for non-union vending machine service techs is about $8 an hour. This can go as low as minimum wage and as high as $16 to $18 per hour, and over $20 an hour for union members. As more machines are placed into service in all kinds of locations, the job outlook for vending machine techs keeps getting better.

Who should I contact to learn more?

Nat. Automatic Merchandising Assoc.
20 N. Wacker Dr., Ste. 3500
Chicago, IL 60606-3102

> Remember, any occupation in which less than 25 percent of the workforce is female is nontraditional.

Unlimited Opportunities for Nontraditional Girls

This is just a sampling of the cool jobs waiting for you; there are lots more career alternatives to choose from. If none of these interest you, contact one of the agencies listed in this chapter for more options (like sheet metal worker and roofer). Remember, nontraditional doesn't mean just "blue collar" or "trades."

Talk to your school's career counselor, or visit the library and check out the latest copy of the government's *Occupational Outlook Handbook*. Get all the facts before you commit to any kind of training, education, or employment— that way you're more likely to choose a job or career that will make you happy. And that, not a skyrocketing paycheck, is what makes it all worthwhile.

Endnotes

1. U.S. Department of Labor, Bureau of Labor Statistics.

2. U.S. Department of Labor, Women's Bureau, 1992 statistics.

Chapter Five

INVEST IN THE STOCK MARKET

Why should someone who's probably got another fifty years or so until retirement start thinking about investing? I mean, you've got all the time in the world before you have to start worrying about real estate in Florida and plane tickets for the grand-kids, right?

Maybe so, but investing your money is about more than retirement villages. It's about sending yourself to college, backpacking through Europe, or driving a rad convertible instead of your parents' hand-me-down minivan. It's about having enough money to be an independent woman and get your own place (how many girls do you know who are way beyond legal age and still living at home?). And it's about working to make a better world.

Don't see the connection? Aside from the benefits of learning how to prepare for your own financial future—not to mention making a chunk of change—investing your dollars now is a great way to support a company's business practices. Until recently, most people hadn't really thought much about who's behind what

they buy. For example, do you know who owns your favorite soft drink? Do you know how that company treats the environment and their workers? Ten years ago, you might never have thought about these things at all. But as this century draws to a close, our sense of responsibility to both the Earth and its inhabitants is intensifying. Partly because of the work of activists, partly because of the explosion of information that has landed at our fingertips by way of the Internet, we're all becoming a lot more educated—and ultimately more concerned—about what goes on in the world around us. So we're starting to ask some questions:

What are the oil companies doing to preserve the environment and ensure that we don't have a repeat of the Exxon oil spill that destroyed our coastline for miles?

How are we, as a free nation, responding to the poor treatment of workers in underdeveloped countries who work like slaves to bring us stuff like overpriced sneakers and clothing?

What are we willing to sacrifice or change about our lifestyles to stop the worldwide abuse of animals in the name of scientific research and product testing?

In today's society, the most powerful vote you have isn't cast in a voting booth, but at a cash register. When you vote with your dollars, you purchase products produced by companies whose business practices you feel are ethical and fair. You know that a particular shampoo manufacturer does not test products on animals. You're a staunch supporter of animal rights, so you go out of your way to buy that brand of shampoo. Great! But why stop there? You can take your support a step further and support that company even more directly by investing in them; that is, by purchasing their stock.

A lot of people, especially investment bankers and stock brokers, might read a statement like that and take great exception to it. They'll tell you, "Buying stock isn't about charity, it's about making money." That's true—the primary reason for buying stock in any company is to make money, and there's nothing wrong with that. In fact, becoming a more financially independent girl can only work in your favor, and it can bring you a lot of things that you've always wanted, including a new world. That said, if you know that you want to invest in the stock market to make money, why not invest with a conscience? Your first objective can still be to turn a profit, but if you can

do that and contribute to a cause you believe in at the same time, then it's that much easier to make a difference in the world around you.

Let's say that there's this new shoe you've seen in a catalogue that you get in the mail now and then. It's not like anything you've ever seen before, sort of a cross between a clog and a sneaker, and you decide that you absolutely must have a pair. They're pretty inexpensive, so you take out your handy-dandy credit card and order a pair.

When these shoes arrive on your doorstep, you fall completely in love with them. They fit like a dream, and the design is too cool. Not only that, you're the first girl on your block to own a pair, and this makes all your friends totally green with envy.

But wait, it gets better. One day when you're sitting around with your feet up, admiring your new shoes, you notice that the brochure that came with your shoes says that they're made from 100 percent recycled materials. Not only that, it also says that this shoe company donates 5 percent of its profits to community-based homeless shelters in your state. Wow! Shoes with a conscience! This is where the wheels should start spinning in your brain.

You love your shoes, and you are sure that these shoes are going to be the rage this season. Not only that, but the manufacturer of these shoes actually seems to have a social conscience. They're not displacing large numbers of indigenous wildlife to produce these shoes, they're not manufacturing them in sweatshops, and they're not robbing the Earth of precious natural resources

DO THE MATH

Comfy shoes + cool design = shoes you must have

shoes you must have = shoes your friends must have

shoes your friends must have = lots and lots of shoes being sold

lots and lots of shoes being sold = lots and lots of $$

Therefore, comfy shoes + cool design = lots and lots of $$

just to cover your feet. You also know from your political science class that it's finally becoming politically correct to have a social conscience (what with the ozone being depleted and the rainforests being decimated at record rates), and usually, anything that becomes politically correct also becomes profitable for someone, somewhere.

So it occurs to your shrewd girl brain that this company is probably going to do well in the coming years with these ecologically sound and fashionable shoes. Congratulations! You put two and two together. Now you're ready to consider the implications of buying some stock in this company.

So you call a broker, buy 100 shares in This Cool New Shoe Company, and before long you see Tyra Banks wearing your shoes in the pages of *People* magazine. Pretty soon they're spotted on such celebrities as Claire Danes and Uma Thurman, and the stock you purchased for $1 per share is selling at $2.50 per share. Could life get any better than this? In a word, yes. This Cool New Shoe Company is on a roll. They can hardly keep up with the demand, so they build a bigger factory and triple their workforce. These shoes are everywhere all at once! The stock climbs within an eight-month period to $4 per share, and, on paper at

least, you're flush. Your initial investment of $100 has risen in value to $400 and you're riding high and thinking about borrowing some money from your grandma to buy a few more shares of stock.

Then the slam comes. The fashion magazines declare that heels are out, flats are in! With that declaration, hundreds of orders from around the country for the fabulous clog/sneakers are cancelled in favor of the more seasonable, but eco-unfriendly, flip-flops. Somewhere, a factory full of recycled clog/sneaker heels begins to gather dust. To make matters worse, whatever meager clog/sneaker market remains is being gobbled up by the megadiscount store that sells copies of those groovy shoes at 50 percent of what you paid for yours. This is not boding well for your financial future. The stock that carried you to new heights of teenage wealth starts to drop in price.

The price is now $3 per share. You figure you're still ahead. Surely, the groovy shoe-buying public out there will find their individuality once again and reject the fascist beauty standards of mass consumer magazines. Not only that, they'll soon recognize those other cheap knock-offs for what they are and come back to the fold of This Cool New Shoe Company. So you sit tight (albeit a little uncomfortably), as the price drops further.

You're in denial. There's still time to bail out and gather a tidy little profit off your initial investment, but you stubbornly hold on, even as the price dips below $2, to $1.50, then to $1. When it reaches 50 cents, you take your once-lovely shoes out of the closet and try and reintroduce them to the world. But your efforts are in vain, and your friends think you have totally lost your mind. Soon after, This Cool New Shoe Company cannot hold its creditors off any longer and big bad bankruptcy comes knocking on their door.

Suddenly, out of nowhere, the Super Acme Manufacturing Company, one of the biggest clothing manufacturers in the country, sweeps in and buys up This Cool New Shoe Company. They're not that crazy about the clog/sneaker combo, but the prez of Super Acme thinks that little shoe company has potential, darn it, and she's going to make it work! Way to go. Your stock rockets to $6 per share and in a moment of total lucidity, you call your broker and sell, sell, sell! Before the week's end, you've got an extra $500 bucks in your pocket and you're ready to buy more stock.

Of course, this is an oversimplified example of how the stock market works, but you get the point. When you buy stocks, the rewards can be very great, but so can the risks. This Cool New Shoe Company could just as easily gone into Chapter 13 (bankruptcy); in fact, if this were more than a mere fairy tale, it most likely would have gone into bankruptcy. But the point is, buying stocks doesn't have to be a forbidding, frightening

Buying stocks can be a great way to support a company.

thing. It can be profitable, it can be a lot of fun, and regardless of the political or social whims of a fickle public, it can be a way to support a company you believe in—for instance, a shoe company that uses only recycled materials and gives some of its profits to help the homeless. But it's not child's play: Investing in stocks requires a certain degree of sophistication and a lot of attention to detail. It's not something just for old, cigar-smoking men—anyone can learn economics and how to buy and sell stocks. It just takes desire and commitment.

What Is the Stock Market?

Basically, the stock market is the exchange of stock, or shares, of publicly held companies. When you buy stock in a company, you essentially become a part owner of that company, and your ownership is represented by shares of stock. It's like you bought a tiny sliver of a huge pie. You don't own enough of the pie to really be thought of as an owner or principal of that pie—you can't just pull up one day, park your car in the executive lot, and expect to get a warm welcome—but as a shareholder, you do have more than a passing interest in that company.

Companies issue (sell) shares of stock to raise money so that they can expand and become even bigger and more successful. That means success for everyone concerned, because as the success of the company you've invested in increases, so does the value of their stock, meaning that what you bought for $10 a share could end up being worth $20 a share, giving you a 100 percent profit.

When This Cool New Shoe Company first started out, it was probably owned by one person and financed purely by her own savings account and spare change discovered between the cushions of her sofa. As the company's sales grew, the owner probably realized that she could increase her sales if she could increase her production. To do that, she would need more employees and equipment. If she didn't have the capital, or cash, to expand her operations, she could raise some by selling shares of her company to friends or family members.

That's basically how it works, except that the companies that offer shares of stock to the public are doing millions of dollars a year in sales, and they're not selling shares just to Uncle Bob or Sister Sue. When a company goes from privately held to publicly held, stock in the company is offered to the public. This is called an Initial Public Offering (IPO). A company can go through an IPO only once, and for some companies, that initial selling price is the peak value of the stock (hopefully, that will not be the case with your stock).

Only publicly held or publicly traded companies can issue stock. Once a company goes public, ownership is then distributed among shareholders (of which you are one). The company is run by a board of directors and the usual executives—the president, vice-presidents, and so on. Often, the founder of the company will retain a controlling interest in the company (at least 51 percent of the stock) to be sure that it continues to thrive on the principles and values on which she founded it.

Even though small, individual shareholders like yourself don't participate in the daily operations of the companies in which they hold stock, they still have certain rights and responsibilities. They have a vote on who will sit on the board of directors, and they can occasionally vote on important company issues. Let's say that The Cool New Shoe Company decided to expand their charitable contributions. Instead of giving only 5 percent of their profits to homeless shelters, the board decides they also want to give 5 percent of their profits to an organization that is fighting for animal rights and welfare. This raises their total charitable contributions to 10 percent. This doesn't seem like a big deal, but an important decision like this would require shareholder approval.

Shareholders also have the right to attend the annual meeting. That's where the company executives, the board of directors, and the major shareholders get together once a year and go over the accomplishments of the past year and talk about their plans for the next. If there are issues to vote on, this is the place to do it. You don't have to attend the meeting to cast your vote; most shareholders vote by proxy, meaning they fill out their ballot and mail it in before the election. In most cases, one share equals one vote. A dozen or so votes may not seem important in a company that's issued two million shares, but that's a matter of perspective, and it kind of depends on how you define "important." It's sort of like voting in a presidential election. One single vote won't sway the election either way, but a couple of hundred thousand people voting on the same ethics and values can have a huge impact on who's going to win—and who's not.

How Do You Make Money in the Stock Market?

There are two ways to make money with stocks: through dividends and capital gains. A capital gain is the profit that you make when you sell your stock at a higher price than that at which you bought it. For example, you shrewdly held onto your shares in This Cool New Shoe Company until the price hit $6—and you had 100 shares—so your capital gains would have been $500.

---

100 shares at $6 each = $600
(the selling price)
100 shares at $1 each = $100
(your initial investment)
YOUR PROFIT = $500

Before you get excited about the cool $500 you just made, remember that you have to pay a federal tax on capital gains. That wouldn't be very much on such a small amount, but when you get the hang of this financial wizardry thing and your profits start to add up, so will your tax liability (and it's your responsibility to report those gains on your income taxes, so be sure you keep accurate records). You'll also have to pay the broker two transactions fees—one when you buy the stock and one when you sell it.

A dividend is an amount that you, as a stockholder, are paid by the corporation, usually on a quarterly basis, as a sort of bonus. Dividends are a portion of the company's profits; it's their way of sharing their success with some of the people who helped them get there in the first place. Dividends are taxed like income, at a lower rate than capital gains. Not every company that sells stock will offer dividends; usually they are paid only by very big, successful, and profitable companies. Some people buy stock in companies solely for the purpose of getting regular dividends. The amount of the dividend you receive is proportionate to how much stock you own.

Who Can Buy Stock?

Anyone can purchase stock, but there are specific rules and regulations for how you go about it. You can't just pull your car up to the drive-up window of This Cool New Shoe Company and order 100 shares of hot stock. As an individual investor, you have to go through a broker. It may not seem fair that you need a broker to handle the mechanics of buying or selling your stock, but if everyone were allowed to buy stock directly, the market would be in total chaos! Brokers and others involved in the daily operations of the stock market are heavily regulated by the Securities and Exchange Commission (SEC). That's what keeps it all fair. See, there are some people out there who would be more than willing to take advantage of you and your money, and the SEC keeps them in line. If regulatory agencies like the SEC were abolished, fraud would skyrocket.

The exchange of stocks is basically a private transaction; to do this yourself you would need a seat on one of the exchanges (the highest price ever paid for a seat on the New York Stock Exchange, or NYSE, is $1.2 million), and it's doubtful that you could afford it. Chances are, your broker wouldn't be able to afford that seat either, but the firm she works for can, and that's what's behind the partnership between you and your broker.

There are basically three different kinds of brokers, and which kind you choose to work with depends on what level of service you want and how much money you're willing to spend for that service.

Full-service broker: Let's say that your rich auntie left you $50,000 in her will, and you've decided that you want to invest that money in the stock market. Problem is, you don't have a clue about how the market works, much less how to pick a winning stock. In this case, you might take a walk through the yellow pages and start looking for a full-service broker. These brokers are aptly named, because they give you the most service available to private investors. Not only will they handle your stock transactions, they'll also help you formulate and maintain an investment strategy that's designed to help you achieve whatever financial goals you've set your sights on. They'll also keep a close watch on your portfolio (your collection of investments) for its performance, and make recommendations as needed. Having all this wonderful attention, however, does not guarantee that the advice of your broker will always be good. With a full-service broker, you can still lose your money (just some of it, or maybe even all of it).

While it's true that these guys put the "full" in full-service, their attention and expertise does not come cheap. Their

commission can cost $80 to $90 per transaction, and unless you have a lot of money to begin with, you probably won't be able to afford their services. Generally, full-service brokers are for people who are investing a lot of money or who are simply too busy (or have no desire) to study the market and do their own research.

Discount broker: Discount brokers are fairly new to the market scene; they were established in 1975 when the SEC eliminated the minimum price structure that brokers used to charge fees to individual investors. You may think at first that this would have the same result as opening the barn door and watching all the chickens run amuck, but removing pricing restrictions actually has had the opposite effect: lower prices stir up competition among brokers and sometimes create a price war, which gives people a bigger pool of brokers from which to choose.

The biggest difference between full-service and discount brokers may not be the prices they charge (a discount fee would run around $30 to $40 per transaction), but the services they provide. While a full-service broker will carefully monitor your investments and make recommendations that are designed to improve your financial outlook, a discount broker's role is to handle your transactions and leave it at that. If you have a question about a particular stock, your discount broker may have an opinion about it, but she will not be inclined to offer you any advice either way. She's not rude; it's simply not her job.

That doesn't mean your discount broker will toss you to the dogs, either. Most are a pretty decent lot, and if you choose a stock that is clearly, obviously, most emphatically going to be a disaster for you, she would probably say something, much the same way that even a disinterested pedestrian would comment, "Hey, your car's rolling over that cliff." But don't count on recommendations from your discount broker—deciding which stocks to buy, and which to pass up, is up to you.

It obviously takes a little more thought to pick your own stocks than it does to pick up the phone and speed dial your full-service broker. But don't let that scare you. Once you get the hang of how the market works, you'll probably find that making these decisions is kind of fun, not to mention empowering.

Remember that brokers make their fee on a per-transaction basis. That means if you buy shares of This Cool New Shoe Company at 9:00 AM and sell them by 4:00 PM, you'll be charged twice: once for a purchase and once for a sale. This is one good reason why you have to learn to pick your stocks carefully and resist the urge to dump a stock when you see it go down a point or two in a short time.

Discount brokers don't always act solely as vehicles for your stock transactions. While they don't really get into guidance and advisement, many do offer other valuable services to small investors, such as news and research on companies that you're interested in. Of course, any additional services such as these increase the commission price you'll pay, but even so, it will still be substantially less than a full-service broker will charge.

Deep-discount broker: Think of it this way: There are three hair salons on your street. The first is absolutely lavish; when you go in for your appointment, a hostess

> **If you're not afraid to cut your own hair, you shouldn't be afraid to pick your own stocks. It's as simple as that.**

greets you with champagne and truffles. A styling consultant meets with you to decide just what sort of mood you want to evoke with your new 'do. Once you both arrive at a decision, the hostess ushers you to a cushy chair where your hair is lovingly shaped by a French stylist named Jean Claude. Your total hair experience costs about $90, including shampoo and blow-dry. That's full service.

The second one is nice, but not quite as nice as the first. You're greeted by a hostess/cashier who offers you a can of soda. As you settle yourself onto a nice cotton couch, she hands you some year-old issues of *Vogue* and *Glamour* to flip through to find a haircut you like. When you finally decide what you want, the next available stylist (who, we might add, is very competent and was probably trained in some big city) gives you the great cut you told her you wanted. Maybe it will look good, maybe it won't. If it doesn't, she'll try and fix it up a little before you leave. You look nice, and it set you back only about $30. You saved quite a bundle, didn't you? That's a discount stylist.

At the third place, you enter an unmarked door and fork over ten bucks to a guy sitting behind a counter who barely looks at you. He promptly hands you a comb, a mirror, and a pair of very sharp scissors. You close your eyes, hold your breath, and go for it. That's a deep-discount haircut.

A deep-discount broker is purely an agent for your transactions. Some don't even have offices; you conduct all your business either on-line or on the phone. They're not shady operations, they're just streamlined to keep expenses to a minimum, so they're able to pass those savings in commissions on to you. To use a deep-discount broker, you should know exactly what stock, and how much of it, you want.

If you're embarking on a serious strategy of saving and investing, using the stock market as only one method of achieving those goals, then you would probably choose a discount broker. However, if your whole reason for reading this chapter is to learn the mechanics of how to buy one particular stock (and you have no intention of becoming very involved in an investment plan at this stage of your life), you could just as easily purchase the stock through a deep-discount broker and be done with the whole darned thing.

Be sure you understand the commission fees **UP FRONT.**

Regardless of which kind of broker you choose, choose carefully. Get some advice from someone who already uses a broker's services; find out which services they value and which they don't. By talking to lots of people who already deal with brokers every day, you'll think of some good questions for interviewing one for yourself. It's important to find a broker

you trust (after all, you're going to be giving this person your hard-earned money), with a good track record of both investing and customer service. If you come across a broker who's more concerned with pushing his or her own investment strategies on you, even after you've explained what you're looking for, then pass.

Above all, be sure you understand the commission fees before you put down any money. If you don't fully understand how this works, you're liable to spend your money in a fury, trading stocks daily like you're some kind of Wall Street magnate only to get a very unpleasant bill at the end of the month. Think of your broker like a cellular phone (you know how those calls "just to say hi" really start to add up?); use this person with discretion and only when absolutely necessary.

How Much Money Do You Need?

One of the biggest misconceptions about investing in the stock market is that you need lots of dough to do it. Sure, it would be nice if you had an extra $25,000 sitting around that you could tinker with, but you probably don't. That doesn't mean you're going to be barred from playing the stocks; it doesn't mean that brokers all over town will shriek with laughter and hang up on you when you tell them how much money you have to invest. When you're determining how much money you need to get your feet wet in the market, there's only one question you need to ask yourself: How much money can I afford to lose?

Harsh, but true. No matter how much of a good thing you think you might have, no matter how high your biorythms spike the day you call your broker, lurking around every corner is always the possibility that you could lose every cent you put into your new venture. There's no such thing as a sure thing in the stock market; that's one of the rules you have to accept before you play.

Don't be frightened off too easily, though; it's not all that bad. Like any risk, there are degrees. Investing all your extra cash in a brand new company with no proven track record is obviously riskier than putting your money in an established, successful company like IBM. Of course, the IBM stock will be more expensive, and will probably not have as much potential for rapid growth.

The basic principle of the stock market is risk versus reward. How much you decide to risk depends on how much you want to get back.

Take a good, hard look at your finances when you're deciding how much money you can afford to stash away in some stocks. The higher the risk, the higher the (potential) reward; but the converse is also true, the lower the risk, the lower (and maybe slower) the reward.

Do you have any outstanding debt, like a car payment or credit cards? If so, you should pay those bills before you invest. As long as you have outstanding obligations, you really can't afford to lose any money. And whatever you do, never, ever take an advance on your credit card to buy stocks. That is the worst financial decision you could make.

Most brokers would advise against putting all your money into one stock; the

real key to building wealth, they'll tell you, is diversification—to have your money spread out over a number of investments, like mutual funds, stocks, bonds, and so on. If you own 100 shares of a stock that goes bad, you've lost all your investment. If you own 50 shares of a stock that goes bad, and 50 shares of a stock that doesn't, then you've lost only half your money (and if the stock that isn't doing too badly actually performs well, your gains may offset the loss you had with the 50 shares of bad stuff). That's the logic behind diversification, and it makes sense. But what you decide to do is up to you. Regardless of what everyone says about putting your eggs in one basket, if you're buying stock for the first time and just want to purchase some shares of This Cool New Shoe Company, go ahead and do it. You can always branch out later.

How much money you'll need for your initial investment also depends on the stock you're buying. A huge, multinational company's stock might be worth over $100 per share; a small, local company's might be worth only $5 per share. That doesn't mean that the $5 per share stock is a bad deal, or is somehow inferior to the $100 per share investment. It's a smaller, maybe riskier investment, that's all.

The price of stock in a company is determined by the profitability (or potential for profitability) of that company, and by the demand for the stock. Profit and demand are linked; that is, the higher the profit, the higher the demand. The trick is to get in on that stock before everyone else becomes aware of its profitability and demand goes up. Then, after everyone else catches on and their fevered buying frenzy drives the price of the stock up, you sell. That's called buy low, sell high, and it's what the stock market is all about.

How Do You Choose Which Stock to Buy?

Good question. If you find the answer, you're guaranteed to make a million (several times over) before you reach age 25. Knowing which stock to buy, when to buy it, and when to sell it is at the heart of every stock market seminar, how-to book, and infomercial out there. The bad news is there's no set formula for success in choosing stock, but the good news is that there are ways to get pretty good at it. Choosing stock is a three-step process:

1. Identify a general area of interest
2. Narrow your search to a specific company
3. Determine if this company is a viable prospect

Identify a General Area of Interest

As soon as you start to develop an interest in the stock market, you should learn to develop a taste for it as well: A good way to do that is to start reading financial magazines and newsletters. You don't have to go hardcore right out of the gate and subscribe to *The Wall Street Journal* and *Barron's*. Start with more user-friendly, and more consumer-oriented magazines like *Money, Inc., Worth,* and

others. These magazines aren't stock market specific, but that's okay (when you're first starting out, columns and columns of stock quotes have a funny way of numbing your eyeballs). They feature a variety of articles on investing—everything from saving for college tuition to planning for your retirement—and although you may go into this with the goal of learning more about the stock market, getting a good overall understanding of our economy and how financial markets work will only help you.

Getting a feel for which companies have a better chance of being successful than others can be as simple as taking a good look around and carefully observing the trends in your community.

Another way to become a more effective investor is to learn to spot trends in the market that may affect the economy. Most of us believe that picking successful stocks is this huge mystery. How many people would be millionaires today if they had noticed, some 15 or 20 years ago, that personal computers would soon find a home on nearly every desk (at home and at work) across the country? Did you predict that shopping malls would soon be found at practically every intersection?

Social trends usually mean economic trends, and while it's true that some turn out to be pretty big losers (pet rocks come to mind) and others seem never to get off the ground (solar heating was supposed to be the boom of the eighties), you can, by keeping your eyes open, become a savvy investor.

If you'd like more specific help, there are a few books and magazines geared toward gen-X'ers and younger people, new investors like yourself, that would definitely be worth a look. Check out your local library and bookstores; you'll find plenty to get you started. If you're on the Net, surf to your heart's content—there's enough there to keep you busy for months, if not years.

Narrow Your Search to a Specific Company

Once you have a general idea of the type of stock you want to buy (maybe you've narrowed it down to a particular industry or product), you can narrow your search even further by considering your secondary reason for investing: to support a company, a goal, or a principle. When you're working with a full-service broker, you can pretty much tell her what kind of companies you're interested in, and she'll provide you with lots of viable alternatives. But what if all you can afford is a discount or deep-discount broker?

This will take a little research on your part. It would be great if you could look in the financial section of your local paper and find two columns: "good companies" and "not so good companies." However, the line between good and bad gets a little fuzzy when you try and apply everyone's individual values and agendas to a company's business practices. That's why you have to do the digging for yourself and make up your own mind.

More and more people are starting to find ways to integrate their value system with their daily lives. Recycling used to be reserved for school fund-raising drives and extremists who lived in communes on the outskirts of the city; today, thousands of cities across the country have enacted community-wide recycling programs, and sorting the glass from paper products seems to have become a way of life for most of us. That's just one example of how people can make small changes in their lives and have their actions be more consistent with their beliefs.

Another way new investors can achieve the same goal is by integrative investing, or Socially Responsible Investing (SRI). By participating in SRI, you're putting your money to work; not just for you, but for your community, your society, even your planet. You do this by making your stock purchases according to a certain criteria: eliminating companies whose practices you don't condone (for example, a paper company that clear-cuts forests) and choosing companies who you do support (such as beauty products manufacturers who do not participate in animal testing).

Integrative investing is a great way for you to not only express your opinions about positive social change, but also to help enact change.

There are currently over 40 mutual funds that could be characterized as socially responsible, and with a little research, you can find lots of publicly held "green" companies (those that practice responsible Earth-friendly policies).

A number of private and nonprofit organizations publish lists and directories of companies that are kind to both the

Earth and its inhabitants; getting your hands on such a list could help you narrow your search even further. For example, the National Anti-Vivisection Society (NAVS) prints a comprehensive directory that lists which companies participate in animal testing, and which do not. If animal rights is one of the criteria you want to use to pick a stock, then you'd start with a list like theirs, or a similar one from People for the Ethical Treatment of Animals (PETA).

DO YOUR HOMEWORK!

You can find green and socially responsible companies that share your particular ideology, no matter what that might be. A good way to explore some options is to pick up a magazine like *GreenMoney Journal* or *E: The Environmental Magazine,* and start reading about some of the pro-earth (and pro-people) companies that are out there. Lots of the advertisers in environmental magazines would probably be a good place to start, too. You can also find hundreds of potential investments in Coop America's Green Pages, which is a national listing of companies that don't abuse the earth or its inhabitants. You should also call one of the socially responsible mutual funds listed on page 80 and ask them to send you specific information on what companies make up their portfolio and what kinds of screens they use to judge potential investments.

Becoming familiar with the business practices of a potential investment is something you should get into the habit of regardless of whether or not you're looking for green investments. For example, if you're a pro-choice advocate, wouldn't you want to know if the board of directors (or founder) of a company whom you are considering buying into contributes heavily to pro-life organizations? If a manufacturer that you think is a good investment is being boycotted by human rights organizations because of their treatment of workers in third-world countries, wouldn't you want to know that before sinking your stash of cash into their future?

These factors should also help shape your purchasing decisions. Sure, most of the books with titles like *How to Make a Killing in the Stock Market Overnight* will tell you it's all about price, buying low and selling high. That's true, if money is your driving force. But there's no reason you can't make conscionable decisions and money at the same time.

Determine if this Company Is a Viable Prospect

How do you know if the company that interests you might be a good investment? You do the math. You learn a little about the economy and you learn to read a financial statement (I can sense your eyes glazing over with that 2:50-in-the-afternoon-low-blood-sugar-this-is-the-most-boring-class-I've-ever-had kind of look in your eyes). It isn't that bad, really, and it's essential if you're going to develop any skill at all in picking stocks.

Call the company and ask for a prospectus. This will give you detailed financial information, including income, expenses, profit over the last few years, and so on. Reading a financial statement takes time and practice, so get help. If

INVESTING WITH A CONSCIENCE

Mutual fund managers use a set of criteria, called a screen, to determine if a potential investment is socially responsible. Here are some examples of positive screens (or good points) and negative screens (or bad points). You can use variations on these screens when you're reviewing a potential investment.

POSITIVE SCREENS
LOOK FOR COMPANIES THAT:
treat their employees well
offer equal opportunity for women/minorities
offer employee and family benefits, health care, and child care
treat customers well
have a good reputation for being involved in the community
are concerned about the safety of their products
have a good human rights record
have a good environmental record
are not major polluters
participate in recycling programs
are receptive to shareholder activism
offer smoke-free workplaces

NEGATIVE SCREENS
AVOID COMPANIES THAT:
exhibit discriminatory labor and employment practices
pay excessively high salaries to executives and board members
give a poor response to shareholders
have a human rights violation record
do business with repressive governments
contract for defense and weapons
participate in unethical or questionable business practices
have a poor environmental record
dump hazardous waste illegally
manufacture alcohol or tobacco products
test on animals
use questionable advertising techniques
manufacture products of poor quality
have had a lot of lawsuits filed against them

you don't know anyone who's familiar with the stock market, go to an economics teacher at your school (or the local community college) and ask for help. You'll find everything you need in the financials to determine if this company looks like a good bet, or if you might as well dig a hole and throw all your extra money into it.

Based on the potential for this industry, the values and principles of this particular company, and their specific financial outlook, you're ready to decide if this is where you're going to park your money for a little while.

The Mechanics of Buying Stock

The hard part is over, and the rest truly is downhill (well, it is if you consider handing your hard-earned money over to a total stranger easy). The actual mechanics of buying stock are incredibly simple: first, find a broker; then give her your money. Pretty simple after everything else you've been through, isn't it? To find a broker, look through your phone book or the financial/business section of your local newspaper. Find out whether the broker is full-service, discount, or deep-discount (it should say this in the ad; if it doesn't, call and ask). You can interview brokers over the phone, or you can go down to their offices and talk to them in person. An in-person interview is preferred—you'll be tell if you feel comfortable with them, and besides, you'll probably have to go down there to open a brokerage account anyway. You also have the option of finding and using a broker over the Internet, but you might feel more comfortable using someone you can contact easily and have met in person.

Once you find a brokerage firm you like, go down to their offices and tell them that you want to buy so many shares of XYZ Company. You'll fill out some paperwork, and then they'll take your money. In exchange for your hard-earned dough, you'll get either a receipt or stock certificates. Not many firms issue stock certificates anymore, but some do. If you are offered stock certificates, treat them as if they were gold, because in a sense, they are. (If you lose your stock certificates during that mega spring cleaning that's taking place in your bedroom, it's your tough luck—unless, of course, you photocopied the certificates and can provide your broker with the stock numbers.) This is an extreme hassle, not to mention nerve-racking. If you have a choice, leave the shares with the broker. Not only will this save you a giant headache, it's easier for you to make future transactions. Let's say that you decide later on to sell that stock and buy another; all you do is place a call to your broker and tell her what to do.

The money you get from a sale could be deposited into your account with that brokerage firm, or it could be paid to you directly, closing your account. If you think you might buy another stock in the near future, you might as well leave the

Contact the following socially responsible mutual funds for a prospectus:

Aquinas: (214) 233-6655

Calvert: (800) 368-2748

Citizens Trust: (800) 223-7010

Parnassus: (800) 999-3505

Pro-Conscience Women's Equity Fund: (800) 424-2295

money where it is, unless you really need it. It will be less of a hassle for you when you're ready to trade again (which will probably be shortly, because you're really starting to develop a taste for this high-finance kind of thing, aren't you?).

What Are You Waiting For?

Why sit around and complain about the way things are when you can change the way things will be? These are two good reasons to get our your paper and pencil and start making lists of what you want to accomplish financially, how much money you can afford to start with, and what sort of screens you want to apply to potential investments. Obviously, any investment you make should be entered into carefully, with a lot of investigation and care. So what are you waiting for?

Have a ball—

after all,

it's only money!

Chapter Six

START AND RUN A SMALL BUSINESS

The next time you're sitting around your humble palace thinking of ways to catapult yourself to the top, consider owning your own business. Becoming a captain of industry may make you fabulously wealthy and help you break away from the pack of other would-be world rulers. Take a look at the kind of influence some business leaders have:

Ted Turner, head honcho at Turner Communications, the mega-entertainment corporation, has a lot to do with what you see—and don't see—on his television stations, TNT and TBS. (As far as role models go, you could do a lot worse than Ted. In September 1997, Turner pledged more than $1 billion over a period of ten years to the U.N.)

Microsoft founder Bill Gates, the richest man in America, has led the world on a nineties version of the magical mystery tour with Windows and his dreamy question, "Where do you want to go today?"

It has not escaped me that both of these examples are men; I know there are a lot of women out there in positions of power, but let's face it, it's high time that girls got this sort of influence. Maybe you're not quite ready to found your own communication firm or write the software that will lead to the next Microsoft, but there are lots of ways for you to start a small business and grow it into a medium-sized business (and maybe someday grow that into an empire of your own). Even if you're not inclined to dominate the world right this minute, having your own business is also a good way to make some spending money.

Girl-owned and operated businesses are sprouting up all over the place, and they're more than dog-walking, baby-sitting, and paper routes. Basically, anything you do or make that other people like well enough to pay money for could be turned into a business.

IS THERE ROOM FOR ONE MORE?

If there's room in China for a McDonald's, there's room in the U.S. for another girl-owned business.

Madam C.J. Walker was America's first female self-made millionaire. Starting with just $1.50 she made doing other people's laundry, she built an empire of hair-care products.

"Mama" Laurenzo turned one taco stand into a $75 million business.

Marsha Serlin started her scrap-metal business while she was still heavily in debt, but she turned it into $45 million a year.

Lillian Vernon, the queen of kitschy mail-order, was a college drop-out who went on to build a $238 million empire.

Most of the information in this chapter refers to marketing a product, not a service. However, if your business idea is service-oriented—something like desktop publishing or gardening—you can adapt most of what you'll find here to suit your needs. Selling a service is not that different from selling a product; it's just that you're mostly selling yourself and your skills instead of something you made with your hands.

Does Your Brain Hurt Already?

If you browse any of the hundreds of books that have been written about starting and running a small business, you might be completely discouraged and think that it's a huge enterprise requiring an army of lawyers, accountants, and sales-people. How can you make a million dollars with a business if you need a million to start one? You don't. Even though there are bunches of books about finding investors, applying for a bank loan, hiring attorneys, and finding equipment and building leases, none of these are necessary for you to start your small business. Some of these books have some valuable reference material—stuff on permits, licenses, and things like that—but a lot of the other information is out of your league (at least, for now), and you can get most of what you need for free from the government.

Thousands of girls your age have a marketable skill or product but aren't encouraged to start their own businesses. Why not? Maybe they think that they need to be older to start their own business; that they need some work experience and a nice little savings account to tap into. Sure, you could wait and do it that way. If you think about it, you're at the perfect age for beginning your own business for two reasons. First, you don't have to worry about supporting yourself right now because you're probably still living at home. Second, your free time is still you're own—you're not struggling to handle a full-time job or a full-time family.

What Do You Have to Sell?

Imagine that you make wind chimes (sure, you'd rather make gold-plated jewelry or blown glass figurines or something like that, but you're starting small, remember?). You figured out more than how to beat the boys at softball during all those summers at camp—somewhere along the way, you learned how to make a pretty cool wind chime. Your specialty is a little number with dangly ceramic butterfly figures that tinkle in the wind. You even spray paint the butterflies cool, retro glow-in-the-dark colors.

You love making wind chimes, and your mother loves to show them off—your front porch is a virtual sea of wind chimes, all tinkling in harmony and giving off the weirdest glow-in-the-dark spectacle that anyone in your town's seen since black light posters went out of style. Your friends like your wind chimes, too. They're always pestering you to make some for them, and pretty soon, it occurs to you that the lovely tinkling of all those wind chimes sounds something like the ringing of a cash register.

But before you start buying glow-in-the-dark paint by the gallon, ask yourself these questions:

Do I have a marketable product?

Am I willing to put in some time to make my business a success?

Do I have the support and resources I'll need?

You'll notice that none of those questions ask how much money you have to sink into this new business. While a lot of money up front may help, it's not essential. You can start small and let your income dictate how fast and how far you'll go. Some of the most successful entrepreneurs started their empires with little more than the spare change in their pockets. Who knows? Maybe you'll be the next C.J. Walker.

Make a Plan

The first thing you should do is write a plan for your business. List what you want to do and how you're going to accomplish your goals. For example:

Q: What products are you going to make?

Just wind chimes? Are you going to make them in one style or different styles?

Q: Who is your market?

That is, who do you think will like your wind chimes? Remember, finding people to pay for your wind chimes is a little different than finding people who will gladly accept them as gifts.

Q: How do you plan on selling your product?

Are you going to find yourself a windy corner and prop yourself up in a booth or are you going to take advantage of things like mail order, swap meets, and retail stores?

Q: How would you like to see this business expand?

Is your goal to support yourself completely with the sales of your wind chimes someday, or do you plan to use this money solely as extra cash?

There are no major rules for how you should structure your plan; it's mainly for your own use and you might not ever show it to anyone. You'll read in small business start-up books that a business plan is essential for attracting investors and applying for a loan. That's true, for a bigger business, but your purpose for writing a business plan is to focus your thoughts and help you determine the best way to approach your business. If you need help writing a business plan, there are plenty of examples available at your library or bookstore. However, most of the examples you'll find are for businesses that are starting with capital of over $100,000. Don't stress, just take three or four 0's off that figure and it'll apply to you, too.

"Doing Business As"

This is always the best part. Whether you're starting a magazine, forming a band, or getting a new business off the ground, coming up with a name is something you always anticipate. Choosing a name for a business is a little more important, mostly because you can always change the name of a band or a 'zine, but your business name quickly becomes your identity with the buying public. (Where would Kleenex be if it were called Nose Tissuz one week, and Kleenex the next?)

"Really," you may think to yourself, "how important can the name be? My little wind chime business is just a small sideline gig; it's not like it's going to be splattered on thirty-foot billboards or anything." Maybe so, but lots of people make their purchasing decisions based on name alone, and having a catchy or memorable name will give you an edge over the competition. Make the name descriptive of what you do or sell, make it easy to remember and spell, and avoid overly cute or catchy names (because there will definitely come a day when you are sick to death of hearing it). Make a list of all the possibilities and try them out on your friends; if you're artistic, design some logos to fit the name, and live with those for a little while, too. After a few days, one will probably stand out in your mind as being the best.

If you use a name that is anything other than your legal name, like "Mary Jones' Tinkling Wind Chimes," some (but not all) states require that you file a fictitious business name statement, or DBA (DBA means "doing business as"), with your county clerk. Your DBA is a matter of public record; it tells people who owns your business. Fees vary from county to county, but they usually run from $10 to $20.

One reason that people might need to know who's behind your business is if they have a complaint against you. That's more of a reason not to get a DBA, but if it's required in your state, you have no choice. The county clerk will give you a receipt that shows the business name and your legal name. Most states require that you file your DBA within a certain time period (usually 30 days) of starting your business.

Some banks require a DBA to open a business bank account, but in some states, the bank can give you a DBA for free when you open an account. Check with your local county clerk for the laws of your state. When you're first starting out, you probably won't get a bank account in your business' name; most banks have a minimum deposit requirement for business accounts, and that deposit amount plus the cost of checks to get you started can add up fast. While you're still using your own name, you'll have to make sure that any stores selling your product write checks to you in your name so you can cash them.

DBAs are valid for up to five years—the exact length of time is determined by your county's laws. After your DBA expires, you must renew it immediately if

BIZ TIP

If you receive checks made out to the business name and don't have a business account set up, you can still cash them. Endorse the check as the business by writing the name of the business as it appears on the front of the check. Then below that, sign your own name and write your account number. Deposit the check through the ATM. While a teller might ask you for some business ID or tell you that you need a business account to keep cashing those checks, an ATM will take your money no questions asked, and it's pretty unlikely that the bank will reject your deposit.

you're still doing business. If you go out of business before the DBA expires, there is no need to cancel it. Some counties also require that you file a change of address if you move your residence while operating the business. Check with your county clerk for your county's specific requirements.

Most counties require that, in addition to filing your DBA, you also run an ad in a local paper for up to four consecutive weeks, announcing your filing. Lots of bigger cities have newspapers that specialize in DBAs, and the county clerk's office can usually direct you to at least one. The cost for a DBA announcement also varies, but can run between $40 to $80.

Do you Need to Register Your Trademark?

A trademark is a word, or group of words, that distinguish your company or product from competitors. A trademark can also be a logo. Here are some examples of company names and trademarks.

Business Name	Trademark
Chrysler	Jeep
Apple Computer	Macintosh
Estee Lauder	Clinique

Trademark laws are complex, and trademark searches (a way to find out if any other businesses are using your name) can be expensive. Just the cost of filing your trademark on a federal level is over $200. In the beginning, your business name will be your trademark.

Until your trademark or logo is listed in the federal trademark register, you cannot legally use the trademark symbol ®. You can, however, protect your claim to your name by placing the letters "TM" next to it wherever it appears, like this:

WindSong Wind Chimes™

If you're running a service-oriented business and you're not selling products, you would have a service mark instead of a trademark, and you would use the letters "SM," like this:

WindSong Designs SM

Since WindSong is a pretty small, local company (at least for now), you don't really have to worry about registering

If you'd like to learn more about trademarks, contact:

**U.S. Patent & Trademark Office
Dept. of Commerce
Washington, DC 20231**

your name or trademark. To avoid possible confusion for your customers, though, make an effort to see if anyone else in your community is already using the name you've chosen. You can do this by checking local phone books or asking the county clerk. If you find there's another business with a name similar to yours, you may want to change your name.

WindSong, Inc.: Sounds cool, doesn't it? Sounds so professional, so successful. Unfortunately, it's also illegal. You can't use any of the following words in your business name unless you are a legal corporation or follow specific guidelines: Incorporated, Inc., Ltd., Limited, National, Federal, United States, and Olympic.

Do You Need a License?

Whether or not you'll need a business license or permit depends on what kind of products and/or services you're selling. Some licenses are required by the county, some by the state, and some by the federal government. Dealing in guns, alcohol, or tobacco, or operating a meat-packing plant (I hope you aren't doing any of these things) requires a federal license. State licenses are granted for day care centers, beauty shops, and businesses related to the medical profession. A wind chime business wouldn't need any of those licenses, but if you're unsure about your particular business, ask your county clerk for information about the laws of your state.

If you are marketing a product for resale, you'll probably need a seller's permit, which allows you to collect sales tax from the public on any products you sell. This permit also lets you buy supplies at lower wholesale prices without having to pay sales tax on them.

On your permit is a number similar to a social security number. You use that number when paying the state sales tax you've collected from the sales of your product. You have to collect sales tax on items sold only within the state where your business is located. That's why, in infomercials and other ads, they always add statements like "California residents add 8.5% sales tax." You can get a seller's permit from your state board of equalization; check the government listings in the front of your phone book for the office in your city. If you're under eighteen, your state may require that your parents or guardian have the license and/or permit issued in their name.

Setting up Shop

Before you run out and print 2000 business cards with your especially catchy name all over them, think about where you want your business to be located. Not the physical location of your workspace—that'll probably be your basement, bedroom, attic, or wherever—but the address you want to give out to people. If you don't feel comfortable using your home address, rent a P.O. Box. They're only about $40 a year at the post office; you can also rent a P.O. Box at private mail centers. You can't use a P.O. Box as your address on legal documents like licenses and permits, but you don't have to give your personal address to strangers to conduct business. If you don't want to give out your home phone number, get voice mail. A voice mail box starts at about $20 per month from the phone company, and private companies offer them starting at around $10 per month.

How and Where Can You Sell Your Products?

There are two ways to sell those tinkling wind chimes that everyone loves: wholesale and retail. Retail sales are directly to the public. You collect sales tax on the sale (in many circumstances) and make quarterly tax payments to the state board of equalization. Because you probably won't have a storefront when you're first starting out, for you, selling retail would mean going through flea markets and open-air markets, or selling directly to the public through the mail.

Selling wholesale means that you sell your products to a store or other distributor at a discount—which can range from 30 to 50 percent—and that retailer sells your wind chimes to the buying public. Most retailers mark up the products they buy wholesale by 100 percent. That means that if you can sell your glow-in-the-dark wind chimes to someone for $20, you'll probably get only about $10 for them from a store. You can obviously make more money on individual sales by selling retail, but other costs may significantly reduce your profits.

Selling Retail

Flea markets, also known as swap meets, open-air markets, and public markets, have been around since the days when people traded goats for beaded necklaces. Some flea markets are nothing more than a huge conglomeration of individual garage sales where vendors sell used clothing, appliances, and furniture—sometimes just junk. Others are very professional and businesslike. There, vendors usually sell new and homemade items like crafts, clothing, and furniture. At specialty and hobby swap meets, vendors sell only car parts, for example, or dolls, computer parts, or even fresh produce.

Small, local flea markets are an excellent way to test the business waters; the cost can be relatively low and you'll discover pretty quickly if there's a demand for your product. At most of these, you rent a space for the day. You usually don't have to pay the owner of that space a percentage of your take; it's all yours. Rental rates vary depending on the size of the market, where it's located, the type of merchandise sold, and the range of income that you can make in a day. Rates are as low as $15 per day to hundreds of dollars. Just keep in mind that in order to make money, the rental fee has to be offset by how much money you make in a day, so when you're first starting out (and don't really have an idea of how much money your wind chimes are going to bring in), start out with as inexpensive a space as possible. You usually have to provide your own furniture—things like display tables, chairs for you to sit on, signs, and other stuff—but at some larger meets these will be provided at extra cost to you.

You can probably find lots of local markets in your area. Some are open every day, while others operate only on weekends. Do some research before you sign up anywhere. You don't want to get into a situation where you spend $50 to rent a booth and then sell only one or two wind chimes.

Spend a few weekends browsing the flea markets in your city; check out some smaller and cheaper ones as well as some of the more expensive locations. Ask one of the vendors for information about the price of a booth and who you should contact. Unless you're in direct competition with that vendor, she or he will probably be more than happy to help you out. While you're there, check out the booths of vendors who sell products similar to the ones you make. Get an idea of the quality of merchandise being sold at that particular flea market and how much it costs. By looking at some other booths, you also get ideas for decorating a booth on a tiny budget.

Arts and crafts fairs are like swap meets for artists; you'll usually find lots of photographers, sculptors, painters, jewelers, and probably a few wind chime makers. The price of a booth at an arts and crafts fair will probably be on the high side (they can often be $1000 or more); the advantage is that the people who come to that fair are usually coming to buy exactly what you're selling: homemade crafts. Some fairs hold competitions with a cash prize.

Selling retail can sometimes be a pain; you have to deal with picky (and often complaining) customers, and you have to remember to collect and set aside the proper sales tax. On the other hand, working a flea market on an occasional Sunday can be a relatively easy way to raise a nice little chunk of change—if you can find one at the right price and with the right clientele. It may take a little time to find your niche, but once you do, you can make a good profit.

Selling Wholesale

If you decide you don't want to sell directly to the public, you can concentrate on wholesale sales. This works in two ways: either the store buys your products outright, or you sell them on consignment. The difference is that when you sell on consignment, the store pays only for the merchandise that they've sold, and they pay you only after the products have been paid for. Consignment is an excellent way to get your products in the door with reluctant store managers. There's virtually no risk at all for the store or for you, and you both stand a chance of making some money. This is most likely the way you'll start.

When you start thinking about stores where your products might sell, think small. You won't be able to walk into a huge store like Macy's or Sears and get much of a reception. All the merchandise in big chain stores is purchased by a national buyer, and she usually buys at industry trade shows. Look for small, locally owned stores. Go to places where they already know you.

Be creative. If you make jewelry, don't limit yourself to boutiques. Try some vintage clothing stores; even CD stores sell crystals, pendants, and handmade jewelry. Once you find a few stores you'd like to approach, call first and get the name of the manager or the person who does the buying. Then call her and ask for an appointment. Tell her about your product and why you think it would suit her store. When you present your products, make them look as attractive as possible. Get a case to carry them in and show them off. Put price tags on everything and take a wide variety of samples.

BIZ TIP

For more professional-looking price tags, get a rubber stamp made with your logo or company name. This costs less than $20 and you can use different color inks to make your tags look more appealing. Then take some cool recycled or colored paper, cut it into small pieces, fold it, and stamp the outside with your logo. Write the price of the piece on the inside, then attach the homemade price tag with colored embroidery string for a professional, but not stuffy, look.

If the manager likes your merchandise but is reluctant to take a chance on you, offer to leave your products on consignment, then check with her every week or so to see how it's going. If they sell out, great! You can drop off some more merchandise and get paid for what she sold. If the products aren't selling, the store may ask you to come and get them. That's okay; it might take some time to find a store that's right for you.

Keep very accurate records of where you left your merchandise, with whom, and how much of it you left. You also need to agree beforehand on the discount the store will receive for the merchandise. Remember the example: If your best wind chime goes for $20, the store will probably want a 50 percent discount, giving you only $10.

How Much Should You Charge?

Knowing how much you should charge for your product is difficult, but it's the key to making money. The perfect price is low enough to attract buyers, but high enough to ensure a profit. It's hard to price items you made with your own hands. Of course, the girl who knits pencil cozies is sure that they're valuable—the craftsmanship and quality alone makes each one worth at least $20, right? That may be what she thinks, and it may be what her mom thinks, but if she wants to sell any of them, she's probably going to have to come down from her cloud and drop her price.

Pricing is tricky when you have no experience, and you're probably going to have to make some adjustments along the way. A good starting point is to take the cost of making the product, add the cost of labor, then add the profit margin you want.

Let's say the wholesale price for the materials needed to make a wind chime runs about $2. It takes you about 30 minutes to put the wind chime together and another 30 minutes to paint it, so your total labor takes about an hour. You're going to be generous and allow yourself a salary of $10 an hour (you may not think that's very generous, but for a brand new business it is). Here's an example of how your costs might look:

materials:	$2
plus labor:	$10
equals wholesale cost:	$12
plus profit margin:	$8
equals retail price:	$20

GROWING YOUR BUSINESS

Lots of successful business people will tell you that one of the keys to their success is constantly thinking about ways to improve: your product, your service, your sales, your advertising, anything you can think of to boost sales and expand. Here are some ways to keep your business (and your interest) growing:

Keep checking out the competition. Stay on top of changes in the market; if you see a competitor selling a lot of musical wind chimes (mind-boggling, yes, but it could happen), consider adding a few to your product line.

Target your advertising so that you get the most for your dollar. When you place an ad, add some kind of code to tell you which ads people are responding to and which they're not. For example, in your local alternative paper, you might add the code "Dept. A" to your address. In another ad you've placed in a trade magazine, you might add the code "Dept. B." Now you can keep track of where people are seeing your ads and how you can more effectively spend your advertising dollars.

Keep building your mailing list, and more importantly, use it! A list made of existing customers is like a gold mine to a retailer, because everyone on your list has either already purchased a wind chime or asked about one. As your business grows, use your mailing list to keep in touch with your customers—send them postcards on upcoming sales or new product lines; offer summer discounts and price breaks for referring others to your business. Send customer surveys to the people on your list, asking them what they like about their wind chimes and asking for suggestions. Get the survey typed or printed on a postage-paid postcard so they'll be sure to return it.

Get on the Web. You're a lot luckier than your great-grandfather, who had to push his fruit and vegetable cart for miles to build a business for himself. Your generation has the Internet! The Web is good for a lot more than research on spider monkeys and meeting people in chat rooms. You can easily build a Web page that highlights your product and gets it out to potential buyers all over the world.

If that price is in line with similar wind chimes you've seen, then you're on target. If it's lower, you can either raise your price and maybe make a little more profit, or you can leave your price a bit lower than the competition to give yourself an edge. But if the price of your cool wind chimes is a few dollars higher than the competition's, you're going to have to cut your expenses, labor, or profit margin.

You have a lot more latitude with price if you're selling directly to the public than you do by selling wholesale to stores. If someone at a swap meet offers you $15, you'd probably take it. A retail store doesn't have that kind of bargaining power. That's one reason a lot of craftspeople sell through a combination of retail and wholesale. You'll eventually find what works best for you.

The Business of Business

No matter how small you may think your modest little wind chime enterprise is, in the eyes of the government (namely the IRS), it is subject to the same requirements, like taxes, that other businesses are. That's why it's important to keep accurate records of money coming in and money going out. You don't have to get complicated and you don't have to hire an accountant; just get a ledger from the stationery store and set up a simple bookkeeping system.

The format of your ledger doesn't matter. Just keep track of everything you sell, including tax for sales within your state. You may want to put the money you collect for taxes in a separate column. You also need to keep detailed records of what you spend for your business, including

---

THE BEST PUBLICITY IS FREE

Donate products to raffles, giveaways, and local charities.

Offer to teach a free class in making wind chimes (or whatever craft you do so well) at the local elementary school or senior center.

Write press releases about your new business and send them to local papers (the novelty of teen business owners attracts a lot of newspapers on the lookout for human interest stories).

Offer to speak to local groups (like clubs and schools) about becoming an entrepreneur.

---

supplies, fees you pay for booth rentals, anything that is related to operating your business. Be sure to keep accurate records of your expenses because you can use these to offset any income tax you'll have to pay. And keep the receipts for everything you buy or spend that is business-related, like crafts magazines. Keep the receipts in a separate place, like a shoe box, so they're easily accessible at tax time. Once your sales begin to rise, go into one of the chain-store accountants like H&R Block or Sears and consult with someone about how to set up your books. They sometimes hand out free ledger books to keep track of expenses and mileage.

You also have to make regular sales tax payments to your state board of equalization. If you fall behind on this, you could be hit with penalties. You may also have to make estimated income tax payments on a quarterly basis, based on how much money you're making. Self-employment income is taxed at a slightly higher rate than money you would make working for someone else, so be sure you keep accurate records to reduce the amount of your tax liability. It may seem like every single dime you make is going to be swallowed up by taxes, but it won't. In fact, you may find out that the taxes you have to pay on your business are negligible.

If you're in doubt about any of the taxes you have to pay, and when, visit the nearest state or federal office and pick up some brochures or talk to some clerks. A few hours of research is better than finding out at the end of the year that you underpaid taxes, or skipped them altogether, and are now facing back taxes and penalties.

Selling Through Mail-Order

Selling through the mail can be extremely profitable, no matter if your company has one employee (namely you) or one thousand employees. It's especially good for small companies because you don't need to maintain an office or storefront to show off your products, and you can reach a wider clientele than if you were restricted to a store. After you hook up to the Internet and build yourself a Web page to showcase your products, you could be sending products around the world!

Big companies like L.L. Bean and Avon do a huge mail-order business. Most of their sales come from one of two places: advertising they've placed in a magazine or newspaper, or through a direct mail campaign. Both methods can be effective, but both can also waste your money if you're not careful. If you want to

try some ads, place classified ads first (they're much cheaper than display ads) and see if you get any response. Let your advertising budget grow with your sales. It's easy to get carried away with advertising and start placing ads everywhere in sight, but this adds up fast.

Direct mail might be cheaper, if you target your mailing carefully. Huge, national direct mail campaigns are

> With the proper planning and just a little motivation, you could easily become the next Mrs. Fields or Mary Kay. In fact, there's no reason you can't be the next Bill Gates.

expensive—the cheapest list rental is about $500, and when you add the price of postage and printing catalogs, pretty soon you're spending a lot of money you haven't made yet. But you can take advantage of mail order by using your own list. Keep a record (the name and mailing address) of every person who buys one of your wind chimes or even expresses an interest in them. As your list grows, use it to keep in touch with customers and potential customers. Make a small catalog and mail it out regularly, or just send a note to say hi and thanks. Add anyone to your list who you think would like to receive info on your company (if you're not sure, add them anyway). Use postcards, if you can; they're cheaper to mail than first-class letters, so you can mail to a larger list for the same cost.

Can the Businesswomen's Hall of Fame be Far Behind?

There's a lot more to forming a business than deciding what you're going to sell.

You may not know a thing about mailing lists, pricing structures, tax laws, marketing, and profits at this stage, but after a few months of running your own business, you'll either pick it up and run with it, or decide it's not for you and move on. Just plan each step carefully and resist the temptation to throw money at every problem or situation that comes up.

Just think of it: soon you'll be earning massive sums of money, employing staggering numbers of people, and realizing incredible amounts of profit! You'll be able to fund progressive, positive social programs, like youth employment and company-paid day care; your ecologically sound and animal-friendly business practices will be the model for other new businesses for decades to come. You'll be a mover and shaker, right? And forget about being invited to the White House, you'll soon be redecorating it yourself with those little glow-in-the-dark wind chimes that started the whole thing.

One Angry Girl Takes Over the World

Because many of you still might think that you don't know enough about anything to start your own business, it might help to meet Jill Portugal, owner, designer, and all around Rad Chick at One Angry Girl Designs, a company that sells T-shirts with feminist slogans like NOT FOR DECORATIVE PURPOSES ONLY. Jill started her company pretty much out of nothing—all she had was $100 in her pocket and absolutely no business experience. Most of what she

FIVE GOLDEN RULES OF STARTING YOUR OWN BUSINESS

by Jill Portugal
owner of One Angry Girl Designs

1. You have to believe, above all else, that your product is worth selling. If you don't, you're going to crumble the first time someone says they won't stock it.

2. When setting prices, think about what you'd pay. I personally wouldn't pay $16 for a T-shirt unless it had Michael Stipe's sweat on it. You need to make enough money to keep going; don't expect to pay rent out of your profits. You can always raise your price later.

3. You don't need to spend a lot on stationery and stuff; make it on your computer. Keep it simple. I buy business cards at the machines you see in bus stations and hardware stores. They work fine.

4. When you write your press releases, remember that modesty will get you nowhere. Say that you have the most fabulous product on the planet. Say you are gaining strength and power by the day, and by the end of the month you will rule several continents. No one can prove it isn't true; plus, it gets attention.

5. Don't pay for business advice. The government has tons of information and volunteers to help you. Lots of women-in-business organizations can answer your questions, too. Go to the library instead of buying books.

Jill Sez

The best things about having my own company:

It is the funnest thing ever.

Nobody gets to tell me what to do, and I get to make all the decisions myself.

I get to look at my shirts and think that they would have never existed if not for me.

Doing something O.A.G.-related makes me happy when I am not especially happy.

It makes me feel like my life has more meaning than it did a year ago.

Customers write me nice notes and tell me I'm cool, and generally sound pretty psyched to be ordering my stuff.

I get to find out about and talk to a lot of cool women who are doing great things, and I would have never met any of them if I hadn't done this.

It's better than sitting around whining. Remember, if you're not part of the solution, you're part of the problem (I can't believe I just said that).

I suddenly can do all these things I never did before, like interview prospective vendors and talk marketing strategy and get business cards and write press releases.

I feel like I'm part of something bigger than me—is that cheesy?

Office supplies! Office supplies! Office supplies!

It cheers me up when I'm unemployed.

I get to impress (and frighten) people who ask, "So what do you do?"

I like to think I'm helping American girls in some itty-bitty way.

It's something I never knew I could do, and here I am. It gives me a really strong, almost impregnable kind of confidence.

I get to be interviewed, which I adore.

It makes me feel like I can do whatever I want and take the company in whatever direction I hope.

It's a nice respite from working in corporate environments.

The worst things about having my own company (don't stress, there are only six!):

It often feels like me against the world.

People in stores are not all that delightful to deal with.

People I thought for sure would be psyched to help me, have not, and that's somewhat disillusioning.

It's hard to do everything at once—plus the things that I enjoy the most tend to get done at the expense of things I don't like to do.

Rejection can suck.

There's no one to blame but myself when things go wrong.

learned, like how to find stores to carry her merchandise and how to determine a price, she learned by making mistakes and trying different things.

Jill started her mini-empire after coming up with a few slogans and deciding that they'd look cool on a T-shirt. She approached a few T-shirt companies, and after finding one she liked, placed an order for twelve shirts. "The first place I went was a 'zine store that took four on consignment," she says. "I had no idea how to price the product, so I called the women's bookstore; they said they usually do a 60/40 split. I made more if I sold to friends or friends of friends—I could charge ten or so and keep half for myself. We'd put them on the walls at our parties with a price tag that said, 'Ten bucks, see Jill,' and I sold about six that way."

Although she wasn't exactly making enough money to quit her day job, Jill was on her way to building a name for her company. After a couple of months, she registered her business name ("it cost $12, no big deal") and filed for a DBA and a separate business account. "My advice," she says, "is to get two wallets! If you borrow money from your business to buy food because you're too lazy to go to the cash machine, make sure you write a note saying exactly what you owe your company, or else you will forget."

She got a big break when *Ms.* magazine rofiled her with a short paragraph in one of their issues. "I got about 75 calls, and about a third of them have ordered so far. Plus every girl who called is cool, and now I have a mailing list which I secretly consider my small army." She also started to grow her company by learning more about marketing and advertising. "I took

books out of the library on marketing and skimmed them. They were minimally helpful because when they talked about 'marketing on a shoestring,' their shoestring was something like $2000. But it was also encouraging because some of the stuff they said to do was stuff I'd already done, so I felt pretty smart. I also talked to the people in the stores for advice."

Today, One Angry Girl is still growing. Although it's not yet supporting Jill full-time, she's busily plotting not just for material success, but the kind of butt-kicking influence that any girl who wants to rule the world desires. "My ultimate dream is to expand One Angry Girl beyond T-shirts and become a major cultural force," she says. "First I want a full line of shirts, then maybe I'll move into bumper stickers and posters and other merchandise. Then I want to network all my girls together into a big revolution. I want to be the girl they call for a comment when some kind of national event happens and they need a feminist's opinion."

Jill admits, "I had no earthly clue how to run a business; I just wanted to do it. I wrote myself a little mission statement that was something like, 'I want to start a business called One Angry Girl. I have $100. I might lose my money. I might do something really stupid, but that's okay. It's only $100. Everything will be okay.'"

To learn more about One Angry Girl Designs, write to Jill at P.O. Box 675, N. Cambridge, MA 02140, or call (888) ANGRY-11.

PART THREE

SHAPE YOUR CULTURE

Culture—uh-oh, there's that word. How important can it really be? I mean, you know that when money talks, people listen. You also know, if you've paid attention at all in world history, that an entire country can easily be inspired and guided by just one politician—if that person has enough charisma. So, adding two and two, as girls are apt to do, you'd naturally come to believe that money and power alone would be enough to rule the world, wouldn't you? Well, you'd be wrong.

Whose literary recommendation alone can send a book straight to the top of the bestseller list? Not Newt Gingrich (his own book fizzled). Not Bill Clinton or Boris Yeltsin. If you guessed television's highest paid entertainer and the world's favorite girl, Oprah Winfrey, you'd be right on the money (literally).

Upset about the ease with which people accepted single-mother Murphy Brown's decision to raise her baby by herself, then-Vice President Dan Quayle publicly chastised her, sending the country into a roaring moral debate and coining the term "family values." No big deal? It actually is a big deal when you consider that Murphy Brown is a fictional character on a CBS sitcom.

What do these people—fictional or not—have in common? They're cultural icons, watched and copied by millions and all but guaranteed a place in our collective memory, not to mention history. I'm not here to judge whether their influence has been good or bad; merely to point out that they all have it. What this means for you is that even if you totally lack funds and force, you can still be the next Queen of the World if you can get millions of adoring subjects to bow at your feet. Nothing influences the masses like the culture in which they live.

Culture is defined as the ideas, customs, skills, and arts of a given people in a given period. That's a pretty general definition, so let's narrow it down a little. Basically, it's what you read, what you watch, what you listen to, and what you do with your spare time. It's *TV Guide*, *Bewitched* vs. *I Dream of Jeannie*, the movie grossing $90 zillion this weekend, the little one-act play down at your community theater, and trashy television talk shows. It's how you act and how your neighbors act (but not how your dog acts, although it is how you treat your dog).

icon like Madonna can get an entire generation of women to wear their bras over their shirts, who knows what kind of influence you could exert if you put your mind to it? Andy Warhol said that everyone would be famous for fifteen minutes. That's a nice idea, but you're going to need more than a quarter of an hour to make it stick.

Historically, girls have not been treated very kindly by the media. We're about to change all that! There are lots of good ways to ingratiate yourself into today's culture: You could create the next

> Tired of all the teen magazines that make you look like a boy-hungry, fashion-crazed (but food-starved), empty-headed girl? Your protests can consist of more than just not buying those magazines—you can join the ranks of the hundreds of other girls who have created and distributed their own magazines.

> Sick of all the *Baywatch*-inspired television shows that portray women as sex objects with nothing on their minds but silicone and calories? Sure, you can take part in television turnoff week, but you can also go a step further by writing, producing, and acting in your own television show and airing it on your local cable network.

Culture consists of absolutely everything around you, and can be counted on to change, sometimes drastically, depending on where "around you" is. For example, the U.S. has a capitalist, consumer culture that is vastly different from cultures of the Middle East, Africa, and China. On a smaller scale, the liberal culture you find in Los Angeles is pretty foreign to a small town like Davenport, Iowa (although that gap is narrowing all the time).

Where, you ask, am I going with this little lesson in sociology? Aside from money and political clout, the next best way to attract attention (meaning followers) to yourself is by becoming a fixture of your culture. Think about it: If a cultural

media messenger and become as powerful and as quoted as *Time* or *Newsweek*; you could write, produce, and star in the next *Ellen*.

Concentrate now, because there are some big shoes to fill. From Mary Shelley, a woman who changed our culture forever with *Frankenstein*, to Oprah Winfrey, the woman in charge of the incredibly popular talk show, to the junior high school girl in upstate New York who sweats blood to get her pro-girl 'zine out there and read, there are lots of examples of girls and women who were and are unafraid to express themselves—women like you who have what it takes to create their own media empire!

Chapter Seven

PUBLISH YOUR OWN 'ZINE

No doubt about it, having your own 'zine (pronounced "zeen") should be near the top of any serious world empress' list of Things I Must Do Today. Aside from the sheer power you can get from being the source of information for the entire world, you also get to write—and read—about things that interest you. Sure, there's always TV and radio, but 'zines are my favorite method of establishing a gargantuan media empire because they're by far the most expressive. They can also be dirt cheap to produce, which is a plus for future media magnates on a tight budget. Although seeing yourself on TV or hearing your voice on the radio is cool, it's over in a second. There's something about the written word that's permanent, almost everlasting. Copies of your 'zine could be discovered 50 years from now in somebody's attic. People could be sitting around in the year 2048, reading your essays and tripping on how you were so far ahead of your time.

Plus, I happen to think that a healthy, diverse alternative press is essential in a democratic society, because what often passes for news is often just celebrity info on who's getting divorced and who's making a million dollars per episode of their lame sitcom. It could be up to you and your 'zine to give the people a perspective that they are definitely not going to get from major media networks and publishing houses.

According to *Factsheet Five* (the ultimate 'zine directory and soon to be your personal bible), a 'zine is defined as "a small handmade amateur publication done purely out of passion, rarely making a profit or breaking even." Until recently, it wasn't only accepted that you would go broke publishing your 'zine, it was a requirement. Kind of like starving artists and suffering poets.

> **Q: How many 'zine publishers does it take to screw in a light bulb?**
>
> **A: Ten. One to screw the bulb in and nine to complain about what a sell-out she is.**

Thankfully, the days of suffering for your art are over. Poverty is no longer cool in 'zine circles, and the whole enterprise can be more than a hopeless hobby. With a little planning, skill, and determination (and the occasional shot of caffeine), your 'zine can be turned into a money-making business, or your segue to a career in publishing.

Currently, tens of thousands of home-made magazines are produced in dark, messy bedrooms all over the world. Of course, some of these are a little slicker than others, and not all of them are scrawled out by the light of a lava lamp (but that does give the genre a kind of romanticism, doesn't it?). From *SCUM*, the Society for Cutting Up Men (the grandmama of modern *grrl* magazines, published in 1968) to the *I Hate Brenda* newsletter, spawned by the wildly popular (then wildly unpopular) Brenda on Fox's cult classic, *Beverly Hills 90210*, 'zines are IT. The accessibility of home computers—and now the Internet—has furthered the cause, and what frozen yogurt was to the seventies, 'zines are to the nineties.

One of the best things about 'zine publishing is that anyone can do it, even if you don't know the first thing about magazines. You can learn all you need to know on the fly. Plus, the financial requirements are minimal (sofa change can work pretty well for this), and there are always ways to cut even those meager corners. At first, self-publishing may seem like a huge task for someone who's never done it before, but if you break it down into smaller, workable sections, it's pretty easy. You don't have any writing experience? So what. You don't have a clue about what goes into producing a magazine? Big deal. You don't need experience, a computer, a degree, or a printing press. You don't need a lot of cash. All you need is desire. Once you have that, the rest is all downhill (well, sort of).

A Little Preparation vs. Many Nights of Agony

The more planning and preparation you do up front, the better your 'zine will look and read, and the greater your chances for success will be. Many 'zine publishers are so excited about getting started, they start banging stories out, taping them down, and stapling them together before they have anything more than a title planned. What you're likely to end up with by using this method are sentences that ramble on for five pages and then suddenly disappear, or diatribes about male supremacy on one page and how to choose a really good red lipstick on the next. While it's true that coming up with a good title is not only one of the most important—and definitely one of the most fun—tasks of 'zine publishing, readers do not live by title alone. Before you begin writing even one word or designing one page, you need to answer one very important question: What is the purpose of your 'zine?

Jill in New York created her 'zine, *Cosmic Peas,* for the sole purpose of scamming tickets to the Rock 'n' Roll Hall of Fame concert in New York (it worked). Some people create 'zines to gain experience to help them someday get a job in publishing or design. Others are on a political crusade—fighting sexism, racism, corporate manipulation, and environmental waste. These are girls well on their way to ruling the world (sound familiar?).

What are you trying to accomplish with your 'zine? What is its purpose? Who's going to read it, or buy it? Is it going to be a freebie, or do you want to score some subscribers and make money? Is this just an expression of your own creativity, or are you in training for a career as a writer, artist, or designer? Every decision you make about your 'zine, from what you put in it to what kind of paper you put it on, will be determined by the answer to this question. A 'zine that you create to hand out to a few friends is a totally different project than one you plan on distributing through bookstores or by mail order.

You probably already know at least a couple of people who have produced a 'zine. There are new ones popping up, and dying out, every day. Many never see the light of day beyond their debut issue; they disappear into anonymity before the ink is even dry. While it's true that some people plan on issuing only one copy of their 'zine (in publishing, these are called one-shots), most failures are due to something other than eccentricity. Most out-of-print 'zines, and out-of-work publishers, were put there because of poor planning.

Before you begin work on your 'zine, write up a brief plan. Include answers to the questions above, and as much other information as you can think of. Make a wish list, too, and write down all the things you want to do with your 'zine, no matter how outrageous or unattainable (being featured on *Oprah* as the feminist force of the new millennium would be cool). Then, every time you're faced with a decision about your 'zine, review your plan. For instance, how much you should charge (if you want to charge at all) could be determined by who your target audience is (yuppies with lots of disposable cash or starving students).

Dredging up the Stuff in the Back of your Mind— and What to Call It

Once you have an idea where your 'zine is going to take you (or vice versa), you should come up with a name. A lot of people think this is backward, and say that you should spend a little more time with your 'zine and get to know it a little better before you title it. My feeling is that if you don't title your 'zine until it's ready to go to press, you will probably end up with a 'zine called *My Three Months in Hell* or *Publishing Is for Suckers.* It's best to come up with a title while your mind is fresh and you can still dredge up some enthusiasm for the project.

Take the pop quiz on the next page (the answers are at the end of the chapter), and you'll see that the title doesn't have to have any relevance to the content at all. In fact, the more obscure your title,

NAME YOUR POISON (ER, 'ZINE)

BELIEVE IT OR NOT—WHICH OF THESE 'ZINES ARE FOR REAL?

My Disease   Believe it   Not
"You could wake up tomorrow with a brain tumor....it could be there now and you wouldn't even know it."

Home Sick   Believe it   Not
"TV trash shows and recipes with stuff your mom will never miss."

Popcorn Feet   Believe it   Not
"Everything you love about your dog but are afraid to admit to other people."

A New Miserable Experience   Believe it   Not
"A variety of issues from a student's perspective."

Dead Budgie   Believe it   Not
"Things from my childhood that scare me still."

Armadillo Droppings   Believe it   Not
"Games, toys, stores, and miniature figurines."

Asian Girls are Rad   Believe it   Not
"Interesting zine about...life and obsession with Asian women."

Beagle Mania   Believe it   Not
Written by a "proud beagle owner."

Hangnail   Believe it   Not
"Things to do and look at during Spanish class."

Harass Me   Believe it   Not
"A political guide to being pissed off."

Chip's Closet Cleaner   Believe it   Not
"A neat story of the time he was a spy for the laundry lady."

John's Hair   Believe it   Not
"How he gets it to stay like that is a mystery to me [and] other weird things I've seen."

Blonde Brains   Believe it   Not
"Not as lightweight as brunettes think."

Pulled Mints   Believe it   Not
"A list of all the evil things about Richmond, Virginia."

Macaroni 'n Cheese   Believe it   Not
"Pop culture and girl news."

Taco Supreme   Believe it   Not
"Cool things that you never appreciate when you have time."

It Seemed Logical at the Time   Believe it   Not
"Will try to apply logic to politics, daily life, and religion."

(Answers are on page 117.)

the higher your intrigue level. And intrigue is a definite plus when you're listing your 'zine in a directory like *Factsheet Five,* which is already crammed with hundreds of titles. If you want your 'zine to jump off the page, you're going to have to come up with something that's really out there. A 'zine called *Fishwrap* really speaks to you, doesn't it? It begs to be ordered (just so you can find out what it's all about). Sometimes a less flamboyant and more descriptive name does more for promoting your 'zine; for instance, *Hip Mama* says it all: young, hip motherhood.

Once you've chosen a name, you've conquered one of the toughest parts of self-publishing. So take a minute to pat yourself on your back. You'd better get used to those self-congratulatory pats, because as most seasoned 'zine publishers will tell you, this can be a lonely, thankless job. But remember that you're on a quest for world power, and it can be lonely at the top.

Veggie Recipes, Political Rants: What to Write About?

Topic is pretty much like title—wide open. If you've never written much before, try sticking to things you know something about: sports, music, or a political agenda that you can get behind (this is a great time to dust off all your conspiracy theories about a second gunman). Since you're preparing for world domination, use your 'zine to express your own views. This is your chance to be opinionated, authoritative, and just plain bossy!

How about an animal rights/vegetarian 'zine, or one that addresses feminist issues—discrimination in your school, or the media's treatment of women. You could be the brains behind the next feminist agenda, like a mini *Ms.* There's a hot underground of *grrl* 'zines that's growing every day! Your topic can be as involved or simple as you choose. If you skateboard, or even want to skateboard, write about ollies and boards and why boys seem to be so uptight when girls want to skate. Probably the easiest topic to write about (and one that most new 'zinesters choose) is your own life. There have been really wonderful, fascinating 'zines written about personal experiences with death, friendship, mental illness, and love. The best 'zines are the ones that say something new, or say something old in a new way. Just remember, if the writing is good, they will come.

Armed with a title and topic, you're ready to maneuver your way through the minefield of late nights, depleted funds, and paper cuts we love to call self-publishing. Way to go! There's this one small detail you still need to work out: exactly what you're going to put in your 'zine. Don't worry. This can be the fun part (really). There's more than one way to express yourself—there are words, pictures, poems (there's haiku, and if you choose that, more power to you).

If you're not used to writing and creating, there are a couple of ways to help get you started. Music and movie reviews are the staples of 'zine publishing. They're to your 'zine what a pair of sturdy black shoes and a favorite pair of jeans are to your closet: Maybe you don't wear them everyday, but they're great to fall back on when you just don't want to think that hard about getting dressed. Lots of 'zine publishers count on these to fill pages, and it doesn't matter if the theme of your 'zine is music or not—you can review girl bands for a feminist 'zine, right? Keep your reviews short, and run three or four in one column. If you can score an interview with a local band, that's even better (you might be able to wrangle a paid ad out of their label).

The editorial page, a kind of "from the publisher" section where you get to talk to your readers one on one, is another staple of 'zine publishing. This is where, in teen magazines like *Tiger Beat* and *Bop,* the editor talks about all the cool celebrities that visited her offices that month for a photo shoot. If you run into Kate Winslet on a shopping trip, then by all means, this is the place to brag about how oh-so-nice she was to you. If you don't happen to meet many celebrities in your little town, or if celebrity worship turns you off (do we honestly need another magazine dedicated to the rich and famous?), then this is a good place to introduce your 'zine to your readers, to tell them what you're trying to accomplish and what you want them to get out of reading your 'zine. After you've published one or two issues, it's where you'll most likely be publishing the "I'm Sorry it's Taken So Long to Get This Issue Out" editorial, a column you can find in most 'zines.

EXPRESS YOURSELF

Rants are another feature you see a lot of in 'zines. A rant is like an essay that is seriously getting something off its chest. *REAL Girls* had lots of rants about Barbie and why she is so evil. Most 'zines contain at least three or four rants on everything from world politics to an intolerable high school classmate. Some 'zinesters have used entire 'zines to rant about someone they know or an irritating brother or sister. A word of warning, though: Just as the legacy of your groovy poetry will live on for the next fifty years if you put it into print, so will those nasty feelings about someone you may make up with as soon as tomorrow! Of course, if you're sticking with the program and are on a true quest for world power, then your first article will naturally be your manifesto. This is where you hit your readers with what you really think about patriarchal societies and the violence of the meat industry.

Most of the stuff you see in 'zines is original material—stuff that was written specifically for the magazine. Lots of 'zine publishers also rely on other sources (namely, their friends) to fill empty pages. That's okay. Get as much help as you can. You may have friends who will write for you for free. But some of the material you read in 'zines is reprinted from other sources.

Reprinting other material is generally not a problem if you're quoting another source, but it is frowned on (not to mention highly illegal) to lift articles from other magazines and reprint them as your own. If you come across something in another 'zine that you love and you think would be perfect in your brain child, then do the right thing and ask permission. If you get it, give full credit. If you don't, don't use it.

Obviously, if you are producing a few dozen copies of a 'zine that you're going to hand out to your friends, you are not going to get sued for reprinting something that appeared in a well-known magazine. Regardless, you should follow the golden rule of publishing: Never, ever take credit for something you didn't write, and always give full credit to the author or artist for what you publish. Not only is it against the law to plagiarize someone else's work, it also stinks, and you wouldn't want someone doing it to you.

If you are publishing articles and/or artwork created by someone else specifically for your 'zine, then you are most likely receiving permission to publish that material just once. You are not entitled to ownership of their work unless you have a specific, written contract granting you such ownership. If you have friends writing for you, it's important that both of you understand up front what the arrangement is going to be. For example, if a friend of yours writes an outstanding rant for you on animal testing and another 'zine publisher is so impressed by it that they want to publish it in their 'zine, what do you do? Nothing. Your friend holds the rights to that piece and is entitled to grant that permission. You have no reason, and no right, to be insulted if they want to print their work elsewhere.

Unfortunately, when it comes to friends, begging for material is somewhat like begging for money: There's a tremendous potential for arguments, tears, and name-calling. Part of this is the wonderful stress that 'zine publishers thrive on (I'll take some anxiety with my caffeine, thank you!), but a lot of it is due to assumptions that one or both of you have made. You can reduce the confusion by spelling everything out up front and making sure everyone understands what is expected of them. That way, there will be no hurt feelings and no upcoming dates in small claims court.

Assuming you still have friends and assuming you've got some material down on paper, ask one or two of your friends to proofread your work and/or make editing suggestions. Yes, it's hard to believe that not everyone would be interested in a 3000-word article about how your dog got his name, but lots of writers (even experienced ones) can tend to overstate an issue. Aside from proofing for typos and other errors, you should always get a second opinion on anything you've written. A boring 'zine is a dead 'zine. Enough said.

Choose a Style

One important decision that you should make fairly early on in your 'zine madness is format; that is, what page size you want. You'll probably settle on one size or another for financial reasons, but you should consider other factors, like where your 'zine will be distributed (this is where that handy-dandy plan you wrote will help).

The standard format is 8-1/2 x 11, which is about the size of most magazines you see on the newsstand. If you're going to photocopy your 'zine, you'll combine four 'zine pages on one 17 x 11 sheet (copied front and back). With this format, just two sheets of paper will give you an eight-page 'zine, which is a good start for your first effort. The standard format is great if you're producing your 'zine on a computer, because you can print 8-1/2 x 11 sheets out and proof them as they're completed.

Standard-sized 'zines work well on the newsstand, because people can read the title without even picking it up (remember all that intrigue you're going to generate with that title?). Another huge advantage to this page size is that people who have never designed a magazine before find it easy to work with because they're familiar with magazines that are this size. Whether you realize it or not, you probably already have a feel for how much text belongs on a page and how big a headline should be. You can take a look at other magazines for design ideas if you get stuck (don't be afraid about lifting a design right from another magazine; it's done all the time in publishing). One disadvantage to this page size is that beginners find all that blank space staring back at them like cold, bare tundra—it's a lot of white space to conquer.

The common format for beginning 'zine divas is digest-sized, which is an 8-1/2 x 11 sheet folded in half for a final size of 5-1/2 x 8-1/2. The smaller pages are somehow less intimidating, and they just don't seem as difficult to fill as a full-sized sheet. If you get stuck for content, one photo or graphic can easily take up a whole page. It's not that much cheaper to photocopy than a standard format; although 8-1/2 x 11 sheets are less expensive than 11 x 17 sheets, you'll need more pages to hold the same information. An eight-page, 8-1/2 x 11 'zine (which uses two sheets of paper) is pretty fat; with a digest-sized 'zine you need at least twelve pages (four sheets) to keep people

from feeling cheated. Digest-sized 'zines are at a slight disadvantage on newsstands; they tend to get lost on the rack with all the larger magazines crowding them for space. The smaller 'zines are also a little harder to design. If you want a lot of artwork and graphics in your 'zine and you love borders and doodles in the margin, you will probably have a hard time fitting much more than a headline on a small page.

Tabloids are not just for Bat Boy and psychic predictions. The term "tabloid" originally referred to the size of the paper, not the genre. Tabloid-sized 'zines are a lot of fun to design— wide open spaces are just waiting to be filled with graphics and photos and huge 100-point type. The pages are enormous (about 17 x 11), and can hold nearly endless amounts of kitschy artwork and columns and columns of thoughtful, witty prose. A magazine this size had better have good writing, and plenty of it, or you'll be using lots of filler.

Tabloids are best left, however, to seasoned 'zine queens. This format can be pretty expensive, and mostly unworkable unless you can afford to have it printed professionally. If you're laying out the 'zine on a computer, it's difficult to proof pages as you're working on them because most desktop printers won't print any bigger than 8-1/2 x 14. You would have to take your disk to a service bureau to output your pages for you, and that can run $2 to $3 per page.

No matter which format you choose, you should learn how to assemble signatures for reproduction. A signature is a printer's term for a combination of pages that are not consecutive, but when assembled, will be numbered sequentially. When you're working with signatures, your total page count must be divisible by four (two pages on each side, front and back, equals four). To get an idea of how signatures work, take three sheets of 8-1/2 x 11 paper and fold them in half to make a digest-sized twelve-page booklet. Now number the pages. You'll see that page 1 and page 12 are on the same sheet. That's a signature. None of the pages will be in order, except the center (pages 6 and 7).

Never design in signatures, it's too difficult; instead, produce each page individually, then lay the pages down in signatures when you are ready to make a master copy. Assemble them only after your pages are complete. You will probably also have to construct signatures for a digest-sized 'zine. Most copy shops have sophisticated machines to construct signatures for standard-size copies (in some shops this is called the pamphlet mode); all you have to do is give them a master copy with all the pages numbered. Most printers will also create signatures. But if you plan on making the copies yourself to save a few bucks, you'll have to learn how to assemble the signatures yourself.

This may seem like more information than you need, but if you understand the basics of magazine production up front, you'll save lots of time and money in revisions and corrections. Plus, when you walk into a printers or a copy shop and know how to talk about signatures and reproduction, they're going to be less inclined to think of you as a sucker and therefore less inclined to overcharge you (besides, even if they try, you'll know it!).

Designing Your 'Zine

Most of what you learn about laying out a magazine you'll pick up by trial and error, not to mention lots and lots of practice. Use other magazines—even other 'zines—as your guide. You can get inspired by checking out what other girls are doing in their spare time. Notice where the art directors have placed headlines, text, and photos. Keep a file of which layouts you like and which you don't. You can get some great ideas for laying out a story just by flipping through other sources.

After you've designed a few issues of your 'zine, it will be hard for you to read a magazine without noticing how it was all put together.

One skill that will come in handy in laying out your 'zine is copy fitting—that is, determining how much copy you'll need to fit the space you have available. At first, fitting copy is a hit and miss process, and the only way to get better at it is with practice, but a few guidelines will help your first few issues go a little more smoothly. For instance, a standard 8-1/2 x 11 page, with two columns of 10-point type, will fit 250 words. That doesn't include any space for headlines or pictures, so take that into account when planning your editorial content. Use a 9-point to 12-point typeface. Any smaller is too hard to read, any larger (at least for body text) is too large. Headlines can go as large as you like. When you're estimating how much to write (or how much to have someone else write) for a story, always go long. It's much easier to cut copy than to expand it at the last minute. Once you lay out a couple of issues, you'll get better at estimating how much copy you'll need, and you'll also get a good feel for how to write to fit available space. Until then, keep lots of filler (graphics, pictures) on hand. You can also fill space with pull quotes or call-outs.

> An excerpt that is enlarged and placed within the story like a graphic is a call-out.

Once you have an idea of what your content is going to be like, you should dummy, or paginate, your 'zine. This is a small-scale outline showing exactly what will fit on each page. Dummies are an absolutely essential tool for learning how to organize the flow of your editorial. They also help you spot those large, gaping white spaces that you might otherwise not discover until the day your 'zine is laid out and ready to go.

The (Really) Fun Part: Putting it Together

There are two methods of producing your 'zine—on a computer with desktop publishing software, or the "when-dinosaurs-roamed-the-Earth" method of cut and paste. A typewriter would make your life a lot easier, but even if you don't have access to one, don't be discouraged. A handwritten 'zine can look really cool, and sometimes, the more homegrown a 'zine is, the greater its appeal.

The cut and paste method of producing your 'zine is pretty self-explanatory:

You basically write (or draw) things, cut them out, and paste them on a page. You can sometimes get a little more creative with cut and paste than you can with a computer. For example, making collages and borders takes a lot of skill on a computer, and you need expensive image-editing software. One complaint most 'zine publishers have about cut and paste is that it's really messy. You paste things down using either rubber cement, aerosol spray tack (you can get this at any art supply store), or just a plain old glue stick. All these methods work pretty well—sometimes too well. In fact, you'd better be pretty sure that you place stuff more or less where you want it, because once you lay it down you can pretty much forget about moving it, and that's one of the drawbacks of cut and paste.

One of the best things about cutting and pasting is that you'll face virtually no restrictions in working with graphics and illustrations. You can take photos from almost any magazine or newspaper or book; clip art can be found almost anywhere, from old magazines to the latest issues of your dreaded teen magazine. Plus, it's fun. Sure, it's messy and there will be times when you want to chuck the whole thing and take up pottery or something a little less mentally taxing. But most 'zine publishers will say that one of the most rewarding things about working on a 'zine is seeing the tangible results of all their hard work.

If you want to achieve a more professional-looking magazine, invest in a computer and some desktop publishing software, like Quark XPress or Adobe

MAKING A SMART DUMMY

Always sketch out the cover and title, masthead (information about who wrote and edited your 'zine and how to order it), and table of contents first. Otherwise you could run out of room before you get all the essentials in.

Keep the jumps to a minimum (those places where you continue a story at the back of the 'zine instead of on the next page). They're distracting to readers, and it's easy for you to get confused. Besides, you could accidentally cut out the last part of a story.

Leave a space about 3 x 5 on the back page for an address area. If you turn your 'zine into a self-mailer, you'll save a lot of money in postage and envelopes. (Tab it shut with a small sticker, otherwise the post office might not accept it.) If your 'zine is a standard size, put the label box in the bottom right half of the front or back cover because you will need to fold your 'zine to mail it. Don't forget to design a return address.

Pagemaker. You can do cool layouts and trick graphics; you can even scan photos and drop them into your layouts. (The major disadvantage is cost: Quark costs about $800 brand new, which pretty much makes it unaffordable, unless you know anyone who works in graphics and is already using the program.) You can spend as little as a couple of hundred dollars on used equipment to several thousand on state-of-the-art machinery. It depends on what your budget will allow and what you want to accomplish.

With desktop publishing, you build the whole magazine on screen. You can easily add and delete pages and move things from page to page without cutting and pasting. The major advantages are speed, versatility, and polish. Even with the simplest four- or five-page newsletter, you'll get a much more professional look. Some desktop publishing systems are a little complicated to use and take some practice, but you'll be able to pick up the most basic tasks of publishing—like building pages and importing text—in no time at all. Besides, experimenting on the computer is fun, and as you get better at it, your 'zine will show it!

A big advantage to working on a computer is the learning curve. If you have any aspirations at all about working for a magazine—writing or designing or even doing artwork and graphics—you could really boost your career by learning how to use a computer now. Very few mags are put together the old-fashioned way and every day more and more publications go digital. Even writers need to learn how to handle a mouse, because they're often asked to submit their stories on diskette.

Sort of halfway between a cool computer set-up and the old cut and paste is an affordable compromise: a typewriter or small word processor. A word processor will allow you more versatility with typefaces (fonts) and you can get a little more creative with ordinary paragraphs by justifying them or changing the font size for headlines and titles. Just type up what you want, print it out, then cut and paste the pieces where you want them.

If you can't afford a typewriter or a computer and printer, consider renting a computer workstation. Most copy shops have at least a couple of computers—Macs and PCs—for rent by the hour. This can be expensive (maybe $10 an hour, and $1 per page you print), so try to have everything ready in advance and limit the time you spend experimenting.

A Thousand Words and More: Using Photos

If you're going to place photos on a page, and you're not scanning them, get a halftone (a photo converted into a series of small dots). Regular photos can reproduce very badly, making your otherwise stellar-looking 'zine kind of amateurish-looking. You can get halftones at any service bureau (also try copy shops and graphics shops), and they're not very expensive. Halftones reproduce much more clearly, and they don't come out as dark. In this process, you can also have your photo enlarged or reduced to fit available space. Line art (like drawings and sketches) does not have to be converted, although you may want to make a high-quality duplicate of the original to paste into your master copy. Accidents can happen, and artwork gets lost. If your originals are valuable to you (or someone else), you shouldn't take a chance on them getting misplaced or destroyed.

Regardless of what method you use to lay out the pages of your 'zine, you should always end up with a master copy. This is the copy that you'll use for making photocopies or that your printer will shoot to make plates for printing, so

make sure it's as clean as possible. Trim off any excess paper or tape, wipe up any dried glue, and make the surface as smooth as you can.

Photocopying vs. Printing

This decision will also be based almost solely on cost, although there are other considerations, like what kind of paper you want to use, the page size you've chosen, how many copies you need, and the level of polish you want to achieve. Most 'zines are reproduced by plain old, unglamorous photocopying. Although some of the more sophisticated or ambitious publishers print their 'zines on an offset press, photocopying works just fine and is much cheaper. If you (or one of your friends, or even your parents) work in an office, you may be able to score some free (or cheap) 'zines.

It's often a good idea to buy the paper yourself, especially if you're using stock that is heavier than copy stock (20#). Check out the 60# or 70#—they're very common for 'zines. Never, never buy paper in bulk at copy shops or small, local office supply stores—the mark-up is too high. Check out the paper suppliers listed in the yellow pages.

If you're working with a digest-size 'zine, then your sheet size is 8-1/2 x 11 and that's the most inexpensive to copy. You can go virtually anywhere to get two-sided 8-1/2 x 11 copies, so shop around for the best price. You'd be surprised at the range that people will quote you.

When you publish a 'zine, you can hold the results of your work in your hands, show it to your friends, pass it around, and say, "Look at this! I did this!"

When you're calling for prices, be sure to tell them you need two-sided copies made from one-sided originals (it makes a difference). Other services like stapling and collating can make the price of your copies go through the roof, so start planning your folding/collating party now. My favorite recipe for a collating party is three Molly Ringwald movies (with at least one appearance by Judd Nelson), a couple of six packs of soda, a bunch of microwave popcorn, and at least three unsuspecting souls to help. Oh, and you'll need some bandages, too (paper cuts are a standard accessory for the self-publishing set).

Plain white paper is the cheapest and the best suited for most 'zines, because photographs tend to come out too dark on colored stock. If you really want color, use a light grey, beige, or a pastel.

Big chain copy shops are fast and helpful, but they also have the highest rates. Lots of smaller neighborhood shops would be glad to take the work off your hands, especially if it's clean and already laid out in signatures.

Offset printing will give your 'zine a professional look, but at a much higher cost. The price varies from printer to printer and also varies depending on your page size, paper stock, and other factors. Printers charge a fixed amount for the set-up and first run, which can be anywhere from 100 to 1000 copies. Your cost for additional copies will be less. For example, the first 2000 copies of your magazine could cost about $600. That seems like a lot ($.30 per copy), but each additional 1000 will cost about $100 (reducing your per copy cost to $.23). You need to have a handle on your per copy cost, especially when you start to sell or trade copies.

With the 'zine explosion in recent years, a number of printers have started to make it more affordable to have professional, offset printing. Some of these printers will gang-run a number of 'zines together (for example, they'll run ten 'zines all at once, as if they were one). This drastically reduces set-up charges for individual publishers. There are many things to consider when getting your paper done on an offset press; if you're considering a professional print job, you should find someone you can trust who knows the business and get some good advice, or you could get ripped off big time. Worse, you could end up with a paper that looks terrible.

How and Where to Give Yourself Away

You did it; you've created a 'zine! You've spent the last few months sweating and toiling and slaving over a hot keyboard, but you did it, and the hard part's over, right? Not exactly. Producing a 'zine is one thing. Getting people to see your 'zine, and order it, is another. And although it can be satisfying to express your heartfelt opinions, it's much more exciting when you're speaking to an audience and start to get some feedback.

At most larger magazines, there's a circulation department with the sole purpose of getting that magazine into the hands of potential readers. They usually have a budget of a few hundred thousand dollars, and use lots of advertising and expensive direct mail. So how, you wonder, does one power-hungry girl do it? Like everything else you've done so far—with a little planning.

There are two types of circulation: free and paid. Which method you choose depends on where you want to go with your 'zine. Remember that plan of yours? Drag it out and read it over. If you are creating a 'zine just for kicks, then leaving copies in a coffee shop or CD shop might be just fine. If you're trying to launch a semi-serious business, then you have to find a way to make money. You can even choose to do a little of both. Lots of 'zines start out as freebies and as their readership grows and they begin to make a name for themselves, switch to paid circulation. Some 'zine publishers get their copies out through a combination of subscriptions, newsstand sales, and free copies. It's up to you.

The biggest advantage of free circulation is exposure. Giving away copies is by far the best way to generate interest in your 'zine while trying to build a paid readership. The obvious disadvantage is that you won't make a dime off your efforts, so you probably won't want to give copies away forever (although it's true that 'zines are supposed to be done for love, not money, even love has limits).

You might also trade some copies, too. When you list your 'zine in a directory like *Factsheet Five*, you can specify that you like to trade with other publishers. This is a great way to get your 'zine out to people and see what other publishers are doing. You could eventually build a network of 'zine contacts, not to mention a few new friends.

> Leave your 'zine wherever there are people.

There are countless places to distribute a free 'zine: CD record stores, coffee shops, used or vintage clothing stores, school campuses, bookstores, and news racks are a few of the most receptive and successful. But those aren't your only possibilities. Publishers have been known to leave their 'zines in hair salons, bus stations, and even inserted into other magazines on the newsstand (when nobody's looking, of course). Always ask the manager before you leave any copies, because although most stores don't mind an extra stash of 'zines, some people don't carry free papers and they'll toss them into the trash before you've even reached the end of the block. You may find dozens of 'zines crowding one tiny shelf; if so, remember the unwritten (but often broken) rule of 'zine distribution: never hide someone else's papers to show off your own. But hey, it's a dog-eat-dog 'zine world out there, and only the strongest survive. If you do move someone else's 'zines, don't get caught (and don't throw them away, because that is definitely not cool)!

Some people think free papers are somehow less valuable than papers that cost something, anything, even $1. There's a way around that stigma: Before you give any copies away, make a small label (address labels work well) that says, "Sample copy. To order, write (your address)." You can make these on a computer or typewriter. Place the label on the front page, near the title and the price (always put a price on your cover, even if you plan to give copies away). People will pick up the paper and see the price, see the label, and think they've got their hands on a special issue. They'll also be motivated to order another issue because they might think that the freebies won't last. Use a brightly colored label so that it stands out: hot pink or blue work well.

When I started my 'zine, I posted a couple of notices on some feminist mailing lists through America Online. Within eight hours, I had over 80 requests for sample copies. Eventually, I got about 100 subscriptions through those posts. With the price of Internet connections going down daily, this is a great investment—not only for promotion, but for networking. (You can also download graphics and cool fonts for use in your 'zine.)

Paid circulation consists of subscriptions, single copy orders, and newsstand sales. You make more money on direct subscriptions and orders, but the drawback is that you have to do all the fulfillment (taking and filling orders) yourself. Don't offer subscriptions unless you're prepared to keep track of your orders (and you're sure you'll be publishing on a semi-regular basis). Send issues out no more than two weeks after you receive an order. There's nothing more irritating than sending a couple of bucks for a 'zine and not receiving it for three months. That kind of service will give you a bad name and make it hard to attract new subscribers, and keep the ones you have.

To figure out how much to charge for your paper, first figure out how much it cost to produce. Start with the price to print or photocopy your first batch. Then add in the price of anything else you needed to get the issue done: stats or halftones, books or magazines you bought for research, paper (if you supplied it),

phone calls, etc. Also add any shipping charges to distributors or contacts out of town, and estimate how much you'll spend on gas to distribute copies around town. After you come up with a nice, round figure, divide it by the number of copies in your print run. Now add in the price of postage for each individual 'zine. Your cover price should be at least twice this figure. All your expenses may not be justified, and if you come up with a $5 price on an eight-page 'zine, you're going to have to learn to cut some corners. Most 'zines range in price from $1 to $3. Even putting a first-class postage stamp on your 'zine could destroy your profits, so plan accordingly (remember, your 'zine has to weigh less than an ounce to mail at the same rate as a first-class letter).

The advantage to newsstand sales is that all you have to do is make sure the copies arrive, then collect a check and drop off more copies next time. You also get better exposure on the newsstand, depending on who's selling your 'zine, and it gives your title some legitimacy as a real magazine and a thriving business.

Newsstands buy your 'zine at a predetermined discount off the cover price: the average is 30 to 40 percent. For

Try to underestimate newsstand sales at first so that you don't end up throwing a big portion of your print run away. It's better to have to send extra copies if they're needed than to destroy 'zines that didn't sell.

GOLD NUGGETS OF 'ZINE PUBLISHING

Write about something you know or feel passionately about. First crushes are passionate fodder for some new 'zines, but they can be a little dull for the people who weren't actually there to see the way his hair gleamed in the sunlight. Try music, politics, feminism, or animal rights.

Always keep a file of filler copy to close up those embarrassing white gaps between stories. Reviews, commentaries, or cartoons work really well for this.

Always put a price on the cover and use sample labels when giving away free copies. This leads the unsuspecting public to believe they've nabbed a bootleg (hence: valuable) copy.

Number your issues, never date them. That way, you can avoid lengthy—and frequent—editorials about why your June issue is hitting the streets in November.

Copy layouts from your favorite magazine. *(YM* has mastered the layout of the calorie counter table. Just a thought.)

Paginate, or dummy, your 'zine before putting it together on paper.

Design a self-mailer label area on the back of your 'zine—this will save you money in envelopes and postage and it gives you a more professional look.

Always make copies of originals. If you lose that one-of-a-kind charcoal drawing of faeries that your best friend did, it's your funeral.

Make stats, or halftones, of pictures for better reproduction.

Leave sample copies of your 'zine in record stores, coffee shops, and vintage clothing stores. Leave them conspicuously on top of everyone else's (but don't get caught!).

Send each issue of your 'zine out to *Factsheet Five* for review.

Include at least one ad for back issues or subscriptions in every issue of your 'zine.

---

example, if your 'zine sells for $2, you'll receive only $1.20 per copy at a 40 percent discount. They never pay up front, so don't expect an advance. Most pay in one to three weeks after they receive the next issue. For example, you'll be paid for November sales a few weeks after you drop off the December issues.

Some newsstands will return unsold copies to you when you deliver the new batch. Most won't, especially those who receive your 'zines by mail. With your check, they'll send a statement of how many copies were sold, at what price, and how many were destroyed.

If you plan on pursuing newsstand sales, try to get a distributor. There's a lot of paperwork involved—invoicing, delivery of orders, etc.—that you will probably not want to do, much less have time to do.

It's easier to deal with one distributor than 20 newsstand or bookstore owners, so even though they further cut into your profits (you may end up with only 50 percent of your cover price), you'll more than make up for it in volume. Plus, distribution is their job. They'll always be on the lookout for new buyers and they'll probably have a lot more contacts than you do.

You don't need a distributor to sell your 'zine through bookstores and newsstands—if you have some stores in mind, do a small, select mailing and include a copy of your 'zine and a short information sheet with the terms of your sales. Pursue newsstand sales only if you're committed to publishing your 'zine on a regular basis. Newsstands and bookstores don't like dealing with publishers whose production schedules are unreliable and/or infrequent.

Promote Yourself

Whether you give your copies away or sell them for two bucks apiece, a well-planned promotional campaign will create a buzz for your 'zine. The goal is to get your 'zine into the hands of as many people as possible, especially reviewers and booksellers. Just a few well-placed copies could really boost your circulation in a short period of time. When you're planning your print run, always add another twenty or so for promotion, and send them out first. In the beginning, before you get any subscriptions or consistent orders, review copies may be some of the only copies that are going out.

Where you promote your 'zine depends a lot on the subject matter, but no matter what you're writing about,

there are lots of ways to get the word out. For instance, if your 'zine is about animal rights, send it to some organizations like PETA (People for the Ethical Treatment of Animals). If you've chosen feminism as your subject, get a directory of feminist organizations (especially those on college campuses) and mail out sample copies. Use your imagination, and don't discount any idea, no matter how wild it may seem.

One good review or recommendation could bring twenty more orders, and so on.

Remember, promotion doesn't stop with the first issue. Every time you publish a new issue, send it to five more new sources. Keep thinking of new ways to generate interest in your 'zine, and never stop promoting it. This is sometimes the hardest part for a lot of 'zinestresses. It's hard to get excited about the business side of 'zines, but whether or not you like it, it's something you're going to have to get used to, especially if you've got expansion on your mind. Unless you can find a partner to handle all these aspects of your 'zine, now is the time to acquaint yourself with the business end of your magazine.

Advertising

While subscriptions, single-copy orders, and newsstand sales will bring you a little bit of money, the only thing that will turn your 'zine into a real money-making business are paid ads. This is without a doubt the toughest part for 'zine publishers, because it's all business and requires kissing a certain amount of behind.

Following the lead of some larger magazines, like *Ms.*, some 'zine publishers refuse to accept ads. They feel that accepting ads can lead to compromised editorial content. Remember the joke about the 'zine publishers and the light bulb—well, you can bet your Exacto knife that someone wrote that joke after the first ad was sold. But you don't have to throw your ethics out the window completely to be supported, at least partially, by paying advertisers. Just be selective about which types of ads you'll accept.

SELL, SELL, SELL!

You can sell ads in your 'zine yourself if you think you'd be good at it. People who are good at sales share some common characteristics: they're outgoing and friendly, are easy to talk to, can communicate with lots of different types of people, and, most important, have a thick skin when it comes to rejection.

How Much Commission Do I Pay?

What you pay someone who sells an ad is up to you—it could be a percentage of the take or help with homework. It's up to the two of you. Standard commissions range from 15 to 25 percent, but you may want to go as high as 50 percent. Make sure that you charge enough for your ad so that even after paying a commission, you'll still make a profit.

Who Would Advertise in My 'Zine?

Determine which kinds of businesses would benefit from advertising in your 'zine. A music 'zine is a natural for record stores, labels, and clubs. But what if you produce a feminist 'zine? Try some women's bookstores or even clothing stores. Pick up some 'zines at a local bookstore and see what type of ads they're getting, then go after the same type (or the same companies!). At first, concentrate on businesses in your area. Local businesses would be much more receptive to a 'zine that's distributed locally than one that is being seen all over the country.

How Much Should I Charge for Advertising?

The cost of an ad in your 'zine depends on several things—the circulation of your 'zine, the quality of paper and printing, the page size, and the readership.

Take the figure you came up with when figuring the cost of your first issue. Divide that figure by the number of pages in your 'zine. This will give you the approximate cost of producing one page. For instance, if your issue cost is $400 and your 'zine is ten pages, this gives you a per page cost of $40. It's standard to add 10 to 30 percent on top of that. That's what you would charge for a full-page ad. This is only a general guide; for a more realistic idea of what to charge for ads, check out similar 'zines. Find out what they're getting for paid ads and adjust your prices accordingly. You know your prices are too low if you sell out every issue; they're too high if you don't sell very many (or none at all).

The best guidance you could possibly get on selling ads in your 'zine is from people who have done it themselves. Pick up a few 'zines on the newsstand and see what kind of ads the others are running. Then write to the publisher and ask how he or she did it. 'Zine publishers are usually willing to give some advice; in fact, most love the chance to connect with others to trade secrets, tips, and horror stories, and you'll probably get a lot more information than just how to sell ads.

The beauty of 'zine publishing is that it can be whatever you choose to make it. It can be as simple or as complex, as cheap or as expensive as you choose. Get used to making all your own decisions—you're well on your way to ruling the world now, and believe me, you're going to be making a lot of them!

NAME YOUR POISON (ER, 'ZINE) ANSWERS

Believe these:

A New Miserable Experience
Armadillo Droppings
Asian Girls Are Rad
Beagle Mania
Chip's Closet Cleaner
Pulled Mints
Macaroni 'n Cheese
It Seemed Logical at the Time

The rest? Not!

Chapter Eight

PRODUCE A CABLE TV SHOW

Every future world leader wants to win friends and influence people. Can you think of any way you could reach and influence more people than with your own television show? Without a doubt, no medium has more of an influence on what people believe—and who they believe—than that technological wonder of the twentieth century: TV.

There's nothing wrong with wanting to work the airwaves for your own benefit; that's what TV is all about! Whether your goal is to propel your garage band to stardom (it's been reported that 75 percent of MTV's Buzz Clip bands have gone platinum with their first record. Coincidence? I think not), or to position yourself in the voting public's consciousness as the only viable choice for world ruler (both Sonny Bono, of Sonny and Cher fame, and Fred Grandy, who played Gopher on Aaron Spelling's *Love Boat*, made the successful transition from TV to politics), TV is the ticket to millions of minds. It's a natural choice when you're ready to take your act on the road, mentally speaking.

The Vietnam War, which is often called the first war fought in America's living room, was seen by millions on TV.

This was the first time that every American citizen could get an accurate look at what our sons, brothers, husbands, and fathers were facing. Those powerful, violent images drastically changed the public perception of war forever. On the other hand, few things have inspired more patriotism for the old red, white, and blue as the sight of an American walking on the moon. Ancient history, you say? How about the plight/flight of O.J. Simpson? The attention of the entire country was held captive as that white Ford Bronco cruised down the L.A. freeways and forever into TV history. But that was just the beginning. His criminal trial became the focus of a media blitz that might have rivaled the Revolutionary War's, had TV cameras been around to document that.

We can remember where we were when the space shuttle *Challenger* exploded or when the Berlin Wall came down. Our parents remember those first steps on the moon and the night Lucy and Desi had a baby. The power of TV is profound, and as lots of politicians, world rulers, and entertainers have learned (some the hard way), it can make you or break you. Maybe it's time you learned how to harness some of its awesome power for yourself.

Becoming the next television icon doesn't have to be a matter of who you know or who you're related to. You don't have to spend a mint on professional headshots, either. As you know, a few years ago, along came a wonderful thing called cable, and believe it or not, it's good for more than MTV Spring Break and Thanksgiving Day marathons of *The Twilight Zone*. TV has become another way to dominate the world. With the accessibility of cable TV (and some Congressional intervention), you can now command the airwaves for yourself, even if you're not as well-connected as Tori Spelling.

Congress, Cable, and What it Means to You

While cable has been around for about twenty years, access to the airwaves has been freed up a little for We the People for only the last decade or so. As cable grew from a novelty in only a few homes to a 100 percent certifiable mass media, our stake in what was being seen—and more important, not seen—began to grow. And our astute members of Congress (of which you may someday be

one) took note. In 1984, they passed the Cable Communications Policy Act, which basically told cable operators to turn over a couple of those channels to some regular folk. You, me, Joe Blow down the street—regardless of our background, experience, or agenda, if we've got something to say, we now have a place to say it. Produce your own show and air it on TV? Sign me up!

So Congress said, "LET THERE BE CABLE," and there was cable, and it was—well, good. Cable was bestowed on the masses, and communication would never be the same.

With a little digging, we can find good opportunities in the big bad world of TV production for independent, system-bucking producers, writers, actors, and directors such as yourself. The Alliance for Community Media, a national non-profit organization that monitors community access programming, estimates that there are about 1000 access centers across the country (that figure grows by the day), but even that number is said to be on the low end.

Leased Access vs. Public Access

There are basically two ways to get your amateur productions on cable: leased access and public access (also known as community access).

Public access is cheap, if not completely free. Leased access costs money;

you purchase airtime from your cable operator. While your first reaction may be, "Why should I pay for time when I can get it free?" consider the next difference between the two. Leased access allows you to use the airwaves for commercial means; that is, to make money. You might sell commercials to advertisers who will buy a slice of your show; or start a strictly commercial enterprise, like an infomercial for the great new line of jewelry you've designed, or a home shopping channel for thrift store freaks.

You've heard the stories about how much TV airtime can cost—a thirty-second spot during the Superbowl goes for about a zillion dollars, right? Leased access isn't quite that expensive. As a matter of fact, depending upon the time slot you've chosen (or had chosen for you, depending on availability), you could pay as little as $50 for a half-hour slot.

There's a formula used to calculate a "reasonable" fee for leased access cable rates, based on things like the number of people served by that cable system, their normal cable rates, and the length of your lease. Air time is usually sold in thirty-minute increments. If you're interested in pursuing leased access, contact your local cable company. Be warned, though, for some reason this information is not easy to come by—either the employees at your local cable distributor simply aren't trained to know anything about leased access, or your friendly cable company is not that hot on the idea of selling you time (after all, it could be selling that time to someone else at much higher rates). It may take quite a few phone calls and a little digging around before you find the information you're looking for.

Public access is often free, but if there is a charge, it's usually minimal and is in the form of a membership to a local community media center (it could be as little as $10). These fees don't make anyone rich—especially the cable operators—but support the media center by helping offset the costs of equipment and other needs. The fees are regulated, but they vary from community to community, based on things like the number of people served by that particular cable company and other demographic information.

The difference between public access and leased access is like the difference between the History Channel and reruns of *Blossom*. In other words: HUGE.

Public access is not the same as public broadcasting, better known as PBS, which shows things like *Sesame Street* and all those reruns of *Riverdance*. One difference between PBS and public access is funding. PBS gets the bulk of their money from federal grants and corporate sponsors, with private memberships comprising only a small percentage of their incoming dollars. They don't air actual commercials, but most of their programs are underwritten by corporations like Mobil Oil and Pacific Bell—and you probably already know that that kind of financial arrangement makes it hard for some to believe that PBS is any more objective than the commercial-saturated

On public access TV, free thinking is encouraged.

networks. Because public access television is not supported in any way by corporations (remember, most of their funding comes from fees paid by cable operators), there's no pressure to suppress or dilute radical or creative thought.

But the most important distinction between public access and public television is that amateur, aspiring, or fringe producers have very little chance of getting their work shown on public broadcasting. Technically, public broadcasting stations are community-based, and they are an alternative to huge mega-networks like ABC and CBS. But as liberal and cutting edge as these stations may seem next to the huge networks, they're absolutely repressed next to public access. There are usually just a few people at PBS stations who decide what will air, and what will not. They choose from high-quality, professionally produced shows and someone like you or me can't just walk in off the street and get our video shown on PBS. But on community media, like Channel 25, we can.

Channel 25 is run by Berkeley Community Media, a community access center in Berkeley, California, and is a good example of the kind of community access centers you're likely to find across the country. Community access centers

are like mini-TV studios; most have at least a couple of TV cameras, editing and sound equipment, and just about everything else you need to produce professional-looking video. Although the rules and requirements are set by individual centers, most stipulate that in order to use the facilities, you be a member of that community or an organization that serves the community in some way.

You're not experienced? You don't have to be. Most access centers offer members free classes in video production and usage. In fact, many require that anyone who plans on using the equipment at the center first complete a short training course and pass a certification test. Some offer only basic training; others, like BCM, offer advanced training for a small additional fee. (There it is again, the f-word.) Don't worry, that fee is still thousands of dollars less than you would pay for a college or trade school course. After a member receives certification, it's simply a matter of booking studio time and getting busy. Not all community access centers open their doors to just anyone off the street. Some require that members show proof of residency in the city served by that center; others require that members are at least 18 years old.

If you don't qualify for membership or if you're too young to join, there still may be a way for you to show your amateur productions on public access. Many public access stations offer Cablecast services. Cablecast is the free broadcast of non-commercial videos provided by residents or community organizations. Basically, you give them your already completed video, schedule a time for it to run, and then let them do all the work. If

---

> ## CABLECAST BONANZA
>
> *What can you show? How about:*
>
> An educational video that you and your animal activist group made about the health hazards of meat.
>
> A meeting of the young feminist's group that you joined at school.
>
> Video of a demonstration organized on your campus to protest the policies of your elected officials.

you shoot it, they'll show it—as long as it's not commercial. Shows are usually scheduled on a first-come, first-served basis, so unless your videos are specifically produced for insomniacs, schedule your show well in advance.

The Next Seinfeld, or a New Learning Channel?

So what are you going to do with all this very cool information? Training for a career in television production is the most obvious reason for becoming involved with cable TV production, but you can also use it to get some exposure for your activist group. Or how about getting some of those creative juices flowing by writing and shooting your own mini-series? Or (and this is my favorite), you could take that first big step toward serious world domination by airing your decidedly feminist political platform.

Armed with all this knowledge about how to influence the masses, how do you actually get started? First, find the community access center in your area. The best way to do this is call or visit your

local cable company or library. Once you find an access center, give them a call, go down there for a visit, and take a look around. Find out what their requirements are and how to meet them, and what kind of training they provide. Find out if they offer Cablecast services; if they do, get started on your video project today!

If you want to produce commercially oriented shows, contact your local cable company or local city government, and start researching leased access. To find out how much it will cost, you'll have to tell them how much time you want (find out what the minimum is and in what slots they sell it—i.e., half-hour, full hour, etc.). They'll also want to know when you want to show your program. Once you get a price, ask for the formula they used to calculate it (you are entitled to this information; don't let them tell you that you're not), then recalculate it yourself to be sure that it's correct. If the price they give you is out of your budget, consider buying a smaller slice of time or moving it to a more deserted time frame, like the middle of the night.

I would like to believe that, armed with all this valuable information on how to reach and influence people, you will use this opportunity to better your world by helping create a new world order. I realize that you might have other, ulterior, motives: like preparing yourself for a career in TV production or just getting the smiling mug of yours on the TV screen for all to admire and love.

If you're thinking of doing this for a career, consider everything you produce to be part of your résumé. Keep masters of everything, because when you walk the street and hawk your creativity at every

TV station in town, they'll want to know what you've done lately. Build a mailing list of the people you want to impress (station managers, etc.) and whenever you book time for one of your productions, send out a letter or postcard to everyone on your list, giving the date and time.

Of course, once you have something to show, it's important to get as many people as possible tuning in (this might be quite a challenge if you end up with a 2 AM spot). Publicize your showing everywhere you can think of. If your video's theme is political, write letters to the editor of local papers and send press releases, too (don't forget to send info to the local offices of national papers and TV stations—if they pick up your story, you could find yourself on CNN).

One more thing: As talented a dynamo as you are, you're probably going to need help sometime, somewhere along the way. Producing anything for TV is a huge ordeal (look what they go through every year for the Academy Awards and how much complaining everyone does before, during, and after). It's probably not anything you'd want to tackle all by your lonesome. Find other people to work on your show; you can probably connect with lots of other like-minded people at the access center. Another place to find tape heads such as yourself is the audio/visual department of your high school or college. Also try placing a notice on bulletin boards at the library, and check with some local video stores—chances are some of the people who work there are film buffs, director wanna-bes, and others who would love a shot at the big time (even if the "big time" is a half an hour shown at midnight, twice a week).

Choose your dream, and use the power of television to help you achieve it. You could be the next Roseanne, the next Moesha, the next CNN correspondent—or the next world leader. Although TV has been called the vast wasteland, even Death Valley has some interesting characters if you look hard enough.

NEED AN IDEA FOR YOUR SHOW OF SHOWS?

If you showcase local bands with an MTV-type show, you could be responsible for discovering and launching the next No Doubt.

The possibilities for talk shows are almost endless. You could interview local officials, or run a forum where kids discuss the problems they face.

Create an electronic art gallery and give some much-needed (and appreciated) exposure for local artists.

Use your time to spotlight environmental issues in your community, like commercial waste or Earth Day activities organized by students.

Broadcast short films that you and your friends wrote, acted in, and directed.

Read poetry and fiction from your favorite authors or that you've written yourself.

Host a thrift-store fashion show, with no outfit over $5!

On a gourmet hour, cook up veggie recipes or desserts using nothing but difference shades of chocolate.

Chapter Nine

ROCK THE WORLD WITH YOUR BAND

Ever since Elvis twisted his hips and sent your grandmother spiraling into a fit like she'd never felt before, rock stars have been totally cool, and something all of us have wanted to be. For you it may have been different: You don't know about The King, but hearing Blondie's "Heart of Glass" for the first time was a totally life-altering experience for you. Maybe your moment came like a ton of bricks the first time you were able to decipher all the lyrics to Salt 'n' Pepa's wild "Shoop." Whatever the song, artist, or moment, you too were bitten by the bug and you knew, you just knew, you had to get up there and shake your groove thing.

Who could blame you? It's the ultimate fantasy! The possibility of a life spent touring the world and seeing your face on magazine covers from here to London has fueled the dreams of millions of wanna-bes. Dancing around the bedroom in your PJs and belting out "Just a Girl" isn't just a teenage rite of passage, it's a blast!

It's true that becoming the next Gwen Stefani is, for more of us, just another fantasy. While almost all of us have had dreams of being famous enough to have people chase us down the street, the truth is that for every En Vogue out there, there are thousands of other singers and bands who work in virtual anonymity for their entire professional lives (and the only people chasing them down the street are bill collectors). That's not because these girls aren't talented, or because they don't have the drive to make their dreams come true. Sometimes it all comes down to luck: being in the right place at the right time, which we can't all do at once.

So, if so much of becoming a star is part of some great cosmic plan we can't control, why try? Some groups really are striving for the fame, the money, and the glory, and they figure that no matter how long it takes to get there, the payoff will be worth it. And if you get to be as big as Madonna, it is. But No Doubt didn't always live up to their name; it may look like they came out of nowhere to become an overnight sensation, but they were a struggling band for over a decade. Other bands—probably most of them—just want to make beautiful music together.

What's your dream? If it's to be the toast of the town at next year's Grammy Awards, then it might help if your last name was Jackson. But if your heart's desire is mostly to express yourself and have some fun by creating and playing music (and Maybe—notice that's with a capital "M"—to make a little money as well), then it doesn't matter if you've got the connections or not. And you don't have to resign yourself to twenty years of playing only sparsely attended family reunions, because with all the small, independent labels and local clubs that have sprung up over the last decade, the odds of finding an outlet where other people can hear and appreciate your music are better than staggering.

No doubt about it, girls rock! We are one hundred percent groove-approved; we know how to croon, coo, and wail; and we can boogie-oogie-oogie till we just can't boogie no more.

So why wait? If soulful Brandy can do it; if teen country-western prodigy Leann Rhimes can do it; heck, if Tiffany can do it, why can't you start early, too? You say there's this little problem of not knowing how to play an instrument? Well, that didn't stop Toni Braxton or Madonna, either. In this world, there are no rules. The field is wide open!

Sticky Baby: That Sounds Cool!

Finding a cool name for your band is lots of fun and may end up being the one thing that you're best at. In fact, coming up with a cool name could be the catalyst for forming a band in the first place. How many times have you been hanging out with your friends when someone just blurts out, "Sticky Baby! Wouldn't that be a cool name for a band?" And everyone else, in wide-eyed awe, agrees, "Yeah, that's cool, let's do it!"

The only difference between you and No Doubt is that they got off their butts and moved on to the next step—plunking the strings on that old guitar or starting to hum a few bars of an entirely original song. Starting with a cool name is perfectly acceptable. It's no different than writers who are inspired to pen entire novels based on a brilliant title that comes to them in the middle of the night. Your biggest problem will not be coming up with names, it will be getting two people to agree on one. Don't worry; you'll probably change your name a hundred times before you settle on one that fits everybody. Just don't rush out and have T-shirts printed on day one of your big band effort (and speaking of T-shirts, don't pick any name that you wouldn't want to wear on the front of yours).

Misery Loves Company

You can form a band with or without other people; it's up to you. But if you do it without, you're a soloist, not a band,

and you can skip this entire section. Natalie Merchant made the transition from band member (10,000 Maniacs) to soloist pretty well; there's no telling how successful she'd be today if she had skipped the Maniacs in the first place, but it's safe to say that it can't hurt to have others around to share your vision, your success—and your misery.

The most important factor in shopping for potential bandmates isn't always how well they can play an instrument (people can always learn how to play, or they can improve if they're not very good in the first place); and it isn't how great their hair would look in a music video. What really makes a valuable band member is how low they rate on the flake scale (0 being best and 10 being worst). If you find a 0, marry this person, you will never have it this good. If someone is a 10, move on. Getting a band off the ground takes commitment more than anything else, and there's nothing more frustrating than standing around waiting for a drummer or bassist who's late to rehearsal for the hundredth time.

If you have a big family you could go the route of the Partridge Family, the Jacksons, or the Osmonds. But if you're like the rest of us, you and your immediate family probably won't want to spend that much time together, no matter what the payoff. You're going to have to find someone who has no clue about what a total pain in the butt you can be when you haven't had twelve hours of sleep.

If you don't have any friends who are interested (or if your friends think you've gone off the deep end), don't worry. There are lots of trade magazines for musicians and wanna-bes; start with

BAM and *The Music Connection*. There are also a lot of regional papers that cater to a local readership. Check out your local newsstand or music store for the latest issues, then scan the classified ads in the back.

Also try the local alternative press like Southern California's *LA Weekly,* or New York's *Village Voice.* Like the music trade publications, these papers run classified ads for musicians, but because they're local you have a much better chance of finding someone within driving distance. Whenever you meet someone through a personal ad, spend a lot of time on the phone with them before you agree to meet face to face; and when you do meet, make it in a public place. Never go to someone's house or apartment alone when you're meeting for the first time.

If you can find a couple of bandmates who actually play, great! But don't make that a prerequisite for joining. And don't eliminate the possibility of having guys in your band. All-girl bands can be seen as a novelty by some people (although others may go to see you play because you're an all-girl group); if a guy you know really wants to be in your band, then don't go exhibiting any of that gender-bias stuff you hate so much.

Don't worry too much right now about finding the perfect people. By the time you're good enough to perform in front of an audience, you might have gone through a dozen personnel changes. Bands are always forming, folding, and reforming every day. This is a good thing. It's cool to work with lots of different people, and it'll expose you to sounds and styles you might otherwise not have discovered.

Finding Instruments

You might want to keep it simple, at least at first. The most basic set-up is a couple of guitars, a bass, and drums. Sound too easy? It worked for John, Paul, George and Ringo. Of course, your band can have whatever instrument you already play—or want to. Piano, flute, clarinet, violin, cello, anything you like. Orchestra instruments can add a new dimension to your songs and give you a unique sound. That's a big plus when you're competing against about a billion other bands that might sound just like yours.

Guitars are either acoustic or electric. Acoustic is, literally, "unplugged," meaning you don't need an amplifier. Acoustic guitars are great for beginners for a couple of reasons: first, they're not loud, so you'll probably be able to practice a lot more without starting a huge fight with parents, siblings, roommates, family pets, and anyone else who lives in your general vicinity. Also because they're not loud, you're better able to hear what you're playing. People who pick up an electric guitar for the first time tend to slam the strings and just make a bunch of noise. That's okay if that's the sound you want—after all, that's where the entire punk movement was grounded. But if you want to hear some discernible melodies, go acoustic.

Plus, the next big wave in music is already here, and in case you haven't heard, it's led by women. Rock is no longer the domain of boys in tight pants and wild eye shadow—and don't even start that nasty habit of breaking your guitar into a million smithereens after the show; not only is it passé, it's extremely costly! If you decide you were born to make noise, then don't go and blow your entire savings account on some trick guitar that would make Chrissie Hynde jealous. You don't need anything fancy when you're just starting out; in fact, by the time you've gotten really good, you'll have a much better idea of what you want and don't want in a guitar. The best (meaning cheapest) way to get started, and the method that most are forced into whether they like it or not, is to borrow or buy used.

> Women with just a guitar and some soulful lyrics are changing the face of rock. Look to Tracy Chapman, Sheryl Crow, Jewel, or Fiona Apple for inspiration.

If you're lucky, you'll find much of what you need in other people's closets. Try your own house first, then dig through the attic of everyone you know. Your grandparents' garage can be a virtual gold mine of unwanted musical instruments that were, at one time, going to transform your dad into the next Peter Frampton. Don't be too picky about what you get when you borrow; you can always upgrade later.

If you can't borrow, buy used. But before you make any decisions about equipment, do a little research. Visit a local music store, one where you know they carry good equipment, and talk to some of the people who work there. Find someone sympathetic and pick her brain for as long as she will let you without making you buy something. Tell her how much money you have to start with and see what she can suggest. Even if there isn't anything in the store that you can afford, you'll get a lot of good advice about what type of equipment to consider—like brand names of guitars, or how extensive a drum set you really need when you're just starting out. Make time to visit a few stores and get a few different opinions.

Whenever you go to check out a used instrument, take a friend or even the rest of the band along, especially someone who knows anything at all about musical instruments. And no matter how good something looks, always try it out first. Even if you just hit a few chords or notes, you can get an idea of how an instrument sounds and whether you like it or not. Don't believe for a minute that all guitars, or all drum sets, sound the same. They don't. Also check out all the switches and knobs. Even if you don't know exactly what they're for, fiddle around with them anyway. If they produce any change in sound at all, they function at least on some level.

Most people initially ask a higher price than what the instrument is really worth. You can—and should—offer less, then negotiate (unless their ad says "firm") until you find a middle ground and a price within your budget.

Unless you plan on being perpetually unplugged, you'll need an amp to go with that electric guitar. There's no need to buy new; you can get a really decent used amp for less than $75. If you can afford it, get two: one for rehearsals and one for practicing alone (you can get a small amp for as little as $25). There are

WHERE TO GET USED

The classifieds: You can find just about everything for sale in the classifieds, from Les Paul guitars to Mr. Microphones. Check the Sunday editions of the papers in your area and don't forget the local free and alternative presses. (If you know exactly what you want and have a few extra bucks, you can always place an "instrument wanted" ad yourself.)

Pawn shops: They're a little more expensive than garage sales, but still cheaper than retail. Pawnbrokers will usually bargain with you—but remember, they're cash only!

Music stores: Some music stores that offer lessons will occasionally sell instruments that have been rented out. Even though the equipment is used, it's usually well maintained, and probably has gone through a thorough reconditioning before being put up for sale.

Flea markets and thrift shops: These are good possibilities, but you have to be careful of quality. Be sure you give the instrument a practice run right there before you buy. If you're ever told that you can't try out the instrument first, then leave. You will probably get ripped off.

Rentals: This is a good way to go if you have a history of starting cool projects but not finishing them (you know who you are). You can rent by the month, and you won't have to put up that much money to start. Plus, if you lose interest in a couple of months, you won't have wasted a lot of money.

two kinds of amplifiers: a one-piece unit (also called a combo unit) housing all the controls and the speaker in one cabinet; and a two-piece unit with an amp head (with inputs and controls) and a separate speaker.

You'll also need a cable to connect your guitar to the amp. A two-piece amp should come with a cable for connecting the two components. If you can afford it, get two guitar cables: a short one (10 to 12 feet) for rehearsals, and a longer one (20 to 25 feet) for gigs. When you go shopping for amps, take along your guitar or bass and a cord to plug it in so you can check out the sound. Test all the inputs and play with different controls until you get a sound you like. You won't need more than 50 amps of power to start.

Even if the used guitar you bought looks like it's in good shape, buy new strings; you'll definitely hear a difference in sound quality. You can find strings at any music store for $6 to $8, but shop around for the best price. You can negotiate at most chain stores, so don't be afraid to ask. Different sizes create different sounds—for example, size 9 is a lighter gauge and easier to play. Buy at least two sets and a couple of individual strings because they break pretty often, depending on the way you play.

If you find a guitar you like, hold the bottom edge of the body up to your chin and look down the top of the guitar all the way to the tuning pegs. If the neck looks curved or bowed, it's no good. You'll have a hard time keeping it in tune and you may have problems playing higher notes and chords.

Bass players choose their strings by size and type of sound desired. Start with a light gauge string. Ask the salesperson to play a couple of notes on different bass guitars to hear the different sounds that different strings can produce. For a brighter sound, get "round wound" strings. For a more muted tone, get "flat wound." Bass strings last longer than guitar strings, and when they start to go flat you can boil them in water; it'll revive them temporarily (but you can do this only once). Guitar strings have to be changed more often and should always be changed before a gig or recording session. Bass strings are more expensive, averaging $15 to $20 a set.

A full drum kit can be very expensive, even used. If you decide that you absolutely must have the whole set-up, be prepared to invest at least a couple hundred dollars. When shopping for a drum set, tap the cymbals to hear the range of sound you can get from different sizes.

If your band is rhythmically challenged, consider an electronic rhythm machine or keyboard with rhythm capabilities. These portable, inexpensive machines were made popular in the eighties by techno groups like the Pet Shop Boys and ABC; lots of rap artists still use rhythm machines instead of live drums. They've come a long way since they were first introduced with just one or two beats that sounded suspiciously like polka. They've also gotten a lot easier to use, even if you have no experience. Most units have several preset beats to choose from, and more expensive units let you program your own beat.

When you start rehearsing as a group, you'll need a PA (public address)

Instrments are like art: You may not know much about them, but you know what you like.

system. You're probably already somewhat familiar with PA systems—that's what your principal uses to announce such earth-shattering news as changes in the cafeteria lunch menu or warnings about stealing toilet paper from the bathroom.

A PA system consists of speakers, a mixer, and an amplifier. Basic models have at least a couple of inputs for more than one microphone (so those people who thought they were getting out of singing have just been nominated for back-up vocals) and each input can be controlled individually, depending on who has a great voice and who's just sort of filling in. PAs systems are pretty expensive and they're pretty technical, so if you fork out the cash to get one, make sure that someone takes the time to learn how to use it. If you can't afford a PA system, go ahead and plug your mike into the guitar amp. It won't sound as good, but it's better than nothing. Along with the PA system, you'll need a microphone (and stand) for everyone who sings. A new mike costs about $30, not including cord or stand.

As tight as your budget feels, you'll probably want to make room for a few accessories, like a guitar strap. Guitars get

pretty heavy, especially after hours of standing around. Get a wide, comfortable strap that won't pinch your neck. And get a tuner if you can. This device plugs into your guitar or bass and lets you tune individual strings. Either the guitar player or the bass players needs one. It's simple to use and will save you lots of time in tuning your instruments to one another.

Making Noise (and Lots of It)

You've researched your options, shopped around, bargained like a pro, and now you're sitting in your garage surrounded by stuff. Remember when I told you that it didn't matter if you could play or not? It's still true. Do you think Alanis Morrissette was born with a pic in her hand? Besides, a novice musician has one advantage over her more schooled and educated competitors: Her head isn't full of all those "proper" playing techniques that a music teacher would want her to use. There's nothing quite as creative as an untrained musician, so don't be ashamed of that, take advantage of it!

The best way to learn your instrument is to become intimately acquainted with it. Become your instrument's best friend. Hang out with it. Take it for long walks, spend the evenings telling it your fears, hopes and dreams, tell it—wait, maybe that's going too far. Within reason, spend as much time with your instrument as possible, because that's called practice! Practice is different from rehearsal. Practice is what you do alone with your instrument as you discover all the wonderful sounds it can make. Rehearsal is what you do with your band mates as a group. That's where you go after you've

WHAT YOU LACK IN TALENT, YOU CAN MAKE UP FOR IN EFFORT.

taught yourself the basics of how your instrument works. Don't show up for rehearsal until you've had some decent practice sessions all by your lonesome.

You'll soon find out that there's no great mystery to playing a musical instrument. Sure, it requires a certain amount of skill, but you don't have to be a prodigy to pick up the guitar. Because you have a kind face, I'm going to make it even easier by revealing the deepest, darkest secret of rock and roll: Some of the greatest songs of all time have only three chords! It's true. Rock is deceptively easy. If you stick with simple tunes (the Ramones and the Beatles are great for beginners), you can, by trial and error, figure it out. So what if you make a few mistakes? Who cares. Besides, one of your mistakes might be the next MTV Buzz Clip.

If you're a rules kind of girl, several excellent books on the market can teach you in simple, easy steps, how to play the guitar and other instruments. Mel Bay's series shows illustrations of different chords and where to place your fingers; other books come with audio tapes that let you hear what you should sound like. Master the bar chords first; they're the easiest to learn and you'll be using them 99 percent of the time anyway. Bass is even easier: There are fewer strings and instead of chords, you play single notes. Another excellent source for beginners is *The Encyclopedia of Picture Chords for All Guitarists*. It features illustrations and photos of finger placement. Check out your local music store; most have a wide

variety of instruction books for most musical instruments.

A good way to accelerate your learning process is to use sheet music, which you can buy at most music stores. You can get music of most current songs by bands you know and like, and some older groups like Pink Floyd and the Beatles. Songs you know are sometimes easier to play. If you can't read sheet music and are having a hard time teaching yourself, break down and pay for a few lessons. They're worth it for the basics and once you know a few chords or scales, you'll pretty much be able to figure out the rest by yourself.

Getting Gigs

Aside from some family reunions, birthday parties, and the occasional bat mitzvah, you probably won't be able to get a gig until you're pretty polished. If you've been getting a positive response from friends and other people who have heard your stuff, and you feel like you're ready to start looking for gigs, start visiting some clubs in your area to check out the talent they book. Start small; don't set your sights on something like the House of Blues the first time out.

Don't be too hasty to blow off birthday parties and retirement gigs. A gig is a gig, and playing live is the best experience, even if it is for a room full of preteens. You won't sound the same in a room full of people as you did in your basement; and its best to work out the kinks with family members (who will

RECORD YOUR OWN CD, CASSETTE, OR VINYL LP

This is the absolute coolest thing you could do with your new band. Even if you never make it to the next Lalapalooza or Lilith Fair, even if you decide to go into computer programming (where your odds of staying off unemployment are considerably better) and banish your guitar to the back of the closet, try to scrape together enough money to record your own CD. It would be way cool to whip out your own CD in the middle of your next party, and if the quality is halfway decent (and you make some sort of effort at marketing yourself), you may be able to make back the money you invested, maybe more!

A lot of companies offer a range of services, from just packaging all the way up to recording, cutting your CD, and putting the package together (some offer studio services; most offer graphics and production services). The process is easier than you might think: basically, you send them a clean cassette tape of your band, fork over a fee that ranges from a couple of hundred dollars to a couple of thousand (depending on what services you're buying), and you'll get back your first release, neatly packaged, ready to spring on the music-buying public.

For example, you can get 1000 CDs made (including black and white graphics for your cover) for just under $2000. This might sound like a lot of money, but you've got to think big: it's actually less than $2 per CD. If you put some effort into marketing yourself (maybe hook up with a couple of mail-order houses or sell directly at live shows), you could make a decent profit. If you think your listening public is a little technologically challenged, get cassettes; they're cheaper (as little as 500 units for about a buck apiece). You can get nostalgic for the days before you were born and cut records; several companies specialize in 7-inchers (these are the cheapest: you can get one hundred 45 RPMs for about $300).

All companies will provide detailed specs about how to prepare your material for duplication. They'll also give you choices so you can find the package that best suits your music (and your budget). Check out some music trade magazines (and the resource section in this book) for leads on CD and record manufacturers.

probably take pity on you) than in a room crammed with people who paid money to hear you play.

Once you find a club, call during business hours and get the name (and correct spelling) of the person who books shows. Also find out the best time to reach that person by phone. Then get your package together.

Your package will contain your demo tape and a short note, explaining yourself and your music (if you can!), tucked into a padded envelope. Remember, your package will be competing with hundreds of others, so find a way to make yours float to the top of the stack. Some bookers say that their eyes just sort of glaze over in a milky, manila color when contemplating the stacks of packages that arrive on their desks daily, so try something different— use a brightly colored envelope or cover the outside with doodles and designs that'll make it stand out in an overworked memory. Throw in a goodie, like a rubber insect or a cereal prize.

Of course, the most important component if your package isn't the fake tattoos, it's your demo tape. If you can possibly swing the cost, produce your demo at a studio. The sound will be much crisper and cleaner and will give anyone listening to your tape the impression that you have your act together.

After you send your package (or drop it off), wait a few weeks before you call and follow up. Don't nag. If the booker tells you she hasn't listened to your tape yet, ask her when you can call back. If she says she did give it a listen, she'll either tell you that you're great and you're playing next Saturday night, or you're "not right" for the club. Don't take it too hard;

keep submitting your tapes to lots of clubs. If you start racking up rejection after rejection, take that as a sign and head back into the basement or studio or bedroom or wherever it is you rehearse. If you're still in school, hit up your student activities committee for a live appearance. Play a rally or dance. Don't get too hung up on getting paid at this stage. Even at a club, you'll be lucky to make $50 for the whole band for the evening. Most clubs pay by attendance—that means that the more people show up, the more you make (so if you get good enough to play a club, tell all your friends to come). For private parties, you set the rate, but be realistic. The point here isn't to make money (not yet), but to gain experience playing in front of a live audience.

Now that you know all there is to know about forming your own girl group, what do you think? Not much of

THIS IS A STICK-UP

What would a new band be without thousands of stickers plastered across your town? I have it on good authority that Pete is THE guy to contact when you're ready to make your band's presence really known (especially on street lamps, telephone poles, store windows, etc.). Prices are cheap: as little as $36 for 250 stickers.

Sticker Guy!
c/o Pete Menchetti
P.O. Box 204
Reno, NV 89504
(702) 324-3889
E-mail: mench@cs.unr.edu

a mystery, is it? It's not like you had to be blindfolded and led to a dark place. Like any other fantasy that may be brewing around inside that girl brain of yours, you'll eventually discover that the hardest part isn't thinking of what to do, it's getting off your butt and doing it. It's easy to let years (even a lifetime) pass by, all the time wishing we had done this, or tried that. Don't feel stupid if your dream is to be a rock star: Like the lottery, it's gotta happen to someone, right?

The actual mechanics of forming a band (learning to play, making the connections, booking studio time, etc.) take a little effort, but nothing that any girl with a dream can't handle. Much of the work is just running around and making a few phone calls. The key is commitment. If having a band is more than a passing fancy, if this is your burning desire, then you have to keep practicing faithfully. You can't flake, you can't blow the band members off, you can't come up with a bunch of lame excuses like "I have cramps," or worse, "I have a date." You have to show up and keep showing up until you get what you want out of this experience, whatever that may be.

Some days you may sound like a million bucks; some days you may feel like tossing your guitar into the river. If you ever get to that point, please, sell it instead! The next girl with this dream will be forever indebted to you.

PART FOUR

CARE FOR AND MAINTAIN YOUR NEW WORLD

It's time you took a breather. You deserve it, don't you? After all, in just a short time, you've risen to the top of the political food chain, mastered the worlds of high finance and global economies, and lofted yourself from virtual anonymity to become the most beloved icon of the people you now serve. Way to go.

Don't get too comfy with your feet up on the royal footstool, however, because you've neglected something very important in your quest to reach total world domination. Don't be too hard on yourself; it's something most world leaders tend to forget at one time or another during their hectic reign. But if your world order is going to last, you're going to have to spend a little more time and effort.

The key words here are *care for* and *maintain*. This world is no different than that cool used car you have your eyes on: If you don't take proper care of her, then one day she's just going to die somewhere alongside the road and leave you completely stranded.

You've done a lot so far, that's true, but more work still needs to be done. Too many world leaders, having risen to fabulous heights of power, don't bother with maintenance. Now that you're on the top rung of the power ladder, it's your responsibility to ensure that all the good you've done will continue—you know, for your grandchildren's grandchildren, that kind of thing. So don't turn your back on the world you now call your own. Make it a point to become the protector of the Earth and her inhabitants.

Aside from the moral implications of a dying planet, there are business considerations as well. How cost effective can it be to keep taking and taking and never replacing? Remember everything you learned when becoming a financial wizard—profit and loss, supply and demand, stuff like that. If you think of your new world like a business and the planet like your supply cabinet, you can see that you can't open that cabinet door everyday and keep taking out all the pencils and paper and staples and expect them to magically replenish themselves. Sooner or later, you're going to have to either cut down on the amount of supplies you use and get more efficient tools like computers and stuff, or you're going to have to call the business supply warehouse to place an order.

Unfortunately, there's no giant Natural Resources Warehouse in the sky, like some giant Wal-Mart that sells replacements for polluted streams and rivers and contaminated soil. Our only option is to take better care of the supplies we were given in the first place (and recycle them whenever possible).

Same with your employees: If you want to run a successful business, you have to take care of the folks who work for you—give them a vacation once in awhile, make sure they don't fight too much amongst themselves, and fix any radon leaks in your ceiling. If you don't, your company will suffer, and you'll lose everyone who works for you.

Care of the planet has to include care of her inhabitants; if you take care of one without looking out for the other, it's just no good. Either you're left with a pristine planet with nobody around to enjoy it, or a bunch of happy, well-fed people with no place to call home.

The time is right for environmentalism: not just in your vocabulary, not just in your consciousness, but in your practical world as well. More and more jobs and opportunities in conservation appear every day. It used to be that only hippies

ENVIRONMENTAL ROLE MODELS

Don't think that your one small girl voice is going to drown in a sea of eco-politicking—there are lots of natural allies and role models out there already.

Kathryn Fuller, president of the World Wildlife Fund (WWF), has doubled the income and membership of that organization in her few years (so far) at the helm. She's also helped enact an ivory ban and introduced environmental education in middle schools around the country with her program, "Windows on the Wild."

Barbar Dudley, executive director of eco-giant Greenpeace, works to educate small fisherman about sustainable fishing practices.

Debbie Sease, a mover and shaker at the Sierra Club, has spent most of her time fighting the good eco-fight against some big, bad, planet-hungry Republicans in Washington, DC.

Katie McGiney is President Clinton's senior environmental advisor and chair of the President's Council on Environmental Quality.

Ingrid Newkirk, famous for her groundbreaking work in animal rights circles, founded the incredibly powerful PETA (People for the Ethical Treatment of Animals).

recycled and the only reason to plant trees was to celebrate Arbor Day, but now hundreds of colleges across the country offer advanced degrees in environmental studies, and there are all sorts of summer job and internship programs for high school students to get a taste of what it's like to save the planet.

Women are at the forefront of the environmental movement, that's for sure, and there's always room for someone else to lend a hand.

As a whole, the problems of the world seem a little intimidating; so intimidating, in fact, that many would-be activists are overwhelmed by the prospect of everything that needs to be done to save the planet. That's why many people are turning to our communities; instead of working for globalization, we're striving to improve our own blocks, neighborhoods, and cities. We're rediscovering that, even in this technologically grounded world, the best way to get to know a people, a culture, is one-on-one, standing, working, and playing side by side. And the methods we use to build friendships—helping people in need, sharing compassion for all of the Earth's creatures—haven't changed at all.

Conservation and care are the buzz words of the new millennium; they have to be, if we ever hope to celebrate another.

Chapter Ten

GET AN ECO JOB

Want to work to help the environment? Great! You're probably trying to decide where you want to begin. How about the rainforests? Or the desert? How about endangered species or global warming? This might be starting to sound like one of those tricky multiple choice questions. Don't worry; just remember that choice is always a good thing.

Start thinking about what kind of work appeals to you—scientific field studies, activist work like fund-raising, or administrative duties like word processing are a few possibilities. Do you want to work in forestry on solutions for water pollution, or would you like to check out a career in public education and awareness? When you first imagine working as an environmentalist, you may think you'll be out in the field, knee-deep in wetlands, recording the mating habits of some endangered reptile. Or maybe you see yourself doing radical activist stuff—scaling thousand-year-old trees in the forests of Washington State and bringing the lumber mills to their knees.

Many of us have this idealized view of environmental work, but that kind of work makes up only a small portion of the opportunities you can dig up. Working in swamps and forests sounds cool if you're a squishy bug kind of girl—it may be just the kind of thing you're looking for—but if you'd rather wear business suits and high heels to work, you can still make a career out of working for the planet. Environmentalists work as lawyers, accountants, engineers, architects, and administrative assistants. You can train for a specialized career in environmental work, but you don't have to earn a master's degree in biology to work as an environmentalist. Practically any skills you have can be put to use for the cause, even if all you can do is type or stuff envelopes.

You might already have some pretty specific ideas about what you want to do. Maybe you don't; maybe your plans are kind of vague, more like "something outside would be nice." One way to narrow down your choices is to get out and do things now! See what kind of work you like and what you don't. A lot of environmental career guides stress a college degree, and that might be the path you've decided to take. But if you're not really sure what you want to do yet, you probably don't want to invest huge amounts of either time or money deciding. That's okay; for some of these jobs, you don't even need to be enrolled in college! High school students who are interested in checking out environmental work have all sorts of opportunities; many of them as summer jobs, at camps, or in paid internships.

> *Giving you this book and saying, "This is how you prepare for a career working in the environment," would be kind of like taking you into a huge supermarket and saying, "This is how you prepare dinner." We need to be specific! Are you more of a meat and potatoes kind of girl, or are you ready to go veggie? Frozen? Homemade? Instant? The possibilities are almost endless.*

The two groups featured in this chapter, the Student Conservation Association and the Youth Conservation Corps, are both nationally recognized organizations. For decades, they've been helping place students and young adults in conservation and environmentally oriented jobs. Both offer paid positions, as well as opportunities to develop your career further with other environmental organizations.

Student Conservation Association

Student Conservation Association
Conservation Career Dev. Program
P.O. Box 550
Charlestown, NH 03603
(603) 543-1700

1800 N Kent St., Ste. 1220
Arlington, VA
(703) 524-2441
http://www.sca-inc.org

Their brochure says it all: "Surveying endangered marine wildlife by sea kayak in the coastal waters of Alaska, leading hikers through the rain forests of Olympic National Park, or teaching environmental education to city kids who have never slept outdoors in a tent...." Sounds a little intense, doesn't it?

The SCA is an outstanding nonprofit organization dedicated to educating and training young people to change their world. SCA volunteers have helped restore the charred forests of Yellowstone Park after ravaging fires, pieced together the devastated Florida Everglades after Hurricane Andrew, and launched community-wide anti-graffiti campaigns in cities across the country.

Lots of students enter the SCA by joining the Conservation Career Development Program. The CCDP is one of the best ways to get your foot in that environmental door and get some great training to prepare for a lifelong career. The program was specifically designed to encourage African-American, Latino, Asian, and Native American youth (especially women) to consider a career in environmentalism, but eligibility for the program isn't restricted to any of these groups.

The CCDP is a year-long program providing high school students with conservation education, community service activities, career counseling and development, job placement assistance, and mentoring to expose kids to the rewards of working to save the planet. The CCDP acts locally, meaning students get together with others from their community to talk about problems—like how to preserve historical buildings or improve cultural and natural resources—and plan solutions.

The schedule is pretty forgiving for students. During the school year, you'll work on weekends and after school, visiting natural, cultural, and historic sites and taking part in local forums on conservation and social issues. During the summer, you have the option of becoming an SCA High School Conservation Work Crew (CWC) member.

SCA Crews are made up of six to ten students and are supervised by an adult. As a CWC member, you spend five weeks living and working with other students (male and female) who are as committed to preservation and conservation as you are. It can be hard, physical work; in fact, the SCA warns "You will have few amenities. You will hike extensively, be dirty more often than clean, sometimes be wet and cold or hot and sweaty, be bitten by mosquitoes, and will cook all meals over a camp stove." Not exactly a European vacation (in fact, it doesn't even qualify as a rustic summer camp), but it does have rewards that other camps don't. No, you don't learn to make world-class lanyards, but you may learn how to

---

GET YOUR HANDS DIRTY

CWCs specialize in rural construction and maintenance projects like:

Revegetation

Fisheries and stream restoration

Trail construction and maintenance

Wildlife habitat improvement

Building and repairing fences

Construction of structures such as shelters and bridges

---

clear a path through the forest. The results are tangible and immediate. It's not all a grind, though; the last week is like a great big field trip, where you get to take a hike or river excursion through the land you've worked to preserve and protect. If you want to be an agent of change in your world, you have to work for it. This is definitely a place to do it.

You must be at least 16 to join. If you're enrolled in college, you can receive an educational award that can be used to pay past student loans or future expenses; if you're still in high school, you'll receive a small stipend. If you like the work enough to stick with it, you can sign on with the CCDP for up to six years. You don't need any work experience, just lots of enthusiasm and an open mind for new experiences. You must also be in good physical shape and be prepared to meet the challenge of the hard work and the harsh living conditions.

The Resource Assistant Program (RAP) is for high school graduates and college students. You perform the same kind of work that CWC members do, but instead of working in crews comprised of other "novices," you work with seasoned environmental professionals and natural resource managers. Positions last up to twelve weeks and are available in all states, including Alaska and Hawaii.

Some of the organizations who've benefitted from the services of RAP participants are the U.S. National Park and Forest Services, Bureau of Land Management, U.S. Fish and Wildlife Service, the Army and Navy, and the Nature Conservancy. RAP participants gain tremendous job experience as well as college credit. All expenses are paid (housing, food, etc.), but there's no salary—RAP positions are voluntary.

Youth Conservation Corps

Youth Conservation Corps
National Association of Service and
Conservation Camps
666 Eleventh St. NW, Ste. 1000
Washington, DC 20001-4542
(202)737-6272
E-mail: nascc@nascc.org

Over 120 youth service and conservation corps in 37 states are supervised by the NASCC. Youth conservation dates back to the 1930s, when FDR formed the Civilian Conservation Corps (CCC) to help young men find work during the Depression. Things have changed a lot since then—women are now active members of the youth conservation efforts and the opportunities have changed from just busy work into a legitimate and desirable way to get into the field of environmentalism. Dozens of programs have evolved into what exists today: a national network of employment programs for America's youth.

Although almost half the work (43 percent) is in environmental conservation, YC also addresses issues like building renovation, human services, education, recycling, disaster relief, public safety, and health. You may be assigned to help clear brush in fire-hazard country, or you may be asked to help staff a Meals-on-Wheels Program or work in a battered women's shelter. These projects have a tremendous impact on this country—over 22,000

HARD-CORP WORK

Here are a few examples of regional youth corp projects:

The Washington Service Corps' Season of Service Project works to help needy and at-risk children. They've set up immunization programs, established a community garden operated by at-risk children, and developed recreation and education programs for kids living in gang-infested neighorhoods.

The California Conservation Corps focuses primarily on environmental issues. Past projects have included coastal oil spill clean-up, tree planting, clearing rivers and streams, and building and reconstructing over 3000 miles of trails throughout California.

The Milwaukee Community Service Corps worked with the Milwaukee Housing Authority to create an on-the-job training program in urban redevelopment. Their program gives young adults valuable skills to help them get good jobs, while at the same time repairing and renovating housing for low-income residents.

young adults participate annually, providing 12.6 million hours of service.

Positions with the individual youth corps are paid, and lots are residential programs. For example, California Conservation Corps members live in a camp with other corps members. Corps workers range in age from 16 to 25, and they work in paid, full-time positions that benefit both themselves and the communities in which they work. The duration of your service and the amount you receive as payment vary from program to program.

Additional Resources

USPIRG

U. S. Public Interest Research Group
215 Pennsylvania Ave. SE
Washington, DC 20003
(202) 546-4707
http://www.igc.apc.org/pirg

PIRG groups can be found all over the country, from New England to Los Angeles, including Alaska and Hawaii. Their common goal is simple: They're on a Campaign to Save the Environment (in fact, that's the name of their summer internship program).

This is no volunteer program. Working as a summer activist for PIRG, you'll earn between $2500 and $4000 for a summer's work, and you'll pick up skills that are essential to any effective activist: networking, communication, organizing, and fund-raising. But it's not classroom learning—it's education by action. Working with a PIRG affiliate in your state, you could find yourself dealing with a wide variety of issues, like water and air pollution, the threat of deforestation, and hazardous waste management. You could work in the field or find yourself training as a lobbyist to convince Congress to increase funding for environmental programs.

Environmental Careers Organization

Environmental Careers Org.
286 Congress St., 3rd Fl.
Boston, MA 02210
(617) 426-4375
http://www.eco.org

Founded through the Massachusetts Audubon Society in 1972, the ECO is a national, nonprofit organization that works to protect the environment through education and new opportunities. Their Environmental Placement Services Program has placed over 7000 college students in paid internship programs with local, state, and federal environmental agencies. The ECO also works with nonprofit organizations, community groups, corporations, and consulting firms.

In additional to placement services, the ECO also offers a series of career workshops for those aspiring to work for the environment; they provide environmental career information and services to over 50,000 people each year. The ECO also offers conferences and valuable publications for the eco jobseeker.

The ECO is a good place to start if you're just beginning to think about a career in the environment. Write and tell them about your interests, experience, and educational background, and they may be able to help you figure out what kind of work is best for you.

If none of these programs fit your needs, do a little research to find the environmental program that's perfect for you.

Sierra Student Coalition

Sierra Student Coalition
223 Thayer St., #2
Providence, RI 02906
(401) 861-6012
E-mail: ssc-info@ssc.org

The SSC was founded in 1991 by a 17-year-old Sierra Club member in Los Angeles, California. The mission of the student-run SSC is to educate and incite students to change the world around them. Among other things, the SSC helps young activists all over the country maintain contact through their network, and they provide members and non-members with valuable resources and information on a number of timely environmental issues.

The SSC also conducts two leadership training seminars for high school students (one on the East Coast and one on the West). The six-day programs are run by students, for students, featuring topics like manipulating the media for maximum publicity, creative fund-raising, and sexism in the environmental movement. In addition to the leadership seminars, the SSC offers students more opportunities through leadership positions., which are paid staff positions (like Web page designer and fund-raising director) with the SSC.

Student Environmental Action Coalition

Student Environmental Action Coalition
P.O. Box 1168
Chapel Hill, NC 27514-1168
(919) 967-4600

SEAC is a grassroots organization that recognizes the incredible power organized and connected students can wield in their world. When you become a member of SEAC, you achieve just that: strength in numbers. Although SEAC's primary focus has always been the care and maintenance of the earth, they also handle social justice issues.

Since SEAC is an extremely well-connected organization (at last count, they had over 1100 member groups worldwide), they'd be a great resource for you to find opportunities with environmental organizations in your own community, and should definitely be one of your first stops.

Youth for Environmental Sanity (YES!)

Youth for Environmental Sanity (YES!)
706 Fredrick St.
Santa Cruz, CA 95062
(408) 459-9344
http://www.yesworld.org

Since their inception in 1991, YES! has been another extremely effective student-run activist group that works for environmental action and conservation. One of the most effective tools in their work has been their summer camp program for student activists. To date, YES! has held over 28 training camps in seven countries, and has presented their eco platform to over half a million students in high school assemblies.

At YES! camp, students are taught the skills they need to become more effective activists (no pillowcase races or pressed flowers). Campers learn effective fund-raising and public speaking techniques, as well as how to build team spirit and use the media for maximum coverage.

The summer camps aren't free, but YES! organizers try to maintain a sliding fee scale so that as many students as possible can attend. They also offer fund-raising kits (to help you pay for camp) and a few full scholarships.

YMCA Earth Service Corps

YMCA Earth Service Corps
National Resource Center
909 Fourth Ave.
Seattle, WA 98104
(800) 733-YESC
http://www.yesc.org

The Y has some great programs to get students excited about working to help the environment. In their service-learning projects, students are responsible for projects like tree planting, beach clean-up, writing newsletters, and educating elementary school students about the environment and our influence on it. The Y also offers leadership weekends where students gather and learn about how to organize an activist group and develop group communication skills.

Chapter Eleven

FIND A VOLUNTEER JOB YOU'LL LOVE

What comes to mind when you hear the word "volunteer"? Do you think of hours spent sitting next to a bed in a retirement home, or passing out flowers as a candy-striper at a local hospital? If so, think again! Volunteer opportunities haven't been so limited and restricted since the days of *Father Knows Best* and *Leave It to Beaver.*

There are literally hundreds of opportunities, from plain old blood banking to joining an expedition to Africa to help impoverished children. Volunteer corps are no longer made up of displaced homemakers and retirees with nothing to do all day. Young people, your generation, are filling the void that communities around the world are feeling since the government has started slashing social programs left and right. In fact, of college-aged young adults polled by *Who Cares* (a magazine about volunteerism), two-thirds already volunteer in their own community. Fifty-six percent help out in cleaning up neighborhoods, and 59 percent volunteer their time to work with children.[1]

More and more young people have learned that volunteering today means more than just helping others, it's also a way of preparing for a career, learning a new skill, making a fantasy come true, or taking responsibility for our planet's sorely needed repairs. Whether you choose to keep company with patients at a nursing home or take part in an archaeological dig abroad, there are virtually endless opportunities out there. The only limits to what you can do, and where you can go, are in your own imagination!

Think about it: Over the course of your life, you will probably have several jobs, but how many of them will be an expression of your political or social concerns? As you get older, you'll find that it becomes harder to be picky about what industry, company, or position you get. Volunteer work is your only opportunity to have complete control over your job from start to finish. You can decide from the beginning what kind of company you want to work for, what sort of tasks you will perform, and how long you'll be around.

Too many students leave high school with no idea of what kind of work they want to do, or what the work they want to do really entails. They often end up either choosing the first job that comes along (and they may realize very soon that they dislike the work), or they spend years of education preparing for a career they don't know much about and may not even like.

Why Should I Volunteer When I Can Get a Paying Job?

That sounds harsh, but it's not. Volunteer work can't really take the place of a paying job unless your last name is Rockefeller or Gates, but it can be something you do in your spare time. You may think that the only reason people volunteer should be "to help others." While it's true that altruism (a selfless concern for others) is usually the primary motivation for offering yourself as a volunteer, it doesn't have to be the only reason. In fact, having a motive other than just "to do good" will probably make you more successful at the work you sign up to do. Say you want to go to school to become a special education teacher and work with small children. Instead of looking for a

related volunteer position, you sign up to answer phones for an environmental agency. You may be "doing good," but chances are you'll get bored pretty quickly and you'll probably want to quit after a short time. Your intentions were good, but you really haven't helped anyone, including yourself. If you had volunteered to spend a couple of hours each weekend as a teacher's aid at a community day care center, you would have been doing something that you have a personal interest or stake in, plus adding credits to your résumé and college application.

Consider volunteer work if you have personal experience with a particular issue that could benefit others.

If you've been a victim of abuse, you might get a lot of satisfaction answering the phones at a rape crisis or domestic abuse center. If a friend or family member was injured in a drunk driving incident, you might become involved with an organization like Mothers Against Drunk Driving (MADD). People with a personal stake in a particular cause are often the most passionate and effective volunteers.

Consider volunteer work if you want to become involved in your community.

A lot of people, when given the opportunity, would like to become active in their community but just don't know how. Volunteering your time or skills to a

THE CHALLENGES WE FACE TODAY, ESPECIALLY THOSE THAT FACE OUR CHILDREN, REQUIRE SOMETHING OF ALL OF US—PARENTS, RELIGIOUS AND COMMUNITY GROUPS, BUSINESSES, LABOR ORGANIZATIONS, SCHOOLS, TEACHERS, OUR GREAT NATIONAL CIVIC AND SERVICE ORGANIZATIONS, EVERY CITIZEN.

—Bill Clinton, Presidents' Summit for America's Future (1997)

community-based organization, like a homeless shelter or an environmental action group, is a great way for you to start making change on a grassroots level. Community organizations are ideal for volunteers—because the group is local, the logistics of your work (like how far you have to drive or take the bus to get there) would probably be a lot simpler to work out. Plus, it might be easier to identify what things need fixing most if you're working locally, because you live in the area and see the problems every day.

Consider volunteer work if you want to fulfill a fantasy or wish.

You'd love to work with animals, but you have no training. The local animal shelter would love to have you walk and bathe their dogs. Maybe you've always loved the theater and would like to see what it's like to work backstage. You can fulfill your dream by volunteering at a local theater and helping with sets, costumes, and rehearsals. If you have any hobbies that you really love, like riding horses or painting or drafting, you can always find an organization or a company that would love to have you volunteer with them and use your hobby. You'd be an especially valuable worker because you're already familiar with the subject or industry.

Consider volunteer work if you want to influence the world around you.

Every day, you hear news stories about children living below the poverty level. You see people living on the street outside the local mall. You've always wanted to help, but how far does the dollar that you give now and then really go? By volunteering to plan and plant a com-

SEE YOURSELF

Wielding a hammer to help build low-income housing.

Playing nursemaid to a baby mountain lion at a wildlife waystation.

Working as a conservationist in a foreign country.

Giving presentations for the Humane Society at local grammar schools.

Working behind the scenes at a television show for children.

munity garden, you can be an agent of lasting change. Not many people have the luxury of going to bed at night with the satisfaction of knowing that their actions make a real difference in someone else's life. Besides, when you start working for a living, you may find yourself in and out of jobs that don't appear to have any social significance at all. You can fill that void by volunteering for a good cause.

Consider volunteer work if you want to get firsthand knowledge about a career choice.

Volunteer work is a great way to feel out a new career. For instance, almost every girl I've ever known has wanted to work with small children at one time or another. If you don't have any younger brothers or sisters or don't spend much time with people much younger than yourself, how do you know if you'd like it? Volunteer a couple hours of your time after school at a local preschool or day care center. By interacting with the kids—reading them stories, playing games with them, and so on—you can get a good idea of what it would be like to work with them every day. You'll also get a good idea of whether or not you have the qualities that preschool teachers need, like creativity, imagination, fairness, and most of all, patience! This kind of reality check is valuable before you spend a lot of time or money in training or college.

Consider volunteer work if you want to get your foot in the door of a particular business or industry.

Becoming a volunteer can open lots of doors to a paying job at a particular organization or industry, if a position becomes available. Lots of people think it would be cool to work at a magazine or a TV or radio station. These "glamour" jobs are very competitive. In fact, most require that all staff members, even assistants, have a college degree; for every opening, they may have literally hundreds of résumés piling up, waiting to be read. How do you break through competition like that? Volunteer your time at a community paper, regional magazine, or community radio or TV station.

Spend the summer typing, writing copy, or editing articles; you'll gain useful experience in the day-to-day operations of that industry, which can be more valuable than a college degree. By developing a working relationship with management, and proving—at absolutely no risk or cost to them—that you're reliable, talented, and eager, you may snag the next paid opening at that company! Even if you don't land a job there, your experience, and your references, may help you get a job at another company. You may also find that your prospective employers may be willing to forego experience or

educational requirements that they might require of other applicants they don't know personally.

Consider volunteer work if you want to pick up new skills.

You know the story: It's hard to get a job without experience, but how are you supposed to get experience without a job? This can be hard, but not impossible. Maybe a for-profit company wouldn't be willing to put you on the payroll while you practice to increase your typing speed or learn how to paint a house, but a non-profit organization would probably be more than happy to let you indulge in a little on-the-job training while you're working for free, because that allows their tight budget to go a little further than if they had to pay you.

If you want to go to school to learn how to become a vet tech, for example, you could end up spending thousands of dollars, not to mention the time it would take for you to get certification. But if you volunteer to help at a local animal shelter or veterinarian's office, you might get someone to teach you valuable job skills, like how to give injections and apply first aid to injured animals. A lot of the skills you pick up have a cash value if you look at how much trade schools and special classes can cost. Plus, if you prove you are a capable, dependable, and hardworking individual, your employer may pay for all or part of any training you need to become a full-time employee.

Consider volunteer work if you want to bulk up your résumé before beginning a serious job search.

It's sometimes hard to make your stark résumé attractive to prospective employers when the only experience you have is a few part-time and afterschool jobs like baby-sitting and dog walking. Volunteer work is real work, even though you don't get paid. It's a great way to beef up your résumé before you begin an all-out job hunt, especially when you're seeking full-time work.

Consider volunteer work if you want to gain leadership skills.

College admissions offices and employers love leaders! Even if you're not going to qualify for a supervisory position the minute you hit the job circuit, potential employers love to see applicants who have the ability and experience to motivate, guide, and encourage their fellow employees. On a practical level, employees with these skills are often given tasks like opening and closing a store or counting out the day's receipts—that means that they're often the first ones in line when the boss is looking for a new shift supervisor or manager. If you plan on enrolling in college when you leave high school, a résumé with volunteer experience would look pretty good alongside your student transcripts—volunteer work says a lot about a person, and this could definitely give you an edge, especially if the colleges you're applying to are very competitive.

Finding the Right Opportunity

The key to getting as much out of a volunteer assignment as possible is finding the right match. If you take a little time to research all the opportunities—or create some of your own—you're more likely to find an organization you'll stick with, and find one where you can not only give, but also receive. If you're interested in a partic-

---

GETTING NOTICED

Most recent graduates are shocked to see how competitive the job market is. You have to catch an employer's eye in just a few minutes, or even seconds. Volunteer experience can help your résumé stand out.

When you include your volunteer work on your résumé, put it right alongside your paid employment history. Many people list volunteer service separately. But the fact that you didn't get paid for this work doesn't make it any less valuable. Write the job description for volunteer work just as you would for a paid position. Include all the skills you learned and all the tasks you performed. In the detailed job duties section, mention that the position was voluntary.

Include any specific contributions or achievements. For example, were you part of a fund-raising effort that met its annual goal; for instance, raising $25,000 for a community homeless center? Even if the help you provided was administrative support, you were still a part of that team, and you should include that on your résumé.

List whatever skills you picked up. Did you supervise others? Even if you coordinated and supervised other volunteers, that experience is still valuable in training you to make decisions and be a leader.

Your volunteer service and experience is worth more than a few short sentences on your résumé; think about the duties you performed and how they might sound if you had been working at a paying job—you'll find that with a little special wording, you can get a lot more out of the experience than just a good feeling.

ular industry or cause, narrow your search right off the bat. For example, if you want to work in politics someday, become a Nader Raider and volunteer at the local offices of the Green Party. If you have no particular direction in mind, your choices are unlimited. Homelessness, poverty, environmental clean-up, and animal welfare work are a few options. When you're thinking about what kind of organizations to approach, consider these questions:

What skills do you have to offer?

Will you be satisfied doing office work, like typing, filing, and answering phones? These are common needs for most nonprofit organizations. If this seems boring, try looking for something where you'll work outdoors, like a nature conservancy group. If you're a people person or a good listener, you'd be a valuable asset to a crisis center or a hotline, even if you don't know anything about computers or typewriters.

Do you want to use skills you already have, or do you want to learn new skills?

Habitat for Humanity will teach you how to use a hammer and a saw to help build housing for economically disadvantaged families. Those aren't skills that are offered to many young women, but they could lead to a well-paying, secure job.

How much time do you have available to volunteer?

Don't take on the responsibility of an assignment that requires four hours every Saturday if you don't think you'll be able to keep to that schedule. Some volunteer jobs, by their very nature, are long-term; some are shorter and may last only a day.

Once you have an idea of where to start, begin looking at specific organizations. Instead of just rifling through the yellow pages, take advantage of volunteer search firms (most communities have at least one). These groups maintain databases of organizations that need help. They may have only a few dozen listings, or thousands, depending on the size of the city where you live. Their job is to connect volunteers like you with organizations where you'll be of the most value and get the most out of the experience.

Some volunteer search firms can give you details over the phone based on some information from you; some may ask that you come into their offices for a short

Contact the main library where you live, or call an area radio station for more leads—they're always running public service spots for local groups needing volunteer workers.

meeting or browse through their listings until you find something of interest.

Once you find something that interests you, call the group and ask to know more about their need for volunteers. They may mail you some introductory brochures and/or information, or they may ask you to come in for an interview, to fill out an application, or attend an orientation.

An Interview?

You're probably wondering why you have to interview for an unpaid, volunteer position, right? You assumed that they should be thrilled to get you, no matter what your skill level, and that they should be beating a path to your door just for the mere mention of your desire to volunteer. That may be what you think, but it's not exactly fair. Think of it this way: just like you want to find a good match—your skills, goals, and talents with an agency that interests you—they also want to find people who will be dedicated and committed and who truly have something to contribute. After all, no matter what your skill level, the organization you join will have to give you some degree of training. Even if that training is minimal, it's time that an employee must take from his or her normal duties to share with you.

Don't think of the interview as completely one-sided; it's a chance to check each other out. Your priorities are to find out why and when the group needs volunteers, how long the position will last, if transportation is available or if you'll have to find your own ride, what kind of training you'll need, and if they'll train you if you don't have the particular skills they need. They'll be looking at your skill level, your availability, and your interest in their group.

You can conduct a pre-interview over the phone—in fact, exchange as much information up front as possible—but never commit to anything without going to the office, meeting your potential coworkers, and taking a look at the environment. If it's not a good fit, be honest and decline. Otherwise you'll be wasting everyone's time. Some organizations have age limits—they may accept people only over 16 or 18—or may require you have your parent's written consent if you're still a minor. Find this out up front.

What Kinds of Jobs Can You Get?

The best way to answer this question is with another question: What kind of job do you want? The field is wide open. Once you've talked with a search firm or checked out other relief and volunteer organizations in your city, and you still haven't found quite what you're looking for, approach individual groups and companies. It doesn't matter if they haven't actively looked for volunteers; maybe you'll be the first. If you have a strong interest in what they do and can prove that you'd be a valuable asset, they'll probably give you a chance. Not many companies, groups, or agencies are likely to turn down volunteer help, if you're the right match.

There are a lot of great opportunities to be found, whether you're searching on the Net or in your local library. No matter what you're looking for, two of the best places to start are the AmeriCorps programs and the Campus Outreach Opportunity League (COOL). Both are especially geared toward students who want to work for change, and both offer a structured environment that's designed to not only give you a rewarding volunteer experience, but also prepare you for a lifetime of service work—whether as a volunteer or a staff member.

AmeriCorps

AmeriCorps Recruitment
1201 New York Ave. NW
Washington, DC 20525
(800) 942-2677
http://www.cns.gov

AmeriCorps is one of the largest volunteer networks in the country, and a great place to start if you're not sure about what kind of work you'd like to do, or who you'd like to do it for. They're part of the Corporation for National Service (CNS), a joint effort of public and private sources created in 1993 by Congress, the President, and community groups nationwide. CNS' goal is to solve problems like illiteracy, poverty, and environmental decay by taking advantage of our country's greatest resources: its citizens. CNS oversees three national volunteer organizations: the National Senior Service Corps, Learn and Serve America, and AmeriCorps, which is geared toward youth service.

AmeriCorps is composed of hundreds of community-based relief programs with the common goal of bettering our communities and the quality of our lives. Although the individual groups that make up AmeriCorps differ in purpose, size, and location, all the services performed by members fit into one of four categories.

Education: The focus is on keeping kids interested in school (with dropout prevention programs, etc.), but volunteers might also work in adult literacy programs.

Safety: These programs focus on the safety of our communities. Many volunteers work with local police forces, or help form citizen's patrol and neighborhood watch groups.

Environment: Many of these programs focus on redevelopment of urban areas, like neighborhood clean-up, but volunteers are also needed for clean water projects and waste management programs in their communities.

Human needs: This is a broad category including a variety of social programs like HIV/AIDS education, prevention, and care; improved housing for low-income families and seniors; community food banks and shelters for the homeless; immunization of children in low-income areas; and general support for the elderly.

In AmeriCorps, you could find yourself working with a wide variety of existing organizations, such as Habitat for Humanity (which helps build and/or repair housing for low-income families and the elderly), the National AIDS Fund, or the American Red Cross. Crewmembers (volunteers) are as diverse as the issues they work on. Members of the corps represent all racial, ethnic, and educational backgrounds; physical and mental capabilities; and family income levels. It's equal opportunity—regardless of your background, interest, age, or the level of commitment you can make, there's a way to put your skills to use in one of AmeriCorps' three programs.

Although work with AmeriCorps is technically volunteer, meaning that you aren't paid a salary, you do earn money for your service. At the completion of your term in any of the three AmeriCorps programs, you'll receive $4725 as an education award, in the form of a voucher. The voucher can be used to pay for college tuition or put against an outstanding student loan. You can also defer payments on your student loans while you serve. Other benefits available to crew members are health insurance, child care, and as-needed training by AmeriCorps.

For information on the CNS' other programs (Learn and Service America and The National Senior Service Corps), contact AmeriCorps or visit the CNS Web site.

AmeriCorps*USA

The newest and largest of the three programs, AmeriCorps*USA is comprised of over 450 local community relief programs across the country. Volunteers participate in direct service, or supervise other volunteers engaged in direct service. (Direct service means that you do the work yourself—you become a tutor; you work in community wellness programs or clean up wilderness areas; you work with community police officers to keep neighborhoods safe for residents.) Crewmembers work alone or in teams, depending on the type and location of their work.

You must be at least 17 years old to serve, and the duration of your service is usually one year, full-time (some part-time opportunities are also available). You are paid a modest living allowance while you serve, but it's usually just enough to cover some meals and incidental expenses. In most cases, you'll be responsible for the cost of your own living arrangements.

AmeriCorps*NCCC
(National Civilian Community Corps)

NCCC is a residential program, meaning that for the ten-month term of your vol-

unteer service, you live in designated housing on one of five military bases around the country—San Diego, California; Charleston, South Carolina; Washington, DC; Denver, Colorado; or Perry Point, Maryland. The cost of transportation from your home to the camp is paid by the NCCC, as is the transportation home after your service is complete.

NCCC service is open only to 18- to 24-year-olds, and members work in teams of 10 to 15 to identify, plan, and complete service projects for the communities surrounding the camp. No part-time opportunities are available; you work full-time during your ten months of service. Much of NCCC's emphasis is on environmental work, but you might also work in disaster relief, education, public safety, and other community needs as they arise.

AmeriCorps*VISTA
(Volunteers In Service To America)

VISTA, known also as the domestic Peace Corps, was founded over thirty years ago as a long-term solution to poverty. During this time, VISTA members have been helping people on a low income or in a depressed area make positive changes to improve their lives. Service in VISTA is full-time and lasts one year (extensions are available, but the maximum length of service is five years). The program is open to anyone over 18; however, crewmembers must have a bachelor's degree or three years of related volunteer/job experience.

Unlike the NCCC, VISTA is not a residence program, so young people (and others unable to relocate) usually have to serve near their own communities. If you do relocate to serve, you will be responsible for your own food and housing, although as with the other AmeriCorps programs, you'll receive a biweekly living allowance. It's not difficult to find work near your home, though, because projects are located in every state as well as the District of Columbia, Guam, Puerto Rico, and the Virgin Islands.

VISTA volunteers are not involved in direct service; that is, when working for VISTA, you won't become a literacy tutor. Instead, you'll help organize others in the community to do the tasks themselves. The idea is that long after the volunteers have left their position or the community in need, the programs they've helped build will continue under the direction of the community's residents.

It's COOL to Serve

Campus Outreach Opportunity League (COOL)
1511 K St. NW, Ste. 307
Washington, DC 20005
(202) 637-7004
fax: (202) 637-7021
http://www.COOL2SERVE.org/

Founded in 1984, the Campus Outreach Opportunity League (COOL) is a

TACKLING ISSUES LIKE LITERACY, HOMELESSNESS, AND EMPLOYMENT TRAINING FOR LOW-INCOME TEENS AND ADULTS, HIGH SCHOOL AND COLLEGE STUDENTS FROM ALL OVER THE COUNTRY ARE TAKING THE PRINCIPLES OF VOLUNTEERISM TO A NEW HIGH.

national nonprofit organization that helps students organize and run community outreach and volunteer programs in their own cities. Students learn the skills they need from COOL staff members, who visit hundreds of schools and thousands of students every year. COOL also holds an annual student conference that offers not only instruction, but valuable networking opportunities for student activists.

In all their programs and activities, COOL stresses five elements of quality community service: community voice, orientation and training, meaningful action, reflection, and evaluation. Whether you're planning a school-based program, a community-wide initiative, or just exploring some options for your own personal contribution, COOL's programs can definitely give you a step up. Here's a sampling of what they offer student volunteer activists:

Into the Streets: This program's motto is "Try it for a day, you may love it for a lifetime," and introduces students to volunteer service in what you could call baby steps. Participation is on a short-term basis in an area that the student feels comfortable or interested in. The program has been adopted by thousands of schools across the country. Many of these schools have integrated it into other activities like Welcome Week or Homecoming.

COOL Press: COOL produces several books and manuals to help students organize their ideas for social change into a workable plan. They also offer detailed instructions for campuses to create their own Into the Streets programs. Want to start a volunteer group on campus but don't know how? They can help. Want to attract more students to your existing programs? It's covered.

Virtual COOL: Send them e-mail and visit their Web site for networking information, news on COOL activities, and stories of COOL participants and leaders. It's a great way to keep in touch with other student activists across the country.

Networking: Join a vast network of other student social activists through COOL's newsletter, mailings, and e-mail discussion groups. With these networking tools, you can put some serious ammunition into your organizing efforts, even if you're brand spanking new to this whole volunteer thing.

COOL Leaders: For students who have been active and successful at organizing on campus, becoming a COOL leader is a way to improve your skills and increase the scope of your influence in the community.

COOL National Conferences: COOL sponsors several annual conferences where students can get together and network, share ideas, and plan for the future. The 1997 conference offered over 150 workshops and seminars on how to improve, expand, and increase chances for success.

Volunteer Vacations

When it comes to vacations, Disney isn't the only game in town. When you start flipping through travel brochures in search of the perfect vacation, think about giving the happiest place in the world a rest this year and spending the summer not only relaxing and having fun, but also building lifelong friendships.

VOLUNTEER ANYWHERE

Imagine spending your days in a cloud forest (did you even know there was such a thing?) in Costa Rica, surrounded by the intense calm and beauty of one of the world's most diverse ecosystems. There, you'll work with local residents to build paths, construct bridges, and plant trees to create an ecotourism reserve.

Teach a classroom full of Polish elementary school students (who rarely have the chance to take English language classes) how to say "Any girl can rule the world, you know," in English.

Volunteer vacations are a way for you to travel the world and really get to know other cultures, instead of supporting tourist traps that drain local economies and decimate communities and families. As a tourist in a foreign country, you seldom get a chance to connect with people personally and become a part of their culture.

On a volunteer vacation, you travel abroad (although some programs have opportunities in the States) and live and work with residents on a wide range of projects. In Italy, you might teach junior high and high school students conversational English; in Vietnam, you could help build a classroom or playground at a kindergarten. The project you are assigned (or choose) depends on the country you're visiting and the needs of the community. But in all projects you'll be working with local residents, making friendships you'll cherish forever and being an agent of real, lasting change.

You must pay your own expenses in all work camps/volunteer vacations, but many groups help with fund-raising. The cost could be as little as $175 or as high as $2000 or more (all costs are fully tax-deductible).

A volunteer vacation is a great way to put a face to a pinpoint on a map, to develop a deeper understanding of the world's issues outside our own boundaries, and to gain a perspective that few people are lucky enough to be offered.

Volunteers for Peace

The International Work Camp Directory
Volunteers for Peace (VFP)
43 Tiffany Rd.
Belmont, VT 05730-0202
(802) 259-2759
E-mail: vfp@vfp.org
http://www.vfp.org

VFP is a 75-year-old program of international voluntary service. Their directory lists over 800 opportunities in international work camps (for people as young as 15) doing things like farming, building (or rebuilding) communities, and environmental clean-up.

Global Volunteers

Global Volunteers
375 East Little Canada Rd.
St. Paul, MN 55117
(612) 482-1074
(800) 487-1074

Like Volunteers for Peace, Global Volunteers places American volunteers in communities worldwide where they live and work with residents in human and economic development projects. Programs are available in such diverse places as Greece, Vietnam, and China. Domestic programs (at an extremely reduced rate) are also available. Participants under 18 are welcome, but must travel with an adult guardian or family member.

Global Youth Village

Global Youth Village
Legacy International
Route 4, Box 265
Bedford, VA 24523
(540) 297-5982
E-mail: legacy@roanoke.infi.net
http://www.infi.net/~legacy

Global Youth Village caters to youth volunteers (people as young as 11 years old can participate). Young people from over twenty countries converge for a 3- or 6-week stay in the Blue Ridge Mountains of Virginia to share experiences, learn about one another's culture, and forge friendships that cross geographic, cultural, and economic boundaries.

Endnote

1. *E: The Environmental Magazine,* Sept./Oct. 1997.

Chapter Twelve

ACTIVATE YOURSELF FOR ANIMAL RIGHTS

Sometimes, animal lovers get the short end of the stick. In fact, people who aren't familiar with the animal rights agenda (or don't agree with it) often categorize animal lovers and activists as "anti-people." A few years ago, *Hunting Magazine* printed an absurd editorial stating that many vegetarians would prefer cannibalism to eating animals!

That's a pretty extreme case of ignorance, but it's not unusual for people who aren't involved in the cause to misunderstand it or even mistrust the people who do believe in it. But to animal rights supporters, working to protect animals is like working to protect the Earth. We believe that if you're really out to save the planet, you can't stop with the rainforests and the oceans and the sky. If you ignore everything else on earth—all the creatures that swim, walk, fly, and slide across this planet of ours—you'll eventually end up with a perfectly preserved planet, with nobody, or nothing, to enjoy it.

If you see a link between caring for the planet and caring for its inhabitants—all of them—this is a way to make the connection for yourself. You can get involved on a personal level with animal rights, protection, and care in many ways without giving up all your free time or money. Real change, lasting change, can begin by simply being more selective about the products you buy or by taking a few minutes to explain to someone how easily a dog could die locked up inside a hot car.

Here are a few ways you could start to make a difference today. They range in complexity and commitment, between being very involved to activities that require nothing more than a few minutes of your time.

Take Personal Responsibility for the Welfare of Animals

This is not as easy as it sounds. How many times have you been walking through a shopping mall parking lot and seen a dog locked inside a stuffy, hot car with the windows rolled up? You want to do something, but you can't just smash the car window, can you? So you look around and see if you can spot the owner, but if you're like most of us, you end up just cursing them under your breath and walking away, shaking your head. Do you have a neighbor who keeps his dog outside during all kinds of bad weather, like freezing rain or snow? That might be illegal in your city. Do you know of someone who keeps so many cats in her house that none of them are properly cared for or fed regularly? That's probably also against the law.

is acceptable and what is not—not just morally, but legally—gives you real power to create change.

There are certain basic rights afforded to domestic animals. We're not talking about Godgiven rights, although there are many animal lovers out there who believe very strongly that all creatures should be treated with fairly equal degrees of compassion, care, and understanding. The kind of rights you should acquaint yourself with are the laws on the books of your city or county governing the care and treatment of animals. Legislation will vary from city to city or state to state—for instance, if you live in rural Georgia, you may be allowed to keep farm animals on your property, but it's doubtful you can keep a goat in New York City—but all these laws address the basic needs of life and the fundamentals of car-

> If you happen to witness a crime, like an animal being beaten or mistreated, don't just stand there and watch—do all you can to stop the offender. Just your presence may be enough to make someone stop; if it's not, call the police!

You can do more than simply want to help; here's your chance to actually make a difference in one animal's life, or two, or twelve, or even a hundred! If you see a situation in which an animal is being mistreated or harmed in any way, and you want to change that, you can follow these basic procedures.

Learn your city's anti-cruelty codes. The goal of learning the law isn't to turn you into a vigilante; you shouldn't be scouring your neighborhood looking for the slightest infraction of the statues in your city. But gaining the knowledge of what

ing for an animal. For instance, nobody, anywhere, can lawfully deny an animal food, water, shelter, and sanitary living conditions while in their care, and that doesn't change, no matter where you live.

Find the county and state law books at your local library. A librarian can help you narrow your search to just animal cruelty and care laws. These books will tell you exactly what is allowed, and not allowed, in animal care and treatment. Look up individual laws in the index. Photocopy them and take them with you. If you are not taken seriously by the people you approach, remind them that the activities you are bringing to their attention are illegal.

Determine that a crime has actually taken place. If you've heard that someone beats their dog, go see what kind of shape the animal is in (always keeping in mind your own safety and observance of laws—for example, don't trespass onto someone else's property). If there are stories of someone in your town who keeps thirty cats in her house, try and find out for yourself if you've been told the facts or if the stories are an exaggeration. You need to take personal responsibility for discovering the truth behind the rumors. If possible, take a friend with you to corroborate your story, and if you can get close enough, take pictures.

Find out who is responsible for enforcing the anti-cruelty laws in your town, then approach that agency for help. Often, anti-cruelty statutes are enforced by a humane society, city shelter, or the Society for the Prevention of Cruelty to Animals (SPCA). You can find these numbers in the white pages of your phone book under the city listings. If you can't find the people responsible for protecting animals, ask the police or sheriff for more information.

Once you find out who will handle your case, sit down and write a clear, factual statement of the activity you have observed. Give dates and times of the activities. Include copies of the photographs you've taken, and give statements from your witnesses. Also tell them which laws have been broken. Be specific; it is sometimes hard for adults to take young people seriously, but if you

---

CALL IN THE CAMERAS

If you have followed all these steps and are still meeting with resistance from animal relief organizations, city officials, or police, call a local TV station or write a letter to the editor of your city's newspaper. Bringing this kind of glaring attention to your case may step up the efforts of the people responsible for helping these animals in the first place.

---

present clear, hard facts, it would be hard to turn you away. Keep a diary of who you contacted and how they responded, and be sure to make copies of everything you turn over to the authorities (never send originals!).

Keep on the case, no matter how hopeless it may seem. While it's important to go through the proper channels when seeking help from officials, it's also important that they investigate and stop any cruelty you've discovered. If nothing has happened after a day or so, take your complaint and supporting evidence to the supervisors of the people you've already approached. If necessary, go to your local government officials. If you witnessed the act yourself, go to the police and swear out a complaint against the person you're accusing.

Ask a local veterinarian to testify on your behalf. A vet can testify to the effects of the abuse on an animal; for example, how a cat being swung by its tail suffers both physically and emotionally. The testimony of a vet or other animal expert can help swing the case in your favor, so don't be shy about finding as many supporters as you can.

Keep an activity log of your case. It's important to keep a detailed diary of everything that happens, including all the contacts you make and the results of those contacts. Animal cruelty, as obvious as it may seem to you or me, isn't always that easy to prove to the police or to a judge. By keeping a documented account of everything you've seen and everything that's been done, you greatly increase your chances of being taken seriously by officials and proving the abuse, and ultimately bringing an end to it.

Let the Fur Fly

It's true: Fur is dead. There seems to be no crueler irony for the Earth's most exquisite creatures than to be tortured and killed for the very thing for which they are admired—a beautiful coat. The anti-fur movement has reached new heights, and every year more high-profile campaigns splash across billboards, TV screens, and magazine pages. Now that supermodels and TV stars have gotten into the mix, it's finally becoming uncool to buy fur.

The chances of legislating the end of fur trapping and farming are pretty remote—this problem is bigger than a mere letter-writing campaign can fix. But that doesn't mean it's hopeless. On the contrary, you can make a dent in the fur trade in lots of ways. Where compassion, kindness, and even the law cannot prevail, one thing can: money. Trapping and farming will end when the demand for their products end; that is, when people stop buying fur products.

It isn't enough for you alone to turn your back on fur, you must also educate others about the cruelty and torture so

> More than 4.9 million raccoons, coyotes, otters, beavers, and other animals are trapped and killed every year in the U.S. alone! That number doesn't even include the animals bred on fur farms across the country.

that they too stop spending their money on such senseless, useless items. Sounds easy, right? But how do you do it?

Design and photocopy a small flyer that tells the grisly facts about trapping and fur farming. Keep a small supply with you and, when you see someone wearing fur, approach them politely, give them the facts, and give them a flyer to take with them. Ask them to consider the pain and suffering the animals must endure simply to put a coat on their back. Be polite and don't harass fur wearers—remember, a lot of people truly believe that these animals are killed humanely. As angry as they might make you, a hostile attitude will only alienate them from you and your cause.

If you own any fur products or garments, donate them to PETA or another animal rights organization for use in their anti-fur campaigns. Any donation to a nonprofit organization is tax deductible (include this information on your flyer and suggest that the wearer donate her coat).

If you hear of any contests in which the prize is a fur coat, write to the organizers and ask them to reconsider their prize. Suggest that they substitute a nonviolent award, like a gift certificate or a trip.

Learn about the trapping laws in your state. Visit the library, or contact an animal rights activist group to get as much information as you can. If trapping or hunting is a big sport where you live, generate negative publicity for the "sport" by writing to newspaper editors or calling radio shows and giving people the facts about what really happens when an animal is trapped. Write to your legislators and demand an end to these barbaric practices!

Approach the management of stores in your area that carry traps and ask them to stop. You might be able to put enough pressure on a store that the owners or managers will change their inventory.

Go Veggie

Think that most vegetarians are tie-dyed hippies who eat nothing but mung beans and alfalfa sprouts? Think again! That outdated stereotype doesn't even hold spring water—today, more than 20 million Americans are vegetarians, and statistics show that the Americans who do still eat meat are reducing their consumption.

Vegetarianism isn't just an animal rights issue, although the incidents of animal abuse and cruelty in slaughterhouses across the country are well-documented. Links between meat and life-threatening diseases like cancer and heart disease are a big motivation for lots of people choosing veggie meals these days. Another reason many people are rejecting meat is the growing publicity about the natural resources that are being consumed and/or destroyed just to breed cattle for human consumption.

As people become more conscious of the state of their environment—and

become more concerned with its salvation—more of us are turning to safe, non-violent ways of living, including vegetarianism. Even the food processing king Green Giant has gotten into the game with veggie meat substitutes. Veggie meals are going mainstream and they're here to stay—they're better for our bodies, they're better for the Earth, and they're better for our conscience.

There are five levels of vegetarianism. Each is progressively more strict as to what you can eat, so each higher level obviously becomes harder to maintain. But the change from each level to the next can be gradual. In fact, you may already be at level 1 or 2 and not even realize it. Maybe you never made a conscious choice to become a vegetarian, but you just stopped eating red meat one day. You're at level 1, you're a semi-vegetarian. That's how simple it can be.

FIVE LEVELS OF VEGETARIANISM

Level 1: A semi-vegetarian eats poultry, fish, eggs, and dairy products, but no red meat or pork. Millions of Americans are turning to semi-vegetarian menus because of the dangers associated with red meat.

Level 2: A pesco-vegetarian eats fish, eggs, and dairy products, but no chicken.

Level 3: A lacto-ovo vegetarian eats eggs and dairy products.

Level 4: An ovo-vegetarian eats eggs, but no other dairy products.

Level 5: A vegan eats only plant foods, and will not eat anything that contains animal products of any kind.

You don't have to start at level 5; it's doubtful that you would be successful at it anyway, even if you did decide to give it a try. That's only because starting a veggie diet isn't the hard part, but sticking to it can be. Cooking veggie takes a little more thought and planning than it does to just throw a burger on the grill; you have to find interesting, delicious recipes that are inexpensive and easy to cook. A lot of people who decide to go vegetarian simply eliminate meat from their diet without replacing it with something else; after a few weeks or months they get bored and go back to eating meat. That's also bad for your body. When you eliminate anything from your diet you must be certain that you are replacing the lost nutrients. If you take the time to discover new recipes—buy a few recipe books or subscribe to a vegetarian cooking magazine—you'll discover hundreds of low-cost, low-fat, healthful, and delicious meals that will keep your taste buds interested for years to come. Do your body, and your conscience, a favor: choose veggie. Here are some ways to help you get started.

JUST THINK

Over 6 billion animals are slaughtered every year in the U.S. alone for meat. Just think, if every household across the country replaced one meat meal a week with a veggie meal, we could reduce the number of animals being killed for dinner by millions! That's an incredible impact to make on the world—and cooking veggie one night a week would hardly be noticeable to most of us.

Begin by cooking one veggie meal a week, without any meat or dairy products. Make this meal a special weekly event for your family, and slowly introduce them to the veggie life.

Subscribe to veggie magazines. *Vegetarian Times* and other magazines are full of delicious, easy-to-make recipes; they also feature great articles on nutrition and other natural ways of living.

Hang in there. Most new vegetarians lose their willpower the first time they walk into a fast food restaurant. When you're out with your friends, order a veggie burger—that's a burger with everything except the meat! Some restaurants may even give you a discount for ordering meatless items.

Pressure your principal and school board to get at least a couple of meatless items on the menu at your school. For information on how to organize and lead a veggie coup on your cafeteria, write to PETA.

Use soy margarine and soy milk. The next time a recipe calls for milk or butter, substitute these for the animal products you would normally add. Soy milk lasts a lot longer in your fridge than cow's milk does, and it comes in different flavors, like honey, chocolate, and vanilla. Soy margarine has no cholesterol, and reduces your chances of a heart attack.

Try one of the new veggie deli meats. Some larger chain grocery stores now carry meatless alternatives. There's a wide variety of flavors to choose from— Canadian bacon and pepperoni are two new choices—and all of them taste just like the meat products they replace.

Respect, Don't Dissect

Animal dissection has been a staple of middle and high school biology classes for longer than most of us—or even our parents—can remember. But does the fact that something has simply been around a long time make it right? Classrooms also have a history of treating girls as second-class citizens, and we're working to change that, aren't we? In our new age of earth consciousness, most of us realize that we should be looking for ways to change the old (bad) habits of disrespecting life. One way we can change is to stop using animals in ways in which they were not intended—that is, to be killed inhumanely, cut open, and placed under a microscope.

Aside from the moral issues of dissection, there are many other reasons to oppose this outdated method of learning. One of the most convincing arguments against vivisection is that, with our advances in computer technology, these experiments are simply no longer needed to teach anatomy and biology. The "labs" of the future feature computers, not scalpels, and sophisticated software programs in place of formaldehyde.

Within just a few short years medical students will be able to study and perform simulated operations on the computer and will no longer have to use real human bodies. If a Harvard medical school student doesn't need a real body to learn more about the digestive system of human beings, then does it make sense that middle-school students should still have to cut up frogs and pigs?

Every day, we're given an even greater chance to learn about the beauty of nature without killing and dismembering innocent animals.

Student objections to classroom dissection are becoming more and more common—from middle school to college and even beyond (many veterinary and medical school students have protested the use of live animals). In 1987, Jenifer Graham, a high school student, took her case to court and eventually to the California legislature, where students were finally given the right to not participate in animal dissections. Three other states (New York, Pennsylvania, and Florida) now guarantee students the legal right to oppose dissection without compromising their grade.

Even if you live in one of the 46 states that has not addressed this serious, and especially timely, issue, there's still hope that you won't find yourself on the business end of a scalpel if you don't want to be there.

Two major organizations, the American Anti-Vivisection Society and the National Anti-Vivisection Society, are dedicated to ending the practice of vivisection and help students find kinder, gentler alternatives to lab experiments. Both organizations offer excellent materials for students, parents, and teachers and school administrators.

Help Increase Adoptions at Your Local Animal Shelter

The best kind of animal shelter is "no-kill," which means that no matter how old, sick, or unwanted an animal may be, the shelter will not put it to sleep. No-kill shelters can be run by a local government, a humane organization, or private individuals—you can usually find at least one in your city (most SPCAs have a no-kill policy). San Francisco was the first no-kill city in the United States.

Every year, millions of cats and dogs are put to sleep in animal shelters across the country. Countless more are turned over to research labs for cruel, painful experiments and die soon after. Animal rights proponents and organizations are working diligently to reduce these figures. In recent years, many shelters have adopted mandatory spay/neuter policies for pet adoptions, and more and more corporations are abandoning their decades-long histories of animal testing. That's encouraging, but there's still a long way to go before all animals are granted the right to live a peaceful, nonviolent existence. But what can you do in the meantime?

One way to reduce the numbers of animals that suffer in shelters is to help make people aware of these animals' plight and increase pet adoptions. You obviously cannot take on the responsibility of finding loving homes for all the unwanted animals that crowd the animal shelters across the country, but you can

One of the most effective weapons against animal cruelty and abuse is the slow, steady gains made by changing one mind at a time.

make a big difference on a small scale at your local shelter.

A great disadvantage all shelters have is that they have to wait for people to come to them. It doesn't matter how beautiful, well-trained, or cute and cuddly an animal is: If nobody sees it, nobody will take it home. Founders of no-kill shelters

use mobile pet adoptions to find homes for their animals; which is an effective way to match loving families with equally loving pets.

You might have seen a mobile adoption before; they're often held in pet food stores and shopping malls on the weekends. The organizer of a mobile adoption must find volunteers to bring the animals to the site, and to sit with the animals during the day so they can show them to prospective owners and answer any questions people may have regarding its background, personality, or care.

The organizer of a mobile adoption also has the responsibility of finding a suitable location for the event. Pet food stores are great, because the people who come to that store already have at least one pet; maybe all the encouragement they need to add another to the family is the sight of a cute face or a wagging tail. School fairs are another fantastic opportunity for a shelter to connect a lonely animal with a new family. I attended a dog adoption at an elementary school fair one Saturday and saw about a dozen animals go home with new families that day.

Running a huge project like a mobile pet adoption all by yourself may be more than you can handle, but you can certainly start the ball rolling by making the suggestion to the shelter administrators. And you can be on hand to enlist volunteers (friends? family?) to help find an adoption site (do your parents have a store? do you know any local merchants?) and to help oversee the event.

Even if the shelter administrators are reluctant to let you set up a mobile adoption (some may have insurance policies that forbid it), there are still ways to get those animals moving. Design and write a short newsletter (just a few pages), featuring photos and short biographies of the animals in need of a home. You can distribute the newsletter to schools, through pet stores, in shopping malls or coffee shops, anywhere there's likely to be people to see it (especially children).

How about a pet adoption TV show? You've seen those thirty-second public service announcements that show the Pet of the Week at the local animal shelter, right? Those are great, but thirty seconds is hardly enough time to showcase all the wonderful, talented, obedient, and adorable cats and dogs waiting for homes down at your shelter. Produce your own half-hour show featuring available animals. You can shoot the video yourself and show it on public access cable TV.

Finally, take it upon yourself to educate others about the dismal future awaiting most animals who are taken to a shelter. It's heartbreaking to hear of people paying hundreds of dollars for a pure-bred dog when there are thousands of unwanted animals waiting in line to go home with someone—sometimes for free! Animals raised by breeders will not, under any circumstances, be put to sleep. Breeders have a great financial investment in these puppies and kittens; there is no threat of death for an animal that has American Kennel Club (AKC) papers. However, the clock ticks for the animals who have been turned over to the shelter. Sometimes they have only days, or hours, left for someone to rescue them.

Mixed breed animals are nothing to be ashamed of; on the contrary, it's been proven that pure-bred animals often suffer tremendous physical and emotional disabilities because of inbreeding. Bulldogs and pugs suffer from terrible respiratory problems; Jack Russell terriers are prone to skin problems and allergies.

Mixed breeds are often more intelligent and healthier than a dog costing hundreds of dollars more. Lots of shelters are starting to improve the public's perception of their hand-me-downs by putting their dogs through short behavioral courses, and some even give the dogs a degree when they complete the course!

If you know someone who's in the market for a cat or dog, direct them to the nearest animal shelter.

You don't have to march down Main Street to be an effective animal rights activist. You don't have to be a protester in some high-profile demonstration and be seen on TV resisting arrest, and you don't have to commit unlawful acts, like breaking into a lab or vandalizing fur coats.

Do you know what the most valuable weapon in the fight for animal's rights is? It's not money. It's not political power, and it's not control of the media. The most powerful weapon in the fight against animal abuse and cruelty is your mind. Because with your mind, with your ideas, your thoughts, and your passions, you can change other people's minds.

The second most valuable weapon in the fight for animals is time, and that's something that is definitely not on our side. For the animals who are suffering right now at the hands of experimenters, time is running out. For the animals who will die tomorrow in the

Small ideas, efforts, and hopes **have a way of GETTING BIGGER.**

name of someone's surf and turf dinner, time is running out. But there's still your time, and that's where you can make biggest contribution.

All animal rights activist groups operate under a tight budget. Almost all are run by volunteers, and they're always looking for committed activists to join their ranks. Whatever your ability or talent, there's sure to be at least two dozen organizations who could use someone just like you. And don't worry about not having any particular "talent" to offer. If you can type, answer the phone, walk dogs, write letters, sweep the floor, or just make sure all the animals have clean water and a dry blanket to lay on, you've contributed much more than you'll ever know—not just to the animals, but to the Earth, to all of us.

Organize a Blanket Drive for Your Local Humane Society

One cold and blustery day in the dead of winter, I decided that I wanted to collect and distribute blankets to the homeless animals at the East Valley Animal Shelter (EVAS) in Van Nuys, California. This idea sort of just came to me, like when you wake up in the middle of the night and you're convinced you have the definitive answer to some perplexing

problem (like how platform shoes ever got so popular). Only the next morning, this idea didn't fade out like some weird dream that didn't make sense in the morning (like how platform shoes got so popular). It stuck with me.

Organizing and running a blanket drive looks a lot harder than it really is, and it's actually much more rewarding than it looks—especially for a die-hard dog lover like me. Once you know the logistics of how to actually set it up and follow through, those weird dreams might go away for you, too (but you might still occasionally feel the need for three-inch heels).

You may be thinking, "Hey, I'm for change and *grrl* revolution and all that, but how can a few blankets here and there change the world?" Good question. They can't. At least, not on such a huge scale. But if you've learned anything from reading this book so far, you've learned that small things—whether those things are ideas, efforts, or hopes—have a way of getting bigger. And really big things can grow out of the sometimes small efforts of just one girl—specifically, you! Okay, you can't change the world by providing a few comfy blankets to some stray cats and dogs. But you can change their world. And sometimes, that's how change has come. One person—or one dog, one cat, one living thing—at a time.

What's a Blanket Drive?

It's no cake walk, that's for sure. Basically, organizing a blanket drive means collecting and distributing clean blankets to the animals at your chosen animal shelter. Sounds great, doesn't it? There's a great potential for the warm fuzzies here, but there's one small catch: These blankets you're collecting start out clean, but if you've ever been around animals for any length of time, you know that they don't stay that way for long. A big part of keeping this blanket drive going is maintenance. Simply put, you also have to wash the dirty ones. (There you have it; that's as bad as it gets and if you're with me still, kudos to you—you have real empress potential!)

Once you know what's involved in getting a blanket drive off the ground, you can tell why not many people do it. But one stroll through the concrete hallways of your local animal shelter will show you why more people should.

If you're a little unsure about your ability to organize and run everything by yourself, keep in mind that you don't have to go for the whole enchilada. If you love animals, your heart is in the right place, and you want to make a dent in the world, then just volunteer a few hours a week. You might be able to find a shelter with a similar program already in place. That way, you could just volunteer a little time but still make a huge difference.

Organizing a blanket drive by yourself isn't hard, but it is a lot of work. Not only do you have to keep the shelter in a steady supply of clean blankets, but you also have to supply things like detergent and bleach, and most important, money! Plus, you need some kind of transportation to keep the whole thing moving back

and forth. There are ways to find other people to help you, but the primary responsibility for keeping it going will ultimately rest on your shoulders. Know what you're in for, and think about it carefully before you decide to give it a shot.

Choose a Shelter and Make an Offer

Your first task is to find a shelter that needs you. If you've never been to your local shelter, go there. Look around. See how the animals live. If you don't see blankets in their cages, ask someone at the desk if they are provided. If not, you've found the place. If they do, maybe they could use your help.

If you don't know where your local shelter is, look in the yellow pages or the city listings at the front of the phone book. Local city shelters are different than SPCAs (Society for the Prevention of Cruelty to Animals); some larger citites may have both, or several. If there isn't an animal shelter in your city listings, check out neighboring communities.

The next step is to get the name of the person in charge at the shelter. If someone asks why you want to know, say you're interested in starting a volunteer blanket program and you want to send him or her a letter about your idea. You might encounter a little resistance from this front-line person, something along the lines of "We tried that and we're not interested," or, "We're not allowed to do anything like that," or some other smokescreen. Thank them politely for their input, but tell them you'd still like to make the offer, and then get the contact name.

Once you have a contact, write and introduce yourself. Introduce your idea, but don't get too specific. For example, don't commit to how many blankets you're going to provide and on what days of the week. There will be plenty of time after they accept your proposal to work out all the details of your plan. Keep it simple (see the sample letter on page 181).

About a week after you send the letter, follow up with a phone call to eintroduce yourself and your idea. Be polite, even if you feel that you're being blown off (they're usually just really busy). Remind the director that you're "that blanket girl" (a description I was happy to fit at the East Valley shelter) and would like to know if they've considered your offer. Try to arrange a personal meeting because you won't be able to iron out all the details of your program on the phone, and you might have to do a little persuading to get them to accept your idea.

What? They Don't Love It?

Don't be too surprised if their initial response is something like "thanks, but no thanks." It's no reflection on you, your idea, or even their interest in helping the animals in their care—it's more likely that they just don't know you and aren't sure about what you can really do for them. People volunteer to work at animal shelters all the time—they may visit, get a hefty dose of all those cuddly cute puppies and kittens and decide they want to spend their Saturdays cleaning poop out of cages, right? But it takes more than good intentions to make a difference, and many show up once or twice and are never

If you answer all their concerns, one by one, until there are no more left, the only answer left will be YES.

heard from again. Basically, the shelter employees don't want to get excited about some really cool thing that someone is going to do for them just to have that person flake three or four weeks later. You really can't blame them, can you? That's why it's so important to go into something like this with your eyes wide open.

Another reason for their resistance might be that they've never done anything like this before and they're just not sure it will work. When I approached the EVAS about organizing their blanket drive, the director of the shelter was enthusiastic, but the head veterinarian was not. He was afraid that the blankets just wouldn't come clean, and that his dogs and cats would transmit parasites and infections to one another.

If you get a response like this, don't be discouraged. If it seems like they're worried that you're too young for such a venture or won't be able to keep it up, show them how serious you are by giving them more detailed information about your plans. Show them that you've thought it out and planned it through—you can do that by knowing how many blankets you're going to provide, how often (weekly? biweekly?), and how you're going to transport them. Let them know that you've thought about how much money it will take, and tell them how you plan on funding a blanket drive (we'll cover the specifics of this later in the chapter).

If they're concerned about disease and infection, show them how it's worked for other shelters. When I hit this wall, I contacted the Berkeley Animal Shelter for help. I'd seen their postings in coffee shops, asking for donations of blankets and bedspreads, so I knew they already had some kind of program in place. They told me that they washed their blankets in hot water and disinfected them by adding lots of bleach and that those methods had proven really effective.

This was just the kind of evidence I needed to convince the vet at East Valley to give it a try. The folks at the Berkeley Animal Shelter were kind enough to write a short "reference" letter for me, stating their methods and results. I forwarded a copy to the vet at East Valley, and that helped a lot. If you need a letter of reference like this, try calling around until you find a shelter that provides blankets and has their own laundry service. Or call a veterinarian's office—most vets have washers and dryers on the premises, and they'd probably be happy to give you some tips to sway the shelter.

Just a couple of weeks after I sent my first contact letter, my blanket program began at the EVAS on a trial basis, and I began collecting blankets to hand out to the sick and injured animals in the hospital portion of the shelter. The reason they started me out on a sort of probation is that there were fewer animals (maybe a couple of dozen in the hospital versus over a hundred in the main shelter), so my initial responsbilities would be lighter. In hindsight, I could see that this was terrific planning on their part—it was a way not only for them to see if I was serious about my commitment, but also their way of letting me increase the scope of my responsibilities slowly, and at my own pace.

WHERE DO YOU GO FROM HERE?

It's Official Now

Congratulations! You may think you haven't done anything yet, but you have. In fact, you've done something terrific—getting permission from an animal shelter for this project means they trust you; they take you seriously enough to bring you into their environment and let you try and change things for the better. That's sort of how world rulers start, isn't it?

Before you start collecting blankets, soap, money, and all the rest of it, you need to have at least some idea of how much stuff you're going to need. One box of detergent is not going to cut it, but how can you tell how much you'll use? First find out approximately how many animals will use your blankets. If you're starting on a trial basis, your initial outlay will be smaller and easier to handle.

If you've done your big sell job and provided references, but you're still getting resistance from the folks in charge, suggest that you try your blanket drive on a trial basis. This lets both you and the shelter see how it goes before setting anything in stone, and allows either of you to back out if things don't seem to be working out.

Blankets: Let's say you're initially providing blankets for twenty animals. That means that right off the bat, you're going to need at least forty blankets. The first time you drop off blankets, there won't be any to pick up. Enjoy that while you can, because the dirty laundry begins the next week. If you plan on leaving twenty blankets behind every time you go to the shelter, then you're going to need a spare twenty to leave while you're washing the first load. Don't assume that you're going to be able to pick up the dirty laundry, wash it, and get it back to the shelter all in one day. Allow yourself at least a few days to get through this chore.

You don't need full-size blankets. These are going in animal pens, not on beds. A queen-size blanket cut in fourths will make four terrific dog-sized blankies. With that in mind, you've reduced your initial need from forty to ten. Plain old cotton or synthetic blankets work best. Stuffed bedspreads, like down comforters, don't work well at all. The stuffing goes everywhere when you cut them. You can stitch up the seams with a sewing machine, but they're kind of bulky and hard to wash. Use blankets like these only if you have nothing else. The same goes for knitted afghans and bedspreads—they weigh a ton when they get wet (and believe me, they will get wet), and they're clumsy and hard to wash.

Old bath towels work great, too. They're easy to wash and most are comfy cotton. When I started collecting blankets from coworkers, I got a lot of old baby blankets and sheets sets. They're good because they're nice and soft.

For some reason, you'll probably get more donations of electric blankets than anything else. They work great because they're just the right thickness. There's only one problem—those pesky wires that run through the middle. Yes, you do have to cut them out, otherwise they won't be very comfortable to lay on, and they may give you problems in the washing machine.

Cut the blanket across the middle; you should be able to find the ends of the wires in there somewhere. It may seem like miles and miles of the stuff is crammed in there, but make sure you get it all (it's easier to find the wires once you've cut the blankets down to more manageable sizes).

> Cut queen- and king-size blankets in fourths; cut twin- or full-size ones in half. Then you'll have two sizes of blankets—one for little dogs and cats, and one for big dogs.

Detergent: Forget that measly one-cup formula. These aren't blue jeans you're washing, and that formula wasn't meant to apply to seemingly toxic smells like dog pee. Figure about three cups per load, with no more than five blankets in a load (if you cram too many in, they won't come clean). The number you actually wash at one time will depend on how big and how soiled the blankets really are. At twenty blankets a pop, that's four loads of five blankets each, times three cups per load, so you'll be using twelve cups of detergent. You'll need to get a pretty good-sized box, so go ahead and hit the discount stores. Generic soap will work fine. Don't buy Tide, because they test on animals and that's kind of—well, ironic, isn't it?

Bleach: Even more important than detergent, bleach disinfects the blankets and kills all those germs. It also kills the smell, so don't be stingy when it comes to the bleach. It's cheap (about $1 per gallon), and you'll need about one-third to one-half gallon per load. That's about $2 a week. Believe me, the first time you open a bag of dirty dog blankets, you'll thank the stars above that someone invented bleach, so buy plenty and use it generously.

Money: You'll be using industrial-sized washers, and they run about $2.50 per load. With four loads, that's about $10 a week. Don't forget the dryer. You can probably fit about two loads into a 30-pound washer. They should come dry in 30 to 40 minutes. At 25 cents for 10 minutes, that's $2 per week for drying. That's comes to $12 just for the equipment. This seems like a lot, but every time you hit someone up for a blanket, you should beg them for quarters as well. Remember that these figures are just guidelines. You may find that you can stuff ten blankets into one load and still have them come out clean—it all depends on the size of the washer, the size of the blankets, and how dirty they are.

Plastic bags: You'll definitely need the super lawn-strength variety; two-ply numbers work well. Basically you don't want anything that is in danger of tearing open while in your car or anywhere else within city limits. Go to a nursery or home improvement superstore, and get the thickest, largest bags you can find. They will probably cost about $5, but one box will last you a couple of weeks.

Gloves: Never, ever handle dirty animal blankets with your bare hands. Aside

COMING CLEAN

Choose a laundromat that's not crowded, and go either early in the morning or later at night. Avoid laundromats where the manager is on site.

You're going to make quite a scene arriving at the laundromat with rubber gloves and tons of smelly laundry, so you want as small an audience as possible. What you're doing is not illegal—think of it as washing dozens and dozens of baby diapers all at once—but some laundromat managers may give you a hard time if they see what's in your bags.

Shop around for a laundromat ahead of time. Go during the day at first, scope it out, and be sure it suits all your needs. Don't try to find a laundromat the night you're doing the blankets. I found one that was open 24 hours a day, and on Tuesday and Thursday offered free soap! It may seem like a small thing, but it saved me more than $5 per week.

from the sheer nastiness of such a thought, there are some pretty awful things you could pick up. You could make yourself sick, and you could easily pass on these germs to other animals, like your own pets (more about how to avoid spreading germs later). Get gloves that reach all the way to your elbows. Rubber gloves work best because you can wash them off with hot water. Always wash your gloves after you're done handling the dirty blankets. You will never, ever get the smell out of leather or fabric gloves (the kind that you garden with). Get the really thick ones, in extra-large. These will cost about $1.50 for two pairs.

Rope or bungee cord: The best way to transport dirty animal blankets is in the open air. Tethered to a helicopter and air-lifted over the city is the preferred method, but if you can't swing that, the next best thing would be a pickup truck. The back seat of your car (or worse, your parents' car) is the least preferred. If you don't have access to a truck, try and find a way to strap these things to your roof (this is another good reason for getting the thickest trash bags available). Make sure they're secure—it would be very unsafe for anything to come loose and fall off your car into the middle of the road, and if the bag hits the ground and splits open, you'll have a pretty awful mess to clean up while trying to dodge oncoming traffic. If you can't tie the bags down safely, your only choice left is to toss them in the trunk. If you have a hatchback, good luck—get a new air freshener (actually, get a couple) and leave all the windows open. Get the 24-inch bungee cords; they're about $5 at an auto supply store.

The Specifics

One of the first things you need to iron out with the director of the shelter is the terms of your agreement—that is, how often you'll be there, how you'll handle the pick-up and drop-off, etc. It's important to be specific about what you can and cannot do, especially if you're working alone. For instance, if you don't have your own transportation and need to depend on other people for rides, you may have a hard time keeping a weekly appointment. Maybe you would start off on a bi-weekly basis. Weekly drop-offs are best for both you and the animals, if you can work this out. If you wait any longer than a week, you're going to have a huge pile of blankets to wash. The longer times will also require a bigger starting inventory of blankets.

When you're discussing the frequency of your visits and the number of blankets you can provide, be conservative. If it works out well, there's always time to expand and do more. If you overload yourself with too much work in the beginning, you may run out of supplies, energy, or funds (or all three!). Then you'll never know if it would have worked out.

Another thing to keep in mind when discussing terms is the contribution, if any, the shelter could make. Don't force this on them or they may feel they've been tricked, but there's no harm in asking if there are any supplies that they could provide for you, like rubber gloves or garbage bags. The head veterinarian at the EVAS volunteered to keep me in a steady supply of both bags and gloves; throughout the life of my blanket drive he kept his word. Of course it would have been great if they'd supplied cash or something like that, but the contribution they did make helped a lot. Besides, it kind of made me feel like they were working with me and wanted me to succeed.

Ask if you could post a flyer in their lobby to solicit donations from the public. Maybe they'll let you place a collection jar on the counter. Usually, any kind of city agency (even a city shelter) is restricted from helping you raise funds in this way. If you're not sure, ask. Get their ideas.

Get clear instructions about where you should go when you're picking up and dropping off blankets. Ask them to designate an area just for this purpose. Find out how they want you to get your car through the gates, and what times work best for them. Saturday mornings are good; most shelters close around 5:00 so if you have to go to school or work, it might be hard to get there before then.

> As you're laying in bed on Friday night before your first Saturday drop-off, you may be wondering to yourself, "What am I in for?"
>
> In two words: EXTREME SATISFACTION.

When you're setting all these times and solidifying your agreement, keep in mind that this is a commitment of more than a week or so. If you promise to be there every Saturday morning at 9 AM, you can't flake if you get a better offer to go to the beach or something like that. This was one of the hardest parts about keeping my blanket drive going. There were Saturday mornings when I wanted to go out of town or just sleep late, but unless I had someone else to cover for me (this is an excellent test of friendship), I had to make the shelter my number one priority.

Saturday Comes Early

Now you've got all the info, but so far, it's all academic, right? You know what kind of supplies you need, you know how much cash you'll need to get started, and you even have the terms of your agreement with the shelter all lined up. So far, you've heard about the cost, the smell, the responsibility, and all the other things that could scare you off. But you haven't heard about the satisfaction and the incredible feeling you get handing a soft blanket off to a dog who's laying on the concrete with her newborn puppies. I can't really describe that part; you have to feel it for yourself. And you will. Every Saturday. Your first week will be the best, for one obvious reason: There won't be any dirty blankets to pick up. This first time is strictly gravy, so enjoy it to the fullest.

Wear old clothes; pick a couple of things out of your wardrobe that you can use just for blanket runs. And after you've made your pickup, it's very important, especially if you have pets at home, to take these clothes off before you enter your own home. Otherwise you run the risk of infecting your own pets with some disease or germs. Wash these clothes separately from your other laundry and use hot water and bleach. These germs can make you sick, too, so don't handle the dirty blankets with your bare hands, and if you accidentally do get your hands on them, wash with hot water and soap right away. Don't rub your fingers in your eyes, and don't eat until you've washed thoroughly.

Ways to Raise Money and Donations of Supplies

Raising money and securing donations of blankets and other supplies is something you're going to have to work at constantly. You'll be surprised at how quickly

HOT TIPS

Store your supplies (rubber gloves, rope, and garbage bags) in a tote bag in your trunk. That way, you always know where they are and they won't get mixed up with anything else in the car.

If you want to visit the animals while you're there, do it first, before you get any germs on you. Don't touch any animals after you've been handling dirty blankets, and once you take your gloves off, put them in your supplies bag and go straight to the bathroom to wash your hands with soap and hot water.

Don't try and pick up, wash, and deliver blankets all in one day. That's just too much to expect from yourself. A more realistic schedule would be weekly pickups/drop offs and washing the blankets some time midweek. This allows time to work the blanket washing into your schedule.

Don't store the blankets in your car while they're waiting to be washed. You shouldn't bring them into your house or basement, either. You can put them in a garage, if there are windows for ventilation.

A good way to store bags of dirty blankets is inside a rubber trash can. You can get 30-gallon trash cans, with a lid, for about $10 at a garden or discount store, and each can can fit two full garbage bags. Find a place outside for the trash cans—in the alley, next to your garage, etc.—but not near the house. Even if it rains, the blankets won't get wet, and being outside in the open air will keep the smell down.

the money disappears, and not even the blankets will last forever. Some weeks you'll get some back that are torn to shreds; some weeks you'll get some that are so dirty it's easier—not to mention more desirable!—to just throw them away. However, use good judgment on this one; your first inclination may be to toss all the dirty blankets in the trash, but if you do that, you'll deplete your inventory in about a day.

Aside from the obvious sources, like scouring your closets, garage, and attic for blankets, and hitting up friends and relatives, get creative about fundraising so you don't have to bear the entire burden by yourself. One of the most effective ways to raise cash or supplies is to draft a one-page flyer outling your blanket program. Describe what you're doing, give a phone number for the shelter in case someone wants to check your references, list all the supplies (including money!) you need to keep the program alive, and most important, list your name and phone number (or address) so people who want to donate items can contact you.

Your parents may not be thrilled about you listing your home phone number or address; in that case, ask a teacher if you can list the school's number. Maybe your principal will let you set up a designated "donation box" somewhere on the school premises where people can leave their contributions.

Post the flyer at school, in grocery stores and libraries—and especially in pet food stores and veterinarian offices. You can also distribute flyers through your neighborhood, leaving them in mailboxes and on front doors. Keep a short stack of flyers in your car and whenever you see someone walking a dog, hand them your information and ask for a contribution. Ask your parents to take your flyers to work and post one on a bulletin board, or send out a notice through their office e-mail (I received 90 percent of my contributions of both money and blankets at the office).

Another way to get funding for your blanket program is to find a sponsor, someone with whom you could negotiate a trade: PR for assistance. For example, talk to some local pet stores, local vets, or even the manufacturer of pet products, like squeaky toys or dog food. In exchange for their partial support (whether it's cash or supplies), you'll design and post a sign on all your donation boxes (including the one at the shelter) that lists them as a sponsor.

Expansion

Like all good world-domination schemes, there comes a time when your success dictates that you expand. When you've reached the point where you're successfully handling the blankets and the laundry, you've found people to help, and funding to ease the financial burden, then you might start thinking about expanding to other shelters.

Organize volunteers at other shelters; form teams of volunteers to care for all the shelters in a certain area; expand your sponsorship funding to include other non-animal related businesses, like local clubs and organizations; and develop an effective PR campaign through press releases and interviews with local papers.

It might seem like a lot, but once you start getting into the routine and reaping the rewards of making these poor animals' lives a little cozier, the effort isn't going to seem like that much. Even though it can be a pain and there are about a million other things you'd rather do, try and keep your perspective—what's more important? Making the life of an unwanted (possibly doomed) animal more comfortable, or hanging out and watching TV?

Ending Animal Abuse and Suffering is Definitely a Girl's Job

Fully realizing that many of you still think you are simply too busy (with the pressures of school and all) to start getting involved in anything for which you're not going to receive academic credit, I would like you to meet Lisette, a Florida high school student who in 1997 formed a grassroots organizaion called Youth for Animal Liberation. "I had the idea and we had our first meeting. Four people attended," she recalls. "Since then we have grown in size; we have 25 local people (though only about 10 kids are really active) and some out-of-state members, too." YAL works to educate and raise awareness about animal rights issues.

Lisette's created an organization that's much more than a part-time hobby. She works extensively with other volunteer organizations that share her philosophy, like Food Not Bombs (a group that serves veggie food to the homeless), Sprouting Up! (a veggie advocacy group), and a local feminist group. She also has plans to link up with a local environmental group and

Lisette says, "Our first demonstration was at a place called Fur by Flors. We have also had two McDonald's demonstrations and educational presentations on animal rights. We have public tables at different events and hand out literature. But we don't do all work and no play; we also have vegan picnics and events."

form a community center run for and by local youth. "Right now we are working on a booklet that (hopefully) will make it easier for people to go vegan. Lots of times people say, 'I'd go vegan, but I have no idea what to eat.' This booklet will have a sample vegan menu, a list of animal derivitives, some foods that look vegan but have hidden ingredients, and more." If you have some ideas about forming your own local animal rights group and need some advice, encouragement, or inspiration, contact Lisette at Youth for Animal Liberation, 8361 SW 34 Terrace, Miami, FL 33155. E-mail her at Vegan36@aol.com, or visit her Web site at http://home.earthlink.net/~luna9/index.html.

Sample Contact Letter

April 1, 1998

Jane Smith
Director
Valley Animal Shelter
123 Main Street
Los Angeles, CA 99999

Dear Ms. Smith:

I'm writing to volunteer my services for your shelter. I'm sure you'd agree that the animals in your care would be much more comfortable, especially in the cold winter months, if they had blankets for their cages and pens. I know that this can be a very time-consuming and expensive luxury for most shelters, but I would like to make it a reality for yours.

I'd like to offer my services, free of charge, to organize and run a blanket drive for the animals in your shelter. I can provide clean blankets on a regular basis, and I'd also be responsible for washing the dirty ones. I would also provide all the necessary materials, like soap, disinfectant, and so on. I'd like to meet with you in person and explain to you how I think I can make a contribution to the work you do.

You can reach me at 555-1212. Please give my offer some serious consideration. I'll be calling you in a week or so to follow up.

Thanks very much for your consideration.

Sincerely,

Your Name
Your Address

BE A VIRTUAL GIRL

The last invention to have an impact as intense as the development of the Worldwide Web was the wheel. That's how much this medium could change your life. What it boils down to is this: With a computer and a modem, you can add an extra push to your shot to the top of the world.

You can't even turn around anymore without hearing about someone surfing the Net. Forget that! Gidget surfs; Lisa Anderson (one of the world's top seeded female surfers) navigates those waves, and that is where you want to be.

If you choose any topic in this book—producing your own cable TV show, finding a cool volunteer job, or finding ways to market your small business—and use the Internet as one of your tools, it's pretty much a fact of life that you can accomplish whatever you set out to do faster and better.

But best of all, by becoming a virtual girl, you can meet up with other Net-chicks such as yourself and form a kick-butt, take-no-prisoners, political man-eating machine that will chew up the competition and put you, a Girl, squarely at the helm of The New World.

It's estimated that a little over 40 percent of on-line users are women;[1] with allies that numerous (and increasing at what seems like a zillion percent a day), there are already enough voters on-line to change the world tomorrow. All you have to do is get everyone organized and thinking in the same direction—yours. So how do you, a total stranger to technology, get from here to there? Easy (honest). One condition, though: Before I give you all these cool secrets for getting what you need to connect to explore this new world, you have to promise that you will never, ever use the Web for on-line shopping, to read the latest issue of some lame model magazine, or to visit the Style Channel on-line. Not that I want to run your life or anything, but the Internet, in theory, is a really cool, revolutionary concept! To think of being able to access the world's (and the world's government's) libraries with the click of a finger is absolutely astounding! Just imagine what you could do. And even though it's a marketing ploy, Microsoft's slogan "Where do you want to go today?" really does say it all.

But (with a capital B) if we let all the marketers and ad agencies and corporate cheeseballs out there (whose only interest, by the way, is where and how we spend our money) take control of the Net, we're sunk. I mean, they've all but ruined TV and radio, and don't think they haven't already started to dig their greasy fingernails into the Worldwide Web. Some of us think the Web is for meeting people, making change, and learning about our world and ourselves. You know, the obvious stuff. But other people think it's for selling junk—whether that junk is $150 sneakers, cheap vacations to some exploited community in a warm place, or the latest stinky buddy film to come out of Hollywood. Case in point: The head of programming at Entertainment Asylum (a division of America Online), a site designed to bring you such enlightenment as interviews with celebrities, video clips, and customizable TV listings, makes you wonder what he really means when he says, "This could change the world. We're on the verge of a Golden Age."[2] If you buy into what they're selling, what you're really looking at is the Golden Age of Consumerism and Consumption.

Are We There Yet?

So how do you turn your back on all that crass commercialism and use the Net for

---

WHAT TO DO ON THE INTERNET

Find green companies to invest in on the way to your first million.

Get a woman carpenter's firsthand experiences about what it's like to wield a hammer in a male-dominated industry.

Trade e-mails with novice and professional video producers and get their tips on producing a first-rate cable TV show.

Investigate the actions of a company you're thinking of boycotting.

Solicit opinions from thousands of other bands on what kind of guitar you should buy.

Look up more veggie recipes than you could cook in a year.

---

building a political network that will bring the world to its knees? If you're not on-line yet, don't worry; it's a lot easier than you might think. If you're even a little technophobic, I can relate. I was one of the last people I know to get a CD player; I have yet to even window-shop for a cell phone. One of the problems I had with getting up and running on the Net was that I felt like everyone was pressuring me. Everyone told me to stop producing printed copies of my 'zine, *REAL Girls*. "Print is dead," they said; I should get myself on-line and create an e-'zine (an on-line, electronic version). So I did what any girl who's feeling the pressure of outside influences does—I resisted. Plus, I thought that to get on-line, I had to absorb the equivalent of a college-level course in computer science.

With everyone and their grandmother talking about PPPs, HTML, and ISDNs, you may feel like you're the only person on the planet whose invitation to that Great Net Party in the Sky got lost in the mail. You may even feel like that's a party you could easily skip in favor of doing laundry or washing your hair or some other non-mental task. Don't stress. Going on-line isn't some scary, complicated ordeal. You don't have to understand the technology to start using it; besides, once you're on-line you'll pick everything up a lot more quickly, because you'll be learning by doing, which is still the best way to learn anything.

Luckily, lots of resources are geared toward getting more girls and women on-line—you'll be able to find plenty to help you choose a system and software and all those other things that dance like sugar plums in a geek girl's head. But you don't have to do the whole shebang. If you want to become a first class navigator and learn to code in HTML, go for it. Even if all you want to do (for now) is send e-mail to other activists or visit some cool environmental Web pages you've heard about, you still have a right to be in cyberspace alongside the hardcore Web surfers. All you really need to start are a computer, a modem, the software to connect, and an Internet service provider (ISP).

Choosing a Computer

There are basically two types to choose from: Macs[3] (made by Apple) and PCs (made by basically everyone else). The two have entirely different operating systems,

and which you choose isn't really important, as long as you feel comfortable using it. Generally, graphics people like designers, publishers, and artists prefer Macs; they're the simplest to use and they rarely give you software or hardware problems. PCs on the other hand, are usually less expensive than Macs, and they appeal more to tech-types who love to mess around and learn how things work. If you see yourself programming and writing your own software some day, you'll probably lean toward a PC.

As far as system requirements, most browsers (the software that you use to move around on the Web) require at least 8 MB of RAM, but the more you can get, the better, because the RAM dictates how fast your computer can handle stuff like loading images and graphics on Web pages you'll be visiting.

You'll also need at least 250 MB of storage space on your hard drive (where you keep all your software plus all those goodies that you're going to start downloading as soon as you connect).

You don't need thousands of dollars to sink into an expensive system; in fact, if you don't mind buying used, you could find a decent set-up for less than $500. Some computer companies are offering models right out of the box for little more than that.

The price for a new computer ranges wildly, based not only on their capabilities, but all the bells and whistles that come with them. Some home computers come with tons of free software that may seem like a great deal at first, but often it's stuff like games for kids, medical reference, and office programs you may never use. If you're buying a computer for the whole family, that might appeal to you. But if you want it mostly for sending and receiving e-mail and setting up your own Web page, you could probably do without a lot of those extras. Besides, once you get online, you'll be able to download more games, reference materials, and other programs than you could use in a lifetime!

It's important to remember that computer technology tends to change pretty quickly, so before buying anything, talk to a lot of sales reps at different stores; try out the demo models by opening programs and files and working with them. And read up on the technology in some computer magazines. Ask around—see what your friends and relatives are using and how they like their systems. Call the local community college and speak to a computer sciences instructor (or better yet, go down and see him or her). Their advice will probably be a lot more objective than a sales rep who makes a living by selling on commission. This will give you a feel for what's available in your price range; it'll also make you a more savvy consumer, which is always a good thing.

Buying a Modem

Some modems are internal, which means they're built in to the computer. If your computer comes with a phone jack on the back of it, you have an internal modem. But if you're buying a less expensive computer (or an older, used one), you'll probably need an external modem. Modems go from very, very slow (2400 BPS) to very, very fast (56k). A 14.4k or 28.8k modem will be just fine for most people. Modems can also be bought used; just be

sure that yours is in good working order and try it out first, if you can.

Modems operate over your regular telephone line. This means that if you have only one line coming into your house, nobody can use the phone while you're on the computer. This is likely to start some scraps amongst family members and/or roommates, so as you start to spend endless hours searching for a way to quench your thirst for knowledge, you may want to consider getting a second line for the computer only.

The Software to Connect

I'm going to go out on a limb here and risk the wrath of my cybersisters out there in Netland by telling you that the easiest, fastest way to get on-line is through a commercial provider like America Online (800-4-ONLINE) or Prodigy (800-213-0992). One way these services hook you is by making it as simple as possible to dial into their network. They distribute free software that gets you connected and on your way in just a few minutes, and its point-and-click simplicity makes it a breeze to install. This is a good way for techno-phobes to get started because you're accomplishing two things at once—you get the software, and the connection, in one handy-dandy little package. By calling their 800 number, you can request either a diskette or a CD-ROM containing the software and the instructions on how to dial up and set up an account. Most offer a few free introductory hours for new customers (AOL offers up to 50 during certain promotional periods) to introduce you to their service and let you try them out before signing up and handing over your credit card.

When you're just starting out, request free software from anyone who's handing it out. Same goes for free hours. If they're offered, take them. More importantly, use them! Use them to learn how to find your way around the Web, and more important, use them to find a local provider who doesn't censor what you say (or read) and who doesn't plan on invading your cyberspace to deluge you with advertising. One of your first outings on the Web should be to The List (a site that lists over 3100 Internet service providers; see the resources near the end of this chapter for more info on this site). By the time you've used up all your free hours, you should have a good idea of which service you want to stick with, and which you could do without.

> I'm quite sure you don't want to spend your life in a state of not knowing diddly, so don't. Make it your business to learn more every time you log on.

These are the bare bones of what you need to get started, and the information here is by no means complete. There's just so much to know and learn when you're getting into computers, you have to spend some serious time with a few different sources (books, magazines) to get to the point where you know exactly what you want. And with the technology changing so rapidly, be prepared to feel

like you're always two steps behind those "in the know." But don't let that scare you off; remember, you can get on-line and start trading e-mail and checking out Web sites without knowing diddly about computers or how they work.

Where Do You Go?

Good question. If you follow my advice and stay away from the Style Channel, model magazines, and other dives, you'll be spending your on-line time in chat rooms, using e-mail (and following mailing lists), joining newsgroups, downloading cool stuff for your own personal use, or visiting Web sites.

Chat Rooms

They've been getting lots of press since the Web has become a household word, and most of that press has been bad. You've heard the stories where two people meet in a chat room and one of them turns out to be an ax murderer. Or how some young girl is lured into a three-month road trip across the country with some strange guy from another state. Although those particular warnings do seem to be a little overdone, make no mistake: There are plenty of weirdos in chat rooms (although I've never met anyone who's exhibited homicidal tendencies). It's usually my luck to end up in a chat room with a bunch of pre-pubescent boys. No harm done; just exit. If you develop a taste for what passes for chat in lots of these rooms, knock yourself out; there are plenty to choose from. You can't get hurt just chatting, as long as you remember the cardinal rule: Never, never, ever give out your home address or phone number!

E-Mail/Mailing Lists

Trading e-mail with friends is definitely one of the coolest uses for all that expensive computer equipment piling up on your desk. I highly recommend this favorite pastime. If your friends are still low-tech and you're all by your lonesome in cyberspace, don't worry; there are lots of ways to meeting people to correspond with. If you're with a national commercial provider like AOL, you can search for e-mail pen pals all over the world (this is cool—I wound up with two new friends, one in the UK and one who lives about three blocks from me!). Another way to use e-mail to communicate with people on a larger scale is by joining a mailing list.

There are mailing lists on virtually any topic you can think of—from women's rights to the Sex Pistols—and there's no limit to how many you can join. You may want to start off a little conservatively, though, especially if you join a list that is even moderately popular. The reason for that is that the number of members on a mailing list can range from less than a hundred to ten times that, and when you join a list, you receive all the mail that's sent to that list. Say you're on a young feminist's mailing list and the topic is rating girls according to their looks (which, unfortunately, seems to be a growing trend among junior high and high school boys). This is a topic that's likely to generate a lot of heated opinion, so it's pretty safe to say that on any given day, you could log on to discover fifty or more e-mails waiting in your mailbox.

Join just one or two lists at first and get an idea of how much mail is generated every day. If the list seems a little dull,

FINDING A LIST

The sites mentioned here contain hundreds of e-mail lists and newsgroups on practically any topic you can think of (pets, music, gardening, whatever you like). A couple have search engines that let you enter a keyword, such as "women," and target specific lists. When I did this at Tile.net, I came up with 100 lists. From Big 10 Women's Basketball to a discussion list about *Dr. Quinn: Medicine Woman*, and absolutely everything in between, there's more than enough to get you started. If you're signed on with a commercial provider like AOL, you can also search for e-mail lists and newsgroups through their browser.

Tile.net
http://tile.net/

Progressive Activist Mailing Lists
http://www.welcomehome.org/rainbow/lists.html

List of Publicly Accessible E-Lists
http://www.neosoft.com/internet/paml/

spice it up with some comments of your own, or join a couple more lists. But if you end up with a list that generates too much mail, you might have to unsubscribe. Either way, it's important to check your mail regularly.

Usenet Newsgroups

Newsgroups are similar to mailing lists—they're available on nearly any topic you can imagine, and their purpose is to generate discussion. The main difference between the two is that messages that are posted to the newsgroup don't come directly to your personal e-mail box—they just kind of stay "out there" until you go and get them. That definitely has its upside: your mailbox can't get clogged with mail, because it's not coming directly to you. And even if you slack off and don't check your newsgroups for weeks (or months!) at a time, you won't get busted by the mail cops. You may return to find 3000 unread messages, but you can sort (by title) through the ones you want to read, and when you're done you can mark the rest as read, which means they'll disappear and leave you a nice clean slate.

Web Sites

Sites are the coolest thing the Web's got going. Everyone's got 'em, but which should you visit and which should you ditch? You could do a search for any site that is about "girls" or "politics" or the "environment," but don't be surprised if

• •

Many of the Web addresses listed in this book are too long to fit on one line, so be sure you enter the full address to get to the right place. Type these Web and e-mail addresses carefully. If you make a mistake, you probably won't get where you want to go or your e-mail will bounce. Because the Web is constantly growing and changing, many of these listings will change, too. If you can't find a specific resource, go to a Web search site or check out similar sites to get the information you need.

• •

you get a message saying something like "Your search has found 1,937,385 documents related to 'girls.'" Not only is that a little intimidating, it isn't a very efficient way to get things done. Plus, you'll not only get information on legitimate sites relating to girls, you'll also get quite a few unpleasant sites. Check out one of the girl-friendly sites listed here to find more of what you want (and less of what you don't).

Watering Holes and Gathering Sites for Girls Who Are Changing Their World

There are some great aids out there for girls who are getting on-line for the first time, as well as for girls who surf daily. The best thing about many women-friendly sites is that not only are they packed with useful and interesting information, but they're also populated by women who would love to help you out. These are great destinations for newbies (yeah, that term means exactly what you think it does). You'll find all kinds of helpful hints and tips, plus unlimited links to other places.

First Pointers for a Woman's Guide to the Internet

http://mevard.www.media.mit.edu/people/mevard/women.html

From "The Women of NASA" to *Geekgirl Magazine*, this site features almost 50 links (plus mailing lists and women's studies sites) to get you cranking in your trek through cyberspace. Look for "Two by Two," which has a sort of mentoring domino effect where beginners are guided through their new Internet experience, with the stipulation that they agree to teach two more women.

Cybergrrl

http://www.cybergrrl.com

Cybergrrl is one of those things that make it way cool to be a chick. I realize that setting out on a quest to rule your world can be pretty exhausting, so on those rare occasions when you're just too tired to contemplate even one more girl fact, check out this site: you enter Planet Cybergrrl (could it get any better?) and pretty soon you're loving what is clearly an x-chromosome world.

There's an on-line comic, *Cybergrrl*, listing all kinds of girl 'zines to read for inspiration and amusement, links to bands, and more. If you join the Cybergrrl village (where you get your own ID and password), you enter "the zone" where, along with other cybergrrls, you can trade e-mails, enter chat rooms, and leave messages for your girls in arms.

Fem mass

http://users.aimnet.com/~mijo/
Femmass.html

Fem mass is a directory that links you to nothing but other women's personal home pages. It's a good place to visit when you're ready to build your own site; you can look at what other women are doing and see what you like, or don't. This is especially valuable if you're new at this Web thing. Once your page is running, get a link here and increase your visibility.

Femina

http://www.femina.com

Created in 1995 to provide women with a comprehensive directory of links to all things girl and women related, Femina features female-friendly sites in categories like business and finance, education, entertainment, media and publications, and culture. Femina also has a great feature that lets you search their site for almost anything.

Feminist.com

http://www.feminist.com

This Web site has a little bit of everything. Among its other virtues, it's a valuable site for girls seeking allies because it contains a database of tens of thousands of women's resources around the country, including eating disorder treatment centers, homeless shelters, youth organizations, and state and local government organizations. If you're looking for something in your area, you can enter the city and state and the database will give you the name, number, and address of the closest resource. You even get an interactive map of how to get there.

For up-and-coming activists, there are some great tools here: weekly and monthly news updates on a variety of topics, the WOMANSWORD newsletter, classified ads seeking everything from interns to research for upcoming books and articles, a calendar of upcoming events, information on women's health, and almost unlimited links. One of the coolest features is a link to other activist and government sites—you can even send e-mail directly to the White House.

If you're hungry for news, check out two links through feminist.com: Washington Feminist Faxnet (WFF) and Women's International Network (WIN) News provide local, national, and international news by, for, and about women.

gURL

http://www.gurl.com

Technically, this is an e-zine (electronic, or on-line, 'zine) but in reality, it's a whole lot more. gURL is a communications network of women on the Web; that is, a way to talk gURL to gURL. When you join, you find access to members-only areas, like a place to post your own home page, a place to find pen pals, and so on. You can also submit your own writings to the mag and maybe get published in the next issue.

Virtual Sisterhood

http://www.igc.apc.org/vsister/vsister.html

A member organization devoted to getting women on-line and making the medium work for them. Their goal is to create a global network of all women (sound familiar?) and one of their highest priorities is to make the medium available to all women, especially low income and minorities and others who are traditionally excluded from things that have a kind of elitist, male stigma. They have an on-line mailing list for female activists, and offer a multitude of other politically oriented links, including a worldwide directory of women's organizations and electronic communications. Their Web page is available in a whole bunch of languages.

Webgrrls Unite! Women on the Web

http://www.webgrrls.com

No, Virginia, tech heads don't have to be geeks, and they most certainly don't have to be guys! Myth-busting is a favorite activity of every girl I know; that attitude is evident from this site, which works to turn women onto the technology of the Net. This is a place to network, exchange information on lots of things (like job leads and internships), and lots more all-around recipes for success.

Join an existing chapter if you like (they're all over the world, in places like Canada, the UK, Asia, Australia, and the Middle East), or get info on forming your own.

WWWomenWebRing

http://www.wwwomen.com/webring. shtml

This site allows users looking for women-related sites to take a guided tour of the best the Web has to offer. There are three types of tours to take: arts and entertainment, business women's organizations, and women's sports.

You can also search for Web rings devoted to a particular subject. When I entered "girls," I found 196 rings—including one devoted to cowgirls only and several created by and for girls who don't—or those who do!—like the Spice Girls. Once you have your own page up, you can request that your site be included so others can visit you on their tour.

Women's Wire

http://www.women.com

One of the most comprehensive sites for women and girls. Although it's often defined as an on-line magazine, the variety of content makes it hard to classify. This site offers good information on a wide range of topics, from politics—where you can read the day's headlines that are only about women—to careers and health and nutrition. They also have celebrity profiles, and shopping and fashion bits, which we have to forgive in light of all the other great information they provide. Like Femina, Fem mass, and other women-related sites, one of the most valuable aspects of Women's Wire are the incredible number of links to other women-related sites.

Help! I've Strayed, and I Can't Get Out!

All beginners need help at one time or another. If this is your time, check these out. Though not specifically for women, they're great resources.

Beginner's Luck

http://www.execpc.com/~wmhogg/beginner.html

Lots of links to resources, making it easy for you to look for information on finding answers to your technical questions, over a dozen Internet guides and tutorials, links to computer magazines, Web publishing sites, tons of images and clips to add to your own home page, and more! Best of all is a list of starting points for those who are completely green to this Net thing.

The List

http://thelist.internet.com/

If you decide to start your internet experience with a mega-provider like AOL, you should make this your second stop once you're wired. It lets you search, by your zip code, for Internet service providers in your area. You'll find all kinds of relevant info—what kind of services they provide, how much they cost, even the speed of their connection. Plus, the links let you go directly to the provider's Web site and in many cases, you can sign on right from your keyboard.

How to Select an Internet Service Provider

http://www.cnam.fr/Network/Internet-access/how_to_select.html

Written by Rick Adams, president and CEO of Alternet Internet Service Providers. This is an informative site if you don't know beans about choosing a provider and are the type to be attracted to those shiny, shrink-wrapped packages of free software that appear in your mailbox every now and then. This article covers everything from link speeds, the degree of technical assistance to expect, and the range of services they offer.

Endnotes

1. "NetSmart III: What Makes Women Click," a Sept. 1997 survey from NetSmart Research, New York.

2. Scott Zakarin, quoted in *Time* magazine, Sept. 22, 1997, p. 59.

3. Apple Computers has started licensing other companies to market computers using their operating system (OS). They're often cheaper than true-blue Macs.

RESOURCES

I can't decide which is more important: Planting seeds of radical thought in your brain, or giving you as many resources for growing those seeds as possible. I could compile volumes of groups, individuals, associations and organizations, Web sites, and other resources that could each provide you with something valuable in your quest for power and your search for truth, not to mention a better life for your planet.

As an activist and agent of change for any cause or ideal, you should always be seeking new sources of information and inspiration. As you start to become more involved in your community, and begin your world, you'll start to see the value of the alternative press and diverse sources of information. You'll also really come to appreciate the tools of activism that keep your agenda alive and kicking in the minds of others. Keep looking for as many information sources as you can get your hands on, subscribe to a magazine your teachers think is too radical for people "your age"; buy a book from the media section at your local bookstore and read about just how controlling mainstream media is when it comes to what you see, read, and hear; and listen to public radio (and then become a member). Go for it!

The partial list of resources that follows is a compromise (again, I say partial only because there isn't space here to get more detailed than this, so use this list as a starting point). General resources are listed first, with more specific info organized by section. If you run, know of, or belong to a resource that should be included here, write and tell me about it at P.O. Box 13947, Berkeley, CA 94712.

General Resources

Action Agenda
P.O. Box 618
Santa Cruz, CA 95061-0618
(800) 631-6355
E-mail: mediawok@aol.com

A great newsletter published by the media watchdog groups Media Watch and Media Action Alliance, who work to educate people about the hidden messages in media, especially advertising, and promote media awareness for all people, not just girls (although anti-women campaigns are the frequent targets of Media Watch). One thing I really like about this newsletter is the inclusion of pre-addressed postcards to the heads of various companies (different ones each month) who are doing evil things that you will want to protest. All you have to do is sign your name and drop the postcard in the mailbox. This instant activism alone is worth the price of a subscription.

Alliance for Democracy
P.O. Box 683
Lincoln, MA 01773-0683
(617) 259-9395
E-mail: peoplesall@aol.com
http://www.igc.apc.org/alliance/

Basically, those who belong to the Alliance believe that our country is being run not by our elected politicians or the constituency who elected them, but rather by out-of-control corporations whose main interest is their own bottom line, not the welfare of the general public. Think this sounds a little radical? Once you start reading magazines like *Boycott Quarterly* and the *Multinational Monitor,* you'll soon realize just how big a slice of the American Pie a few individual corporations really own—and control.

This is especially true for the media. You may think that the sheer number of TV and radio stations, magazines, and newspapers guarantees that you're given a wide range of information and perspectives, but what you probably don't realize is that most of those information and entertainment sources are owned and controlled by just a few conglomerates.

Through a network of grassroots affiliates, the Alliance works to "free all people from corporate domination of politics, economics, the environment, culture, and information." What a coincidence— these are all the things you're working to wrestle from the grip of those who have been making a mess of it for so long!

Their Web site contains background information on the Alliance, including their constitution and by-laws, as well as action alerts and information on joining or forming a local chapter of the Alliance.

Brave Girls and Strong Women Bookstore
P.O. Box 15481
Washington, DC 20003-0481
http://members.aol.com/brvgirls/index.htm

This site features all kinds of magazines and books that enable girls to reach their dreams—whether that dream is to walk on the moon, or just to walk down the street with their head held high. No matter what you're working for, working against, or trying to do with your life, some of these materials may be just what you need to help you get there.

Center for Campus Organizing
P.O. Box 425748
Cambridge, MA 02142
(617) 354-9363
E-mail: cco@igc.apc.org
http://cco.org

Some student activist groups make noise and some make change. Many of the latter have hooked up with the Center for Campus Organizing (CCO), which strives to organize and connect students working for change across the country. Instead of working blindly in your little corner of the world, dreaming that impossible dream against inequality, you can join the ranks of CCO and kick some serious collective butt.

When you join CCO, you receive their "action alerts," which are one-page information sheets that provide background information on a number of issues. You also gain access to the CCO's vast library of resources, which includes publications like *Agents of Change: A Guide for Student Labor Activists, Little White Lies: The Truth about Affirmative Action and Reverse Discrimination,* and *Raising Hell: a Citizen's Guide to the Fine Art of Investigation.*

CCO's Campus Alternative Journalism Project (CAJP) includes an e-mail network of student editors and journalists across the country, and an article exchange (via e-mail) that lets you swap newspaper articles with others. CAJP also offers a yearly alternative journalism contest, speakers and trainers for your on-campus efforts, advice or help on any topic, and a library of publications like "The Alternative Journalism Internship Guide." Be sure to ask them about joining the CAN-YFN (Campus Activists' Network-Young Feminist's Network) mailing list (it's a great on-line meeting place for young women working for change on their campus).

Infusion is a quarterly newsletter put out by CCO that keeps members all over the country in touch. In this newsletter, you'll find the scoop on what other groups are doing, how their successes (and failures) can help you, and a list of upcoming events and resources.

CCO also publishes *The Campus Organizing Guide for Peace and Justice Groups,* which provides practical information on the nuts and bolts of forming a group and getting it on its feet, including how to attract members and publicize your meetings, the basics of setting up an information table on campus, and methods of nonviolent direct action. Also included is an essential list of publications and contacts.

Center for Investigative Reporting
568 Howard St., 5th Fl.
San Francisco, CA 94105
(415) 543-1200

To get to the who, what, when, where, and why of an issue or company you are investigating, try the Center for Investigative Reporting first. Although they don't provide specialized research, they do have a pretty extensive list of publications and articles that may get you started. Check out *The Investigator's Handbook* by Don Ray, which gives novice researchers detailed information and tools for getting the skinny on just about anything or anyone. Also take a look at CIR's own magazine, *The Muckraker.*

If you're interested in becoming a serious investigative journalist or you're just into muckraking as a sideline, write and ask the CIR about their internship program (for students and non-students; previous publication credits are not required).

Coalition for Environmentally
Responsible Economies (CERES)
711 Atlantic Ave.
Boston, MA 02111
(617) 451-0927

This organization is devoted to promoting the CERES principles, which set standards for corporations' policies and actions as they relate to the environment.

Consumer Information Center
Pueblo, CO 81009
http://www.pueblo.gsa.gov

If you don't know this address by heart, you must have been living under a rock for the past few decades. This is one of the coolest things your government will ever do for you—free publications (mailed to your or downloaded from their Web site) on just about anything you can imagine. In the business section, you'll find things like "Copyright Basics" and "Basic Facts about Registering a Trademark." Publications about the environment include "The Duck Stamp Story" (is this great or what?) and "Why Save Endangered Species?"

If you're not sure what you want, request their Consumer Information Catalog, which lists over 200 booklets from a variety of federal agencies.

Co-Op America
1612 K St. NW, Ste. 600
Washington, DC 20006
(800) 58-GREEN
E-mail: info@coopamerica.org
http://www.coopamerica.org/

For over 15 years, Co-Op America has been helping people change their lives, and their world, through responsible consumerism. That means learning which companies are kind to the Earth (and its inhabitants) and supporting those companies financially by buying their products.

Co-Op America has programs and tools designed to make better use of our natural and human resources, including several magazines and other guides providing alternatives for consumers and businesses. One of their most well-known publications is their *Green Pages,* which is the largest annual directory of socially and environmentally responsible companies (this is a great resource for finding earth-friendly vendors for your new small business or green companies to invest in). They also publish *Boycott Action News,* a quarterly magazine detailing current boycotts and the history behind them.

Co-Op America also publishes the *Financial Planning Handbook for Responsible Investors,* a great booklet with worksheets and tax tips, plus resources for the socially responsible investor or to find more environmentally sound products for your school.

Earth First!
P.O. Box 1415
Eugene, OR 97440-1415
(541) 344-8004
E-mail: earthfirst@igc.apc.org
http://www.envirolink.org/orgs/ef

Earth Action Training Camp
5261 Manila Ave.
Oakland, CA 94618
(510) 658-1430

Earth First!ers (according to their Web site, Earth First! is not an organization, it's a movement) practice the kind of in-your-face tactics and techniques that have earned them a reputation as fanatics. Much of what's said about them is untrue; what is true is that this group is definitely not for the weak-kneed or weak-spirited. If your commitment to saving the Earth is more than lip service, if you're willing to stir things up and take part in monkey-wrenching and #@*% stirring that other activists would shy away from, give Earth First! a call.

For a fee that ranges between $15 (low-income) and $45 (international air mail), you'll receive the *Earth First! Journal,* which keeps you up to date on the activities of Earth First!ers and other radical environmentalists.

Earth First! also offers training camps specializing in forest and urban activism. During three hard days, you'll learn about things like first aid, how to read a map, urban food support and base camp organizing, media skills, and nonviolent civil disobedience tactics. It's only $15, including food! You can also reach Earth First! through their Web site.

Encyclopedia of Women's History
http://www.teleport.com/~megaines/women.html

What began as a classroom assignment to write research papers on women in history has now become a resource featuring dozens of "papers" from students in grades K-12. This Web encyclopedia is handy if you need some short biographical information or interesting facts about women in history. Great for your new feminist group's next rally, material for your pro-girl 'zine, or just interesting reading to inspire and excite.

Envirolink
http://www.envirolink.org

Envirolink is the largest online provider of environmental research information; they're the ultimate resource for anything to do with saving our planet—or its inhabitants! They're a nonprofit organization linking hundreds of organizations and millions of people around the world with one common goal: to save this crazy planet we like to call home.

Where do you start? It's enough to give you an ecological anxiety attack! Check the site map for a list of possibilities, whether you're searching for volunteer opportunities, information on endangered species and animal rights, chat rooms, and absolutely anything else even remotely eco-related.

Envirolink provides info on topics from oil spills to clear-cutting forests, but you can also link to a number of sources that provide nothing but boycott information. Check out the link to *Environmental Action News,* which gives details on current boycotts and links to boycott pages.

Envirolink can also provide you with links to jobs, internships, and volunteer opportunities where you can work for Mother Earth and her preservation.

Essential Information
http://essential.org/EI.html

Just what is says—this site has all the info you need to know if your mission is to save the world from itself. EI was founded by the original consumer watchdog, Ralph Nader, in 1982 and is a nonprofit organization that makes it their business to give us all the dirty little secrets that CBS, NBC, ABC, and their like shy away from.

EI's goal is to create an informed public, which is getting harder and harder to do as fewer companies keep buying up more of the media sources. As part of that effort, Essential Information publishes the *Multinational Monitor,* a monthly magazine dedicated to keeping an eye on the business practices of companies and industries around the world. You can reach *MM* at (202) 387-8030 or by e-mail at Monitor@essential.org.

Another valuable tool offered by Essential Information's Web site is their link list. It currently provides almost 60 links to like-minded sites, like the Center for Auto Safety, Environmental Resources Information Network, and the Media Access Project. The organizations—and possibilities—you can discover through this initial listing can go on forever.

The Feminist Majority Foundation
801 W. 3rd St., Ste. 1
Los Angeles, CA 90048
(213) 651-0495

1600 Wilson Blvd., Ste. 801
Arlington, VA 22209
(703) 522-2214
http://www.feminist.org

One of the country's leading feminist groups, the Feminist Majority offers an extremely valuable networking tool for young feminists' groups through their Feminist Student Network. The FSN is a database of young feminist activists all over the country, whom you can contact by phone, e-mail, or snail mail to get advice or share ideas. It's easy to use, too. Instead of scrolling endless pages of names and numbers, you can search the database using keywords or phrases like

"forming a group" or "fundraising." Out of that search you'll be given links to girls whose profiles meet the criteria you've entered. The Feminist Student Network is a way to meet and greet like-minded feminists who, like you, are bent on changing their world.

While you're on-line, check out the Foundation's newsletter, *The Feminist Majority Report.* It's full of great information for girls into acting up, like news and updates on women's issues from around the world, as well as social, environmental, and cultural issues. Their Web site contains back issues so you can look up past articles and news clips (check out the Spring '95 issue to see one of the first reviews ever of *REAL Girls* magazine).

Also check out the FMF Internet Gateway, another site rich with links of particular interest to women and girls.

Girls Incorporated
30 E. 33rd St.
New York, NY 10016-5394
(212) 689-3700

441 W. Michigan St.
Indianapolis, IN 46202-3233
(317) 634-7546
http://www.girlsinc.org/

Girls Inc. is a fabulous organization that strives to help all girls become strong, smart, and bold. They've been at this for over 50 years, and aside from their cool Web site, Girls Inc. reaches over 350,000 girls through over 1000 sites across the country. The majority of the girls served through Girls Inc. are from low-income neighborhoods, mostly because these girls are given fewer opportunities than just about anyone on the planet. Girls Inc.

sites provide activities and alternatives for girls after school, during summer vacation, and on weekends. Their programs include PEERsuasion, which works to keep girls from becoming substance abusers; Girls Re-Cast TV, which shows girls the truth about the TV role models we've been given (from June Cleaver to Pamela Anderson Lee); Operation SMART, which gets girls excited about careers in science, math, and technology; Preventing Adolescent Pregnancy; and Sporting Chances, which works to give girls equal opportunity in sports.

Girls Inc. offers not just lip service and slogans, but real solutions to the problems that lots of girls face every day. If there's no Girls Inc. organization in your community, write for information on how to start one.

Institute for Global Communications
http://www.igc.org/igc

Here it is, ladies—the mother lode, the big kahuna, and all those other relevant cliches. You may notice that lots of the resources listed in this book begin their Web addresses with www.igc.org/. That's because the IGC is the heart of the Web for hundreds of organizations and individuals working for peace, economic and social justice, human rights, and environmental salvation.

IGC has created five "communities" of organizations and activists—PeaceNET, EcoNET, ConflictNET, LaborNET, and WomensNET. Within each community, you can find boycott information, read action alerts, and get updates on specific campaigns, or link to other organizations and Web sites. Warning: This is not a fluff site—it's

where to go when you are ready to get serious. Be prepared to spend a lot of time investigating IGC.

Journals and Newspapers
http://eng.hss.cmu.edu/journals

This is a great news source for potential politicians, writers, or just well meaning trouble makers. This site provides an alphabetical listing of well known, not so well known, and definitely alternative newspapers and magazines. Not only will this site help you develop a taste for varied perspectives, it'll help you get a much more well rounded view of your world.

The Media Foundation
1243 W. 7th Ave.
Vancouver, BC, Canada V6H 1B7
(604) 736-9401
E-mail: adbusters@adbusters.org
http://www.adbusters.org/adbusters

This is one of my favorite contacts in this entire book, and I think the work they do is some of the most important of our age. You could categorize it as "media awareness," but that doesn't even scratch the surface. By encouraging "culture jamming" among us masses (and through their excellent magazine, *Adbusters*), they work to expose big business (and government) interests by telling the real truth in advertising and by parodying these groups' own marketing and PR efforts.

The best thing about the MF is they don't just tell you what great things they're doing, they give you the tools and information you need to go into your own community and do it for yourself. They sponsor spoof ad contents, "subvertisements," "TV uncommercials," and events like Buy Nothing Day. Check out their Web site for lots of goodies that I would get in trouble for printing.

Adbusters Magazine is the ultimate guide for media activists and alternative media junkies. Aside from some inciteful articles on the effects of media, they provide a great forum for both political and media activists to showcase their work. *Adbusters* also offers several information packets and kits for anyone interested in alternative media and/or adbusting.

National Organization for Women
1000 16th St. NW, Ste. 700
Washington, DC 20036
(202) 331-0066
E-mail: now@now.org
http://www.now.org/

You're probably already familiar with NOWs work; as far as women's organizations go, you can pretty much consider them the heavy-hitters. The organization was founded in 1966; one of the founding members is also NOWs president, Betty Friedan, author of *The Feminine Mystique*. Today, a quarter of a million people belong to NOW; with that kind of membership, there's always the hope that there really is strength in numbers. NOW organizes events, helps women get elected to office, files lawsuits on the behalf of women who have been discriminated against, lobbies tirelessly to get women-friendly legislation enacted, and basically does anything and everything that's necessary to ensure equal rights and equal treatment of women—all women.

If your political efforts are aimed at helping women and girls, consider NOW your first stop. Membership includes access to local NOW activities, a sub-

scription to the National *NOW Times,* action alerts, and inclusion in the e-mail action alert network. NOW also offers a lot of volunteer and internship opportunities for young women.

Progressive Student Network
2526 N. Francisco, #1
Chicago, IL 60647
(312) 278-5376
E-mail: gwpsu@gwuvm.gwu.edu

Although the PSN was formed in 1980, its roots can be traced to the turbulent epicenter of student protest—the group was formed on the Kent State University campus, where four students were shot and killed by the national guard during a protest against American involvement in the Vietnam War.

PSN is a national network of student groups who are all working for social and political change. Through a variety of methods, PSN provides a way for student activists across the country to share ideas and methods, and get help organizing individual campaigns on a local or national level. One of the cool things about PSN is that it allows different types of groups to come together and share ideas. For example, some of the member groups are issue-oriented, focusing on the environment, or the political climate in Tibet; some groups are focused on particular demographics—they might be working for women's rights, or for the concerns of Latin-American students.

Whatever specific goals your group has, you don't have to worry about being a square peg in a round hole with PSN; there's room for everyone. Because of the diversity in the groups that make up PSN, you have the advantage of working with different personalities and different levels of experience. It's great to commiserate with activists who are struggling in their first stages, like you are, but you also have access to seasoned activists who have a better idea of what works and what doesn't.

PSN holds annual conferences in the fall that are designed to bring groups into the fold. They also hold committee meetings during the year, where representatives of member groups meet and discuss policy. Another faction of PSN is the Caucuses for People of Color, Women, and Gay/Lesbian/Bisexual students.

To keep all these people connected and in touch, PSN also publishes the *Progressive Student News,* a paper that's distributed to over 5000 student activists nationwide. It's important to remember that PSN is a grassroots network; they don't have staffed offices with full-time employees who can guide you through the process of starting a group on your own campus. They can, however, connect you with any number of other groups and individuals across the country who probably can give you the level of help you need.

Public Information Network
P.O. Box 95316
Seattle, WA 98145-2316
(206) 723-4276
E-mail: pin@igc.apc.org
http://violet.berkeley.edu/~orourke/
PIN.html

The Public Information Network (PIN) is a nonprofit organization dedicated to the exchange of information on the environment, economics, and human rights. They are an extremely valuable resource

if your group's efforts have anything at all to do with business ethics and practices (or lack thereof) and the subsequent effects on communities, environment, and people. Their goal is to provide information and training that will enable activists worldwide to achieve true democracy, social justice, and environmental balance.

Their End Game Project is an education and action effort that provides detailed information on "corporate welfare" systems. PIN also provides personalized research for individuals and groups and publishes a couple of manuals that no decent corporate activist would be caught dead without. Their *Activist Research Manual: Sources of Information on Corporations* ($10) gives you the tools you'll need for corporate dirt-digging—where to look and how to do the research—whether you're investigating human rights violations or environmental abuses. *The Primer on Corporations* ($10) is full of facts, statistics, quotes and other information on today's corporations. Like the research manual, it also includes valuable resources for corporate investigations and a directory of citizen watchdog groups.

PIN also holds Access and Action Research Workshops, which are designed to give activists the tools they'll need to be successful in their campaign against corporate crimes.

All of PIN's projects are designed to arm activists—whether acting alone or in a group—with as much information as possible. Their theory, much like the basis of this book, is that information is the great equalizer, and without it, you can't get much done.

Rainforest Action Network
221 Pine St., #500
San Francisco, CA 94104
(415) 398-4404
E-mail: helpran@ran.org
http://www.ran.org

The Rainforest Action Network works to protect our planet's rainforests through education programs, grassroots organizing, and nonviolent direct action. One way they keep people informed is through consumer boycott action; if your boycott is focused on environmental issues, RAN can provide you some great background information for your efforts. In fact, they may already have a boycott going that you can join.

You can call, write, or wire yourself to their network and find current boycott information, RAN's action alerts (news updates about current RAN campaigns), information on how to join, and background and research information on specific topics like the giant redwoods. RAN also offers internships for committed student activists in the San Francisco Bay Area. Unfortunately, this group promises to be very busy in the coming years, until some girl comes along and changes the way we do things in this world of ours.

The Third Wave
116 E. 16th St., 7th Fl.
New York, NY 10003
(212) 388-1898
http://www.feminist.com/3wave.htm

The opening screen for this young feminist Web page tells some pretty grim statistics: 1 in 10 adolescent girls suffer from anorexia or bulimia; 8 million girls are sexually abused before they reach 18 years old; young women are 25 percent of today's homeless population. A pretty rude awakening, yeah, but Third Wave uses these facts not to scare you but to rally you with other girls in your fight for rights and respect. They're is a national, nonprofit, multicultural member organization devoted to social change, especially for young women.

Membership fees are pretty reasonable: $1 for every year of your age. For example, if you're 16 years old, your cost is $16; if you're 18, your cost is $18, and so on. Write or visit their site for more information on how you can get on the bus.

US Public Interest Research Group
(USPIRG)
215 Pennsylvania Ave. SE
Washington, DC 20003
(202) 546-4707
http://www.igc.apc.org/pirg

USPIRG is one of the granddaddies of modern activism. With offices across the entire country, they offer a powerful and effective activist network, whether your cause is saving the planet from gross polluters or feeding the hungry and homeless in your own community. Local chapters offer a wide variety of opportunities for part- and full-time activists, but three of their programs are specifically geared toward students.

Free the Planet!, launched in 1995, is a network of student activists whose primary work is in environmental education and action. Through the USPIRG Web site, you can join forces to save the planet by linking to e-mail mailing lists, connect with local activists in your community, and send free political action faxes on lots of topics to elected officials.

PIRG student chapters have existed on campuses around the country for over twenty years, connecting students concerned about social, political, and environmental issues. The really cool thing about PIRG student chapters is that members not only work with other committed activists like yourself, but also have access to seasoned, experienced activists who act as mentors. It's great to chat with other people who are sharing your struggles with a local polluter to end his evil ways, but it's even better to connect with an activist who's been there, done that, and has some real tangible advice to give.

Over 100 campuses across the country have student PIRG chapters; they've registered hundreds of thousands of student voters, helped pass some of the country's most effective recycling laws, helped stop Clean Water Act violators, and strengthened the Clean Air Act. Student chapters also organize community service projects like food and clothing drives, and environmental clean-up. You can also earn college credit for your work with PIRG.

The National Student Campaign Against Hunger and Homelessness (NSCAHH) is a coalition of student activists and residents in communities across the country who use education and direct service to end hunger and homelessness on a local level. Started a decade ago by state PIRGs and USA for Africa, NSCAHH is the largest student activist network fighting hunger and homelessness in the country—more than 600 campuses in 45 states participate.

Aside from the student-specific projects, state PIRGs also offer internships and part- and full- time employment, and few of these jobs require any experience.

Your Say
http://ausnet.net.au/yoursay/home.html

If there are things about the world and the way it's run that upset you, but you just can't put your finger on specific examples, then this is the site for you. Here, you're briefed about some topic, like nuclear testing, then given the opportunity to send any message you like to world leaders. The week I logged on, the topic was French President Jacques Chirac's decision to recommence nuclear testing in the South Pacific. With just a click, you can voice your opinion and send a protest over e-mail, the Internet, or snail mail, or you can make a donation to a relevant organization (this time it was the Anti-Nuclear Fund). They also, thoughtfully, provide you with a complete, ready-to-send letter in case you're having a little writer's block.

Government Documents
http://www.library.yale.edu/govdocs/gdchome.html

Whether your thing is animals, the environment, politics, women's rights, or anything else, you should make it your business to visit this site. Providing a huge array of things like census figures, court decisions, and declassified documents, it's a user-friendly site that lets you search easily, by completing various statements such as "I am looking for..."

JINN Magazine/Pacific News Service
http://www.pacificnews.org/jinn/index.html

PNS features the work of journalists whose perspectives are not usually covered in the mainstream press—like teenagers and immigrants. It's a great source for news that you won't see on any of the three networks, and may be one of the few places you can gather information about your causes. Also features *Yo!*, a politically oriented youth magazine based in San Francisco, and *Jinn*, an online magazine that features the work of young writers and alternative presses.

Progressive Resources Catalog
Donnelly/Colt
Box 188
Hampton, CT 06247

This annual mail-order catalog has great stuff (like *A People's History of the United States*, fabulous history you won't learn in high school, and *Power of the People: Active Nonviolence in the United States)*, as well as a huge array of buttons and T-shirts for whatever cause you're championing. You can even design your own items at a decent price. (These guys sent me a great sticker that says "Girls Kick Ass," which is now firmly planted on my truck's rear bumper.) Owned and operated by a husband and wife (and three children) out of a barn, the Progressive Resources Catalog gives you some great ammunition in your fight against The Man.

Things I Must Do Today
(formerly *REAL Girls Magazine*)
P.O. Box 13947
Berkeley, CA 94706

I started publishing this 'zine as a way to give girls the tools (namely, information) they'd need to take control of their lives. When I was growing up, you just didn't read about things like boycotts (and how to start one, especially against a huge advertiser like a makeup company). Other articles talk about animal rights, becoming a savvy media consumer, and rejecting the female standard as it's presented in mainstream magazines—thin, pretty, stupid, and passive.

A while ago, RG morphed into TIMDT, which is an activist newsletter for young women. Each issue is filled with dozens of things for girls who want to make change in their lives and their world. Join a boycott, adopt a cow, get some rad pro-girl stickers printed—lots of stuff to replace shopping at the mall or figuring out your color horoscope.

Sticker Sisters
P.O. Box 11480
Takoma Park, MD 20913

Like the Progressive Resources Catalog, Sticker Sisters provides a way for you to express your views on sexism and women's rights with stickers, buttons, and more. The company was started by Ariel Fox, because she wants girls to be proud of themselves. She warns, "If you are racist, homophobic, or otherwise unaccepting, my catalog is not for you." Write for a catalog, then order something from her!

Part 1: Become a Strong Political Force

Center for the American Woman and Politics
http://www.rci.rutgers.edu/~cawp/

This Rutgers University-based site serves as a research, education, and public service center, promoting a greater understanding of women's relationship to politics and government. Plus it's got a bunch of relevant info, like who's the highest ranking woman in the U.S. Government right now. (As of this book's writing, it's Secretary of State Madeleine Albright.)

The Electronic Activist
http://www.berkshire.net/~ifas/activist/index.html

They say that success in politics is all about connections—here are yours. This site contains an e-mail address directory, by state, of congressional and state government officials, as well as media contacts. Need I say more? Very cool. Click on South Carolina and up pop Senator Strom Thurmond, Governor David Beasley, and the e-mail addresses of three major newspapers. Click on one of those names and your e-mail window appears, just waiting for those deep, relevant, and socially valuable comments you've been waiting to make. Point and click on the Federal and National link, and up pop (among others) e-mail links to the White House, the Democratic and Republican committees, and Rush Limbaugh.

ForeFront Connect: Political Information for Women on the Web
http://www.ffconnect.com/

Your one-stop source for comprehensive, non-partisan information about women, politics, and public affairs.

League of Women Voters
http://www.lwv.org/~lwvus/

Founded in 1920, this nonpartisan group encourages the informed participation of citizens in government, while seeking to influence public policy through education and advocacy.

National Women's Political Caucus
1211 Connecticut Ave. NW, Ste. 425
Washington, DC 20036
E-mail: MailNWPC@aol.com
http://www.feminist.com/nwpc.htm

A national organization dedicated to getting as many women as possible into public office. If you've been having lingering feelings about that opening in the city council or school board, but just don't know where to take your ambition, try the NWPC. With over 50,000 members nationwide, they train, provide endorsements and support, and even help get women appointed to offices. Don't think for a minute that this group is out of your league—that's precisely the kind of self-doubt that keeps women out of public office in the first place. If you have even an inkling that you want to run for office, contact the NWPC.

Net Grams
http://www.voxpop.org/netgrams

You can set a netgram (like a telegram sent by your computer) to your favorite, or not-so-favorite, politician, indicating your extreme displeasure with how this planet's human population is treating its better half—namely, the women.

Women in Politics
http://www.glue.umd.edu/~cliswp/

Current and historical information about women involved in every aspect of politics in the United States can be found at this site. They also feature a special section on getting women elected to public office.

Activist Group Resources

The Directory of Corporate Affiliations
Reed Reference Publishing Co.
121 Shanlon Rd.
New Providence, NJ 07974
E-mail: mlevenson@reedref.com

An extremely valuable resource for locating the right people to direct your complaints to. Gives detailed company contact information, which will help you target your campaigns more effectively.

Do Something!
423 W. 55th St., 8th Fl.
New York, NY 10019
(212) 523-1175
http://www.dosomething.org

By becoming a Do Something! member, you gain access to any of their numerous programs for student activists, including community programs (like leadership courses, projects, and a community coaches program) that work with existing grassroots activist organizations. The Do Something Grant gives young activists up to $500 to get their projects running, while local Do Something Funds can help support a project already underway. Plus, every year, Do Something! chooses ten outstanding activists (under age 30) and gives them the Do Something BRICK Award for Community Leadership. The national grand prize winner receives a grant of $100,000 to fund the project, the others receive grants of $10,000 each.

The Future Is Ours: A Handbook for Student Activists in the 21st Century
By John W. Bartlett. Published by Henry Holt & Company, 1996 (New York).

Great practical advice on forming a group and planning events, as well as lots of inspirational stories of young adults (and teens) who have already made huge advances in changing their communities (and world).

How You Can Manipulate the Media: Guerrilla Methods to Get Your Story Covered by TV, Radio and Newspapers
By David Alexander. Published by Paladin Press, 1993 (P.O. Box 1307, Boulder, CO 80306; 800-394-2400).

Just having a good cause isn't enough; you need to know how to get your cause, and your words, noticed. This is a terrific resource for devising strategies of sound bites and maximum media coverage.

Resources for Radicals
By Brian Burch. Published by the Toronto Action for Social Change (Box 73620, 509 St. Clair Ave. W., Toronto, ON, Canada, M6C 1C0; 416-651-5800; e-mail: burch@web.net).

An annual bibliography of books and magazines of interest to activists working for peace and justice. From a booklet on tenants' rights to *Ecotactics*, a handbook for nonviolent environmental action, there are dozens of offerings to choose from.

Student Environmental Action Coalition (SEAC)
P.O. Box 31909
Philadelphia, PA 19104
(215) 222-4711
E-mail: seac-office@seac.org
http://www.seac.org

Formed over 10 years ago through a simple classified ad in *Greenpeace Magazine*,

SEAC is a nationwide network of high school and college student activists that provides a helpful shoulder to lean on, as well as resource materials like guidebooks and background research on a variety of topics. Today, they're comprised of over 1500 student groups in all 50 states. SEAC is student-run and student-led, which makes them an especially effective resource for on-campus activist groups.

SEAC's primary mission is to provide information, support, and training to student-run activist groups. They provide a number of tools, including the SEAC Information Clearinghouse, which provides fact sheets, books, action guides, and other materials for student activists; *Threshold*, their monthly magazine; the SEAC Organizer Training Program, a series of workshops that cover all aspects of organizing and activism; and their extremely effective e-mail network, SEACnet. SEACnet includes a number of e-mail action lists, including lists for people of color, women, high school students, activists dealing with international issues, and animal rights supporters.

Boycott Resources

Boycott Quarterly
c/o Center for Economic Democracy
P.O. Box 30727
Seattle, WA 98103-0727
E-mail: boycottguy@aol.com

The ultimate authority in anything dealing with boycotts. Gives detailed information on current boycotts as well as valuable information on brand names, parent companies, and subsidiaries.

Bunny Hugger's Gazette
P.O. Box 601
Temple, TX 76503

Someone puts a lot of effort into this publication, and it shows. *BHG* features boycott information and corporate crime details as they relate to animal rights and animal abuse.

Corporate Crime Reporter
P.O. Box 19405
Washington, DC 20036
(202) 387-8030

1322 18th St. NW
Washington, DC 20036
(202) 429-6928

Basically, they'll get you the low-down on everything you ever wanted to know about that big bad company down the street that's taking over your town.

INFORM, Inc.
381 Park Ave. S.
New York, NY 10016-8806
(212) 361-2400
E-mail: inform@informinc.org
http://www.informinc.org

INFORM is a nonprofit environmental research and education organization that reviews the business practices of industries in general, as well as individual companies, to determine how those practices may be harming our world. They're not an activist group, so they're not involved in any direct action; they can, however, provide you with specific background information on things like toxic waste and industrial air pollution. INFORM has also done extensive research on recycling and solid waste management.

Membership in INFORM is $35 (the membership fee is tax deductible) and includes a subscription to their quarterly newsletter, *INFORM Reports*. If you don't have the facts and figures to back up your claims and justify your demands, you might contact INFORM for help; they might be able to provide you with the ammunition you need to blow your resistors right out of the water.

Internship Resources

America's Job Bank
http://www.ajb.dni.us/

America's Job Bank (AJB) is the national clearinghouse for the Public Employment Service. Their Web page of jobs of all kinds is updated daily. Includes a link to America's Career InfoNet, which provides general information and helps you find out more about careers.

The Back Door Guide to Short Term Job Adventures
By Michael Landes. Published by Ten Speed Press, 1997.

The Back Door Guide includes the who, what, when, where, and how of thousands of positions (the why is up to you). This book has so many opportunites explained in such detail that the hardest part may be picking which one to do first.

Internships in Foreign and Defense Policy
By Women in International Security. Published by Seven Locks Press, 1990 (P.O. Box 27, Cabin John, MD 20818).

A book for girls who want to keep their world safe and secure, compiled and written by Women in International Security,

an organization devoted to supporting women in the male-dominated areas of foreign and defense policy.

USAJOBS
http://www.usajobs.opm.gov/index.htm

The U.S. Government's official site for jobs and employment information, provided by the U.S. Office of Personnel Management. Includes information on the Peace Corps and AmeriCorps, as well as application forms and instructions.

Part 2: Manipulate the Economy

Feminist Economics
Rice University
6100 Main St.
Houston, TX 77005-1892
http://www.bucknell.edu/~jshackel/iaffe/

Published by the International Association for Feminist Economics, for members of the organization. *Feminist Economics* provides an open forum for discussion about feminist economic perspectives. But this isn't just talk—the journal's goal is to improve the quality of life for everyone. While some of the articles sound like college paper topics ("The Prevalence of Gender Topics in U.S. Economics Journals"), you'll get a good idea about what's on the mind of concerned women all over the world.

Junior Achievement
JA New York, Inc.
107 Washington St., 3td Fl.
New York, NY 10006
E-mail: JANY@ja.org
http://www.ja.org/

A nonprofit organization dedicated to teaching kids about business and economics. Their classroom programs, taught by volunteers in over 100 countries around the world, teach kids about free enterprise and how to get a slice of it for themselves.

If you can log on to their Web site, you can get local address and phone information. If you don't have access to a computer, contact the New York office and they can point you to someone in your area.

Nontraditional Job Resources

Create the Job You Love (And Make Plenty of Money): More Than 550 Ways to Escape the 8 to 5 Grind
By Barbara J. Witcher. Published by Prima Publishing, 1997 (3875 Atherton Road, Rocklin, CA 95765; 916-632-4400).

This book lists 550 alternative occupations that will definitely get you out of the traditional 40-hour work environment. Grouped into categories such as communication, sports, and transportation, it describes each position's responsibilities, requirements, and pay.

Illinois Women in Trades Training Partnership
828 S. Wabash, Ste. 200
Chicago, IL 60605
(312) 922-8530
http://www.accessil.com/iwttp/home.htm

This organization provides the information women need to access nontraditional job opportunities, both as employees and potential business owners/managers.

It's a Living! Career News for Girls
Ceel Publishing
1643 Fitzgerald Ave.
Alexandria, VA 22302
(703) 671-1835
E-mail: Ceel@msn.com

Each issue of this eight-page newsletter tells the stories of three women who are working in a job they love. Girls can get first-hand knowledge of what it's like to work as an airline pilot, biologist, or computer programmer.

Tradeswomen, Inc.
P.O. Box 40664
San Francisco, CA 94140
(415) 821-7334

This is a great magazine by, for, and about women working in the trades. Aside from terrific resources for your own career (or educational opportunity) search, the magazine includes personal insights from the women who work these jobs everyday. If you're considering going into the trades, this is an excellent way to network and to join the community of women working in nontraditional jobs.

The Woman's Journal
P.O. Box 82293
Portland, OR 97282
http://www.aracnet.com/~wmnjourn/

The Woman's Journal addresses issues affecting women, and provides useful and meaningful information about women as achievers, trailblazers, and entrepreneurs.

Investment Resources

Clean Yield Publications
41 Old Pasture Rd.
Greensboro Bend, VT 05842
(802) 533-7178

A useful bimonthly newletter focusing on the stock market for socially concerned investors. You'll find profiles of publicly traded companies, reports on the current climate of the stock market (and the economy in general), and updates on the trend toward socially responsible investing.

Eco-Rating International
http://www.eco-rating.com

Sometimes, no matter how much you've researched and investigated, it's hard to know if that company you're interested in is really all that "green." Using a ten-point scale, these guys rate lots of companies on their environmental soundness. Visit them to verify the eco-soundess of an investment you've chosen.

Good Money Quarterly Report
P.O. Box 363
Worcester, VT 05682
(800) 223-3911

Offers objective information for people who want to put money in socially responsible companies and industries.

The GreenMoney Journal
West 608 Glass Ave.
Spokane, WA 99205
http://www.greenmoney.com

Specializing in socially responsible investing, this newsletter is essential for girls who are changing their world as well as their bottom line. In addition to some really useful information, you'll also find valuable links and leads to other resources.

If You're Clueless About the Stock Market and Want to Know More
By Seth Godin. Published by Dearborn Financial Publishing, Inc., 1997.

If I were giving stars, this would get four. The information is detailed but easy to read and understand, and the title says it all: Start with zero knowledge in the morning, and by the evening you could be picking winners.

Shopping for a Better World
Council on Economic Priorities
30 Irving Pl.
New York, NY 10003
(800) 729-4237
(212) 420-1133

Very useful in helping you apply screens to potential investments, *Shopping for a Better World* evaluates corporations and their perfomance as it relates to military spending, fair employment practices, community relations, and the environment.

Social Investment Forum
P.O. Box 57216
Washington, DC 20037
(202) 872-5319

A national association of investment practitioners. Contact them for a comprehensive listing of socially responsible mutual funds and investing opportunities with community development.

Women & Money
1405 Carleton St., Ste. A
Berkeley, CA 94702

Just a year or so old, this is a good resource for all kinds of financial information from—and for—a woman's perspective. You may find the information a little over your head at first, but once you get the hang of the buzzwords and economic lingo, you'll find it really useful.

Your Wealth-Building Years
By Adriane G. Berg. Published by Newmarket Press, 1995 (18 E. 48th St., New York, NY 10017; 212-832-3575).

Because this book is geared toward young adults (ages 18 to 25), it gives you everything you do need to know and nothing of the stuff you don't need. It covers lots of different financial strategies, not just the stock market, which makes it a good resource to keep on hand.

Small Business Resources

American Business Women's Association
9100 Ward Parkway
P.O. Box 8728
Kansas City, MO 64114-0728
(816) 361-6621
E-mail: ABWA@abwahq.org
http://www.abwahq.org/

The ABWA is a membership organization devoted to increasing opportunities for women, both personally and professionally, through networking, education, and recognition. They offer scholarships, educational programs, local chapters, and conferences and conventions. Their magazine, *Women in Business,* covers business trends, ownership, and self-improvement for women who are taking control of their lives, not just their checkbooks.

Even if you think this is more than you and your small business need, take a look at their membership options on their Web site. Check out the Company Connection, a way for women starting their own business (or still planning it) to get valuable information and discounts on products and services.

Their Web site also features some past issues of *Women in Business* on-line for you to read through, as well as links to other resource that may fill your more immediate needs. Just remember, though, when you are starting to excel in your business, joining a pro-woman organization like this one might be a good idea.

Bay Area Business Woman
On Your Marks Publishing
5337 College Ave., Ste. 501
Oakland, CA 94618
(510) 654-7557

Although this paper targets the San Francisco Bay area, you should definitely order a copy even if you and your small business are on the other side of the country. The profiles of local businesswomen, resource listings, and a calendar of events are a useful reference for girls just starting out in business. The editors may also be able to point you to a local paper in your own area.

The Entrepreneurial Development Institute (TEDI)
http://www.bedrock.com/tedi/tedi.htm

TEDI is a national, nonprofit organization that strives to empower youth (especially disadvantaged and at-risk youth) to become productive members of their community and effective agents of change in their own lives. One way they accomplish this is by helping young people create and run small businesses that address the needs of their own communities. The TEDI training plan helps with things like marketing, finance, writing a business plan, and then helping actually get the business off the ground. Some of the businesses that TEDI has helped develop are a student store and a children's book publishing company run by teen mothers. The TEDI Web site even advertises and promotes some of their teen-run businesses.

The Edward Lowe Foundation
58200 Decatur Rd.
P.O. Box 8
Cassopolis, MI 49031-0008
(800) 232-LOWE
(616) 445-4200
http://www.lowe.org/

The purpose of the Foundation is "to champion the entrepreneurial spirit by providing information, research, and educational experiences which support small business people and the free enterprise system." Spend at least thirty minutes at their Web site and you'll be itching to get yourself and your products/services into the marketplace. Their Web site has two areas of interest: smallbizNet, an information clearinghouse for anyone who chooses to access it; and *Entrepreneurial Edge Online,* an on-line magazine about entrepreneurs.

SmallbizNet is one of my favorite resources on the Net: you can search smallbizNet by category or keyword, and what you'll find is a seemingly unlimited library of articles and information for anyone who's contemplating, or running, a small business. Most documents are completely free, and they're more than

just a couple of paragraphs of information. For example, document #1060, "A Pricing Checklist for Small Retailers," is seven pages long and full of valuable information and formulas for determining a pricing structure that works. Looking for background on marketing, advertising, or topics of particular interest to women? Check here. This is like having a whole small business library at your fingertips.

An Income of Her Own (AIOHO)
Business Plan Competition
1804 W. Burbank Blvd.
Burbank, CA 91506
(800) 350-2978
E-mail: aioho@world.std.com
http://www.anincomeofherown.com

AIOHO is a nonprofit organization dedicated to giving girls the tools they need to be economically independent. They've developed workshops, newsletters, mentorship programs, and even a camp called Camp $tart-Up to give budding entrepreneurs a leg up in the business world. Their Web site offers free Web pages for women entrepreneurs under age twenty to showcase their businesses. *Turned On Business* is their newsletter for teen girls featuring news you need to know, contests to enter, and success stories from other business owners. AIOHO can also provide extremely valuable, practical information on how to apply for a patent or a copyright, where to get funding for your small business, or how to develop a marketing plan that will grow your business. Joining AIOHO gives you a valuable network of contacts and information that most people have to pay hefty association fees to obtain.

AIOHO also sponsors a business plan competition, where you could win your own personal business coach for one year and other cool prizes. They also make a board game, entrepreneurial women's trading cards, and other books and materials that a prospective business owner such as yourself would find very helpful.

National Foundation for Women
Business Owners
1100 Wayne Ave., Ste. 830
Silver Spring, MD 20910-5603
(301) 495-4975
E-mail: NFWBO@worldnet.att.net

The foundation provides extensive information, research, and statistics on women-owned businesses and business owners. They're the ones who can tell you that there are now nearly 8 million women-owned businesses in the U.S., and that women-owned businesses currently generate nearly $2.3 trillion in revenues.

No More Frogs to Kiss: 99 Ways to Give Economic Power to Girls
By Joline Godfrey. Published by HarperCollins, 1995.

Covers everything from saving to investing, all designed to give girls the knowledge, resources, and tools they need to become more financially independent.

Small Business Administration
Office of Women's Business Ownership
1441 L St. NW, Ste. 414
Washington, DC 20416
(202) 653-8000

A fabulous organization that offers all kinds of goodies—like free publications on starting and running a small business and access to the National Women's Hall of Fame, which provides, at the very least, some intense inspiration for getting your behind in gear.

Teen Biz Video Survival Guide
TeenBiz International, Inc.
2118 Wilshire Blvd., #1172
Santa Monica, CA 90403-5784
(310) 315-9998
E-mail: markjames@teenbiz.com
http://www.teenbiz.com

Through a series of interviews with teen business owners, this video gives pretty good general hints and tips on how to start and grow a small business. In addition to the video, Direct Media also produces a series of business and economics-related info for teens and young adults.

Part 3: Shape Your Culture

The Alternative Press Center
P.O. Box 33109
Baltimore, MD 21218
(410) 243-2471
http://www.altpress.org/

The Alternative Press Center (APC) is a nonprofit collective dedicated to providing access to and increasing public awareness of the alternative press. The APC publishes the *Alternative Press Index,* a quarterly subject index to approximately 250 alternative, radical, and left periodicals, newspapers, and magazines, including complete contact information.

Institute for Alternative Journalism
77 Federal St.
San Francisco, CA 94107
(415) 284-1420
http://www.igc.apc.org/an/

IAJ is a nonprofit organization dedicated to strengthening and supporting independent and alternative journalism, and to improving the public's access to independent information sources. This organization believes that democracy is enhanced, and public debate broadened, as more voices are heard and points of view made available. The more, the merrier!

'Zine Publishing Resources

BigTop Publisher Services
833 Market St., #602
San Francisco, CA 94103
(415) 974-1544
E-mail: info@BigTopPubs.com

A national magazine distributor specializing in assisting independent publishers with newsstand distribution.

Factsheet Five
P.O. Box 170049
San Francisco, CA 94117

The first and last word in 'zines, from tracking down the last copy of *Chip's Closet Cleaner* to research on what the political right is doing. Aside from the first and best place to get your 'zine, homemade video, or audio tape (or CD) reviewed and listed, you can scour the pages for titles that might help you in your own projects—whether you're trying to connect with other environmentally aware girls or just interested in learning more about liberal politics.

Feminist Bookstore News
P.O. Box 882554
San Francisco, CA 94188
(415) 626-1556

If your 'zine is feminist-oriented, FNB can generate a lot of interest for you with booksellers across the country, which can increase your distribution and influence. Even if your publication isn't about feminism or *grrls*, you can use *FBN* as a resource to find local distributors and presses of women-produced magazines. For $1, they'll send a national listing of feminist bookstores you can contact directly.

How to Do Leaflets, Newsletters and Newspapers
By Nancy Brigham. Published by Writer's Digest Books, 1991 (1507 Dana Ave., Cincinnati, OH 45207; 800-289-0963).

Clear explanations and lots of illustrations on stuff like design, and tips for dealing with vendors and printers.

Market Hill Printing
216 Market St.
Amsterdam, NY 12010
(518) 842-0320
E-mail: mkthill@klink.net
http://www.klink.net/~mkthill

A commercial offset printer, they also cater to a large 'zine publisher list. One of the perks their site offers is an e-mail quote service and a laundry list of information that you need to provide to get an accurate quote from any printer (such as what kind of paper are you using; are you printing the cover on the same stock or cover stock?). Market Hill also offers low-budget prices on services like binding (folding, collating, etc.) and shipping.

See Hear
33 St. Marks Place
New York, NY 10003
(212) 982-6968
http://www.zinemart.com

A mail order and wholesale distributor of 'zines, magazines, and books—everything from *Hairy Women* to *Charlie's Angels.* Write and tell them about your little homemade endeavor; maybe you can get your 'zine into their distribution list. Their Web site features *The Fanzine Reader,* which highlights the best of their catalog.

Small Publishers Co-Op
2579 Clematis St.
Sarasota, FL 34239
(941) 922-0844

A printer specializing in small run publications, like 'zines. Because they gang-run publications (print several at once), they can give you discounted prices on offset printing and photocopying.

The World of 'Zines
By Mike Gunderloy and Carl Goldberg Janice. Published by Penguin USA, 1992 (P.O. Box 999, Dept. 17109, Bergenfield, NJ 07621; 800-253-6476).

Written by ex-editors of *Factsheet 5.* A great resource for 'zine production, especially if you have no background in production, printing, or graphics.

Video Resources

Unplug
360 Grand Ave., #385
Oakland, CA 94610
(510) 268-1100
E-mail: unplug@igc.org

Billed as "the center for commercial-free public education," Unplug is a national, youth-run organization conducting a campaign against the commercially sponsored (not to mention saturated) Channel One and other "sponsored" education materials, like videos lesson plans, posters, and activities like PE-TV (which is PE while you watch TV, all brought to you by way of mega-advertiser, Reebok).

Write for a copy of their newsletter, *Not for Sale* (which refers to you and your gray matter, sweetie); it features great articles and information on the lack of cultural diversity on TV and action kits that can help your activist group fight the tidal wave of commercialism that's coming your way. Unplug also offers a great selection of books, articles, and other resources.

Independent Television Service (ITVS)
51 Federal St.
San Francisco, CA 94107
(415) 356-8383
E-mail: itvs@itvs.org
http://www.itvs.org/ITVS

Through funding by the Corporation for Public Broadcasting, ITVS strives to bring quality and vision to a medium that's dominated by formula programming and dull, unimaginative ideas. Instead of turning their backs on TV altogether (which lots of people are very tempted to do), they work to pump some life back into the boob tube, providing quality programming (and media literacy) for both kids and adults. Their series *Signal to Noise: Life With Television* tries to engage TV viewers in a debate over the state of TV and how (and in fact, if) it should be changed. "Don't turn off your TV," they say, "reclaim it." If you're interested in alternative media of all kinds (books, films, organizations, etc.) contact ITVS for a listing of resources (their *Signal to Noise* mailer unfolds to a poster-sized list of contacts for you to pursue). ITVS also has resources on funding for independent producers.

The Independent Film & Video Monthly
c/o Association of Independent Video and Filmmakers (AIVF)
304 Hudson St., 6th Fl. N.
New York, NY 10013
(212) 807-1400

They provide listings of happenings and events in independent film and video. When you write to them, request a back issue of *Media in the Schools*.

Videomaker Magazine
P.O. Box 4591
Chico, CA 95927
(916) 891-8410
E-mail: editor@videomaker.com

One of the best resources out there for anyone who's into video (whether you're shooting family reunions or an exposé that'll thrill the world); they've got product updates and info, plus great articles on technique.

Zillions
Subscription Dept.
P.O. Box 51777
Boulder, CO 80323-1777
(800) 234-2078
(914) 378-2551

The focus of this magazine is on advertising; it shows how real ads are put together, who they're aimed at, and how they work.

Music Resources

Assoc. of Women's Music and Culture
2124 Kittredge St., #104
Berkeley, CA 94704
(707) 523-8580

This organization for female artists publishes an annual directory of members, a quarterly newsletter, and the Women's Music Calendar, a monthly schedule of women's performances. It could be useful to help you connect with other women in music and the arts, and might give you some hot leads about festivals and other venues where you might get a booking.

CD AND RECORD MANUFACTURERS FOR CUTTING YOUR OWN CD

World Audio Video Enterprises
4-35 Stafford Rd. E
Nepean, Ontario, Canada K2H 8V8.
(800) 928-3310

Healey Disc Manufacturing
58 Antares Dr., Unit 1
Nepean, Ontario, Canada K2E 7W6
(800) 835-1362

United Record Pressing, Inc.
453 Chestnut St.
Nashville, TN 37203
(615) 259-9396

Dixie Record Pressing, Inc.
631 Hamilton Ave.
Nashville, TN 37203
(615) 256-0922

Lady Purple Productions
P.O. Box 15308
North Hollywood, CA 91615-5308
(818) 997-8112

A women-owned and operated business that provides marketing services (photography, press releases, finding producers, management, etc.) for new bands. They might be a little over your head when you're just starting out, but you never know, if you ask politely and they like your demo, they may give you some useful tips.

Note by Note: A Guide to Concert Production
By Redwood Cultural, Community Music and Friends, and Joanie Shoemaker. Published by Redwood Cultural Work, 1989 (P.O. Box 10408, Oakland, CA 94610).

Written for concert promoters, this is a cool book to have on hand if you plan on staging your own events, at least early in your career. At the least, it'll tell you how it's done, which could help you become more savvy when you start to deal with promoters and managers.

The Rock Band Handbook: Everything You Need to Know to Get a Band Together and Take It on the Road
By Kathryn Lineberger. Published by Perigree Books, 1996.

A fabulous reference for anyone who wants more specific information on everything from how to play a guitar to choosing a drum set. The information is accessible and easy to understand. It's also a quick read (you could probably finish it in one afternoon) and it's easy to

finish it with the feeling that anyone (including you and your friends) could form the next hot band.

Women's Music Plus: Annual Directory of Resources in Women's Music and Culture
Empty Closet Enterprises
5210 N. Wayne Ave.
Chicago, IL 60640
(312) 769-9009

Rock music is definitely one of those areas that has been male-dominated, so women need every edge we can get. This is definitely an edge—and a sharp one at that. It lists complete resources and contact info for women artists, and not just rock. Blues, Country, R&B, Classical—it's all here.

Part 4: Care for and Maintain Your New World

Clean House, Clean Planet: A Manual to Free Your Home of 14 Common Hazardous Household Products
By Karen Noonan Logan. Published by Pocket Books, 1997.

It's kind of ironic that many cleaning compounds contribute to pollution. This easy-to-use guide is for everyone who is concerned about the chemicals in cleaning products. Includes simple recipes for natural, non-toxic cleaners that work.

Greenpeace
(800) 326-0959
E-mail: info@wdc.greenpeace.org
http://www.greenpeace.org/index.shtml

In case you didn't know, Greenpeace's goal is to help the Earth nurture life in all forms. Their 43 offices in 30 countries are dedicated to making a green and peaceful world. Look up the latest environmental news on their Web page.

Not in My Back Yard: The Handbook
By Jane Anne Morris. Published by Silvercat Publications, 1994.

Whether you're part of an activist group opposing a hazardous waste dump or a neighborhood organization resisting a convenience store, this book gives you the facts. Discusses identifying and targeting a controversy, doing legal research, managing publicity, and even dealing with intimidation.

Save Our Earth and Make a Difference
http://library.advanced.org/11353/indexframe2.htm

An interactive Web site dedicated to eco-consciousness. Take their eco-quiz, learn interesting (and scary) eco-facts, and get ideas about what you can do to protect your world.

Taking Out the Trash: A No-Nonsense Guide to Recycling
By Jennifer Carless. Published by Island Press, 1992 (1718 Connecticut Ave. NW, Ste. 300, Washington, DC 20009; http://www.islandpress.com/).

Did you know that tires, motor oil, asphalt, batteries, and even car bumpers are recyclable? Recycling is more than just filling up the recycling bin, it's a way of life! As Jennifer Carless points out in this handbook, there is more than one way to recycle. She explains how we've gotten ourselves into such a big trashy mess in the first place and connects us

with the basics of recycling. Also uncovered is what the government is doing. Is recycling some products worth the energy and potential health risks? (Check out the publisher's Web site for more interesting environmental books and ideas.)

Eco Job Resources

Association of Junior Leagues International
1319 F St. NW, Ste. 604
Washington, DC 20004
(202) 393-3364

An organization of women committed to improving their communities—activities include teen outreach, adolescent pregnancy prevention, and middle school programs. They also publish the *Homeless Women and Children's Report.*

Center for Environmental Education
400 Columbus Ave.
Valhalla, NY 10595
(914) 747-8200

CEE is a nonprofit organization that helps teachers, administrators, and students integrate environmental education into their school's curriculum. Their lending library is vast; it includes over 8000 books, magazines, and videos for kindergarten through twelfth grade. CEE covers everything from recycling to pesticide usage, electromagnetic pollution, and environmental regulatory compliance.

In addition to providing excellent educational materials, such as how to pack a zero waste lunch and waste prevention tips for schools, they also offer other student programs that get people involved in not just learning about environmentalism, but practicing it. Their Peer Partners program teams high school and college students who "adopt" an elementary school and then give presentations to kids about environmental issues from rainforests to recycling. Other CEE programs include school-based organic gardening (a "greening partnership" program) where students investigate the environmental conditions at their school as well as team up with local business leaders to research and address issues like energy consumption and recycling.

E: The Environmental Magazine
P.O. Box 5098
Westport, CT 0688

One of the coolest magazines, filled to the gills with informative, interesting, and timely information on everything that affects the state of our planet. Even the ads, screened to feature only eco-sound companies, are fascinating.

The Job Seeker
28762 Cty. EW
Warrens, WI 54666
(608) 378-4290

Nothing but eco-related positions, including temporary jobs, internships, training programs, and permanent jobs across the country.

Volunteer Resources

54 Ways to Help the Homeless
http://www.earthsystems.org/ways

Rabbi Charles A. Kroloff lists 54 concrete ways to help the homeless—ranging from different ways to give food to contacting government representatives for change.

Alternatives to the Peace Corps: A Directory of Third World and U.S. Volunteer Opportunities
By Annette Olson. Published by Food First Books, 1996 (P.O. Box 160, Monroe, OR 97456; 800-274-7826).

This is a great book if you like the idea of serving in the Peace Corps, but aren't yet old enough or don't necessarily agree with a lot of the politicking that organization does. Check out over 80 pages of groups offering domestic opportunities, international service, service vacations, and study abroad options.

Big Brothers/Big Sisters of America
230 N. 13th St.
Philadelphia, PA 19107
(215) 567-7000

Volunteers from this group work one-on-one with kids who are lacking positive role models in their lives. While it's true that when you first think of Big Brothers or Sisters, you think of volunteers who are much older than you are now (in fact, in some programs, people your age are the ones in need of an older, more stabilizing influence). But there may be volunteer opportunities available at your local office, especially if you want to work with younger children. Give them a call and let them know what you have to offer.

Friends in Action Manual: A Model for Establishing a Volunteer Program to Build a Caring and Supportive Relationship with Poor and Homeless Families
By Carolyn Parker. Published by the Community Ministry of Montgomery County, 1992 (114 W. Montgomery Ave., Rockville, MD 20850; 301-762-8682).

If you're already involved with some kind of aid to the homeless, or you and your group want to tackle building a program from scratch, this is a terrific resource for dealing specifically with needy families.

Girls and Young Women Leading the Way: 20 True Stories about Leadership
By Frances A. Karnes and Suzanne M. Bean. Published by Free Spirit Publishing, 1993 (400 First Ave. N., Ste. 616, Minneapolis, MN 55401).

First-hand accounts of girls, from grade school to high school, who have created volunteer opportunities in their own communities. Provides lots of inspiration.

Get it Together: The Video Project
5332 College Ave., Ste. 101
Oakland, CA 94618
(800) 475-2368

Great advice for girls seeking info on starting their own relief and volunteer groups for their communities. How to organize, identify needs, and enlist help are some of the topics covered.

Impact Online
http://www.impactonline.org

What's unique about this organization is that they have an on-line database of opportunities that you can search by type and location.

Internet Nonprofit Center
http://www.nonprofits.org

If you don't know where to begin, start with the Top 40 Charities and narrow your search from there. They also sponsor an e-mail mailing list for donors and vol-

unteers where you can discuss all things philanthropic.

Volunteer Centers and Listings
http://www.dnai.com/~children/volunteer.html
http://rso.union.wisc.edu/wud/web/cs/other.html

Both of these great sites provide a link to agencies seeking volunteers. The listings are grouped by state, so it's easy to find something near you. While the bulk of the links are with domestic agencies, there's also a section linking you to agencies who need help in their international relief efforts, like the Peace Corps and United Nations Volunteers.

Volunteer: The Comprehensive Guide to Voluntary Service in the US and Abroad
Published by CIEE: Council on International Education Exchange (205 East 42nd St., New York, NY 10017; 212-822-2600; e-mail: Info@ciee.org).

A very comprehensive directory of national and international opportunities for volunteers. Sort of along the lines of *Alternatives to the Peace Corps;* if you're looking for international opportunities, order this booklet.

The Volunteer's Survival Manual
By Darcy Campion Devney. Published by The Practical Press, 1992 (P.O. Box 38296, Cambridge, MA 02238; 617-641-0045).

The only book I've seen so far that addresses the practical side of volunteering (like finding the right match for your skills, experience, and goals).

What You Can Do to Help the Homeless
By The National Alliance to End Homelessness. Published by Simon & Schuster, 1991 (200 Old Tappan Rd., Old Tappan, NJ 07675; 800-223-2336).

Includes specific projects and activities that you can organize in your own community for easing the burden of people who have no place to call their own. Whether it's gathering food, providing childcare, or organizing a clothing drive, there are literally dozens of ideas in here.

Who Cares: A Journal of Service and Action
1511 K St. NW, Ste. 412
Washington, DC 20005
(800) 628-1692

A fabulous quarterly magazine devoted to the spirit of volunteerism in young people. They've got informative articles and inspirational stories of others who are into the volunteer thing, too.

Animal Rights Resources

American Society for the Prevention of Cruelty to Animals (ASPCA)
424 E. 92nd St.
New York, NY 10128
(212) 876-7700
http://www.aspca.org/

The Public Information Department of the ASPCA sends out information packets tailored to specific requests regarding a variety of topics such as dog fighting, puppy mills, animal research, factory farming, and volunteering. The Legal Department is a resource for information about laws protecting animals in all 50 states. The ASPCA's Web site includes great information, including a list of pending federal and state legislation affecting animals—write your senator!

Animal Legal Defense Fund
1363 Lincoln Ave.
San Rafael, CA 94901
http://www.aldf.org/

Founded in 1981, ALDF is the country's leading animal rights law organization working nationally to defend animals from abuse and exploitation. ALDF's network of over 700 attorneys is dedicated to protecting and promoting animal rights.

Animal Liberation
By Peter Singer. Published by Avon Books, 1991.

Called the "bible of the animal liberation movement," this book changed the fight for animal rights forever. A compelling, incredible book exposing killing industries like animal experimentation and factory farming. Also provides great, indepth discussion of vegetarianism and animal rights philosophies. According to PETA's catalog, "If you only read one animal rights book, it has to be this one."

Animals
Published by the Massachusetts Society for the Prevention of Cruelty to Animals (350 S. Hungtington Ave., Boston, MA 02130; 617-522-7400).

A subscription to this magazine is less than $20, and for that small amount you get some fascinating reading: from trouble with housepets to what the south African elephants are up to these days.

The Cambridge Development Lab
86 W. St.
Waltham, MA 02154
(800) 637-0047

Offers a variety of computer education software for biology, physiology, and botany, geared toward all students, from elementary through college level classes.

The Endangered Species Handbook
Animal Welfare Institute
P.O. Box 3650
Washington, DC 20007

Contains several options for non-animal lab projects.

Farm Animal Reform Movement
Box 30654
Bethesda, MD 20824
(800) 632-8688
http://www.farmusa.org/

FARM (Farm Animal Reform Movement) campaigns for the rights of farm animals, promotes healthy veggie eating, and encourages environmental consciousness. FARM conducts several national programs, including the Great American Meatout, when thousands of activists across the U.S. and Canada mark the first day of spring by celebrating the life-enhancing effects of meatless eating. Friends and neighbors are asked to "kick the meat habit" at information tables ("steakouts"), public picnics, and food tastings.

Feminists for Animal Rights
P.O. Box 16425
Chapel Hill, NC 27516
(919) 286-7333
http://www.envirolink.org/arrs/far/

Feminists for Animal Rights is dedicated to ending all forms of abuse against women and animals. They believe that the common problem in the lives of women and animals is violence—either real or threatened—and they work in nonviolent ways to change that. In addition to publishing a great semiannual newsletter, FAR has regional chapters in close to a dozen cities across the United States and Canada. FAR volunteers are engaged in a number of ongoing projects, including a foster care program for the pets of women in battered women's shelters.

The Fund for Animals
850 Sligo Ave., Ste. 300
Silver Spring, MD 20910
(301) 585-2591
http://envirolink.org/arrs/fund

Works in a variety of ways to give voice to the animals in their struggles to survive. They run the world's largest low-cost spay/neuter clinic in New York City, the nation's first spay/neuter clinic on wheels in Houston, and famous animal sanctuaries in several states. In addition, the Fund has twenty field offices working on grassroots issues across the country.

In Defense of Animals
131 Camino Alto
Mill Valley, CA 94941
(415) 388-9641
http://www.idausa.org/

IDA's protests, campaigns, and legal actions have ended New York University's cruel monkey cocaine experiments, forced the cancellation of a proposed baby-seal slaughter off the coast of

Africa, and closed down two Mississippi animal dealers suspected of selling stolen family pets to research laboratories. Get involved and see what you can do to help.

The National Anti-Vivisection Society
53 W. Jackson Blvd., #1552
Chicago, IL 60604
(800) 922-FROG

This organization loans out a lifelike bullfrog model, at no charge, for more humane lessons.

Operation Frog
2931 E. McCarty St.
Jefferson City, MO 65101
(800) 541-5513

Operation Frog is a computer simulation of a frog dissection—minus the pain and suffering, not to mention the queasiness associated with real animal bodies.

People for the Ethical Treatment of Animals (PETA)
501 Front St.
Norfolk, VA 23510
Phone: (757) 622-PETA (7382)
http://www.peta-online.org/

People for the Ethical Treatment of Animals (PETA), with more than half a million members, is the world's largest animal rights organization. Founded in 1980, PETA is dedicated to establishing and protecting the rights of all animals. PETA operates under the simple principle that animals are not ours to eat, wear, experiment on, or use for entertainment.

PETA focuses on the areas in which the largest numbers of animals suffer most: on factory farms, in laboratories, in the fur trade, and in the entertainment industry. The organization also deals with other issues, including the killing of beavers, birds, and other "pests," and the abuse of backyard dogs. PETA works through education, cruelty investigations, research, rescue, legislation, events, celebrity involvement, and direct action.

PETA publishes the *Animal Times*, a magazine full of updates on animal rights and abuses, plus campaigns, recipes, and special offers on books and other PETA products. All proceeds go to their groundbreaking work in saving animals' lives.

Vegetarian Resource Group
P.O. Box 1463
Baltimore, MD 21203
(410) 366-VEGE
Email: vrg@vrg.org
http://www.vrg.org/

The Vegetarian Resource Group (VRG) is a nonprofit organization dedicated to educating the public on vegetarianism and the interrelated issues of health, nutrition, ecology, ethics, and world hunger. In addition to publishing the *Vegetarian Journal*, VRG produces and sells cookbooks, other books, pamphlets, and article reprints.

Vegetarian Youth Network
P.O. Box 1141
New Paltz, NY 12561
http://www.geocities.com/RainForest/
Vines/4482/

The Vegetarian Youth Network is a grassroots, Web-based organization run entirely by, and for, youth who support and encourage compassionate, healthy, globally aware, vegetarian/vegan living.

VisiFrog
Ventura Educational Systems
910 Ramona Ave., Ste. E
Grover Beach, CA 93433
(800) 336-1022

VisiFrog is a computer dissection program that can be used as either a lesson or a test. Using an identification game and quiz, students learn about a frog's musculature, cardiovascular system, and respiratory systems.

Volunteers for Animal Welfare
P. O. Box 20061
Oklahoma City, OK 73156
(405) 842-6772
http://members.aol.com/vawokc/
index.htm

Volunteers for Animal Welfare is a non-profit organization dedicated to humane education, proper animal care, pet adoption information, and cruelty and abuse investigations.

When Elephants Weep
By Jeffrey Moussaieff Masson and Susan McCarthy. Published by Dell Publishing, 1996.

An extremely moving, poignant examination of the emotional lives of animals. For every time you've heard someone say that animals have no souls and have been frustrated to come up with a response, here are almost 300 pages of ammunition.

World Society for the Protection of Animals
29 Perkins St.
P.O. Box 190
Boston, MA 02130
(617) 522-7000

WSPA has been campaigning for 40 years to protect all animal life. With offices around the world, WSPA specializes in disaster relief, humane education, international campaigns, and hands-on projects in those countries where the term "animal protection" is seldom heard.

Youth for Animal Liberation (YfAL)
8361 SW 34 Terrace
Miami, FL 33155
http://home.earthlink.net/~luna9/
index.htm

Youth for Animal Liberation is mostly made up of high school and college activists who believe in grassroots change. The main goal of the group is to increase the number of animal rights activists and supporters and to heighten awareness by putting animal rights in the public eye.

DATE DUE